**Teaching Reading
to Handicapped Children**

Teaching
Reading
to Handicapped
Children

CHARLES H. HARGIS

The University of Tennessee
Knoxville

039186

LOVE PUBLISHING COMPANY
Denver · London

Copyright © 1982 Love Publishing Company
Printed in the U.S.A.
ISBN 0-89108-113-5
Library of Congress Catalog Card Number 81-84574

PREFACE

My philosophy of teaching reading emphasizes simplicity. The instructional methods which I advocate are also simple. In his book *Small is beautiful* (1973), E. F. Schumacher states, "Any third-rate engineer or researcher can increase complexity; but it takes a certain flair of real insight to make things simple again." My classroom and clinical experience confirm the need for simple methods for use with handicapped children, and my research has been directed to finding simple methods for teaching reading.

Even though the methods and materials described in this book are relatively simple, practicing the methods and preparing the material take vigorous effort and considerable discipline on the part of the teacher. Nevertheless, the rewards are great. There is nothing so dear to the heart of a teacher as having students on task, completing assignments with comprehension, and finally making progress.

I sincerely hope that this book will be of benefit—not only as a reference work for teachers of reading to the handicapped but to all teachers who must cope with reading problems and disabilities in their classrooms.

ACKNOWLEDGMENTS

Several people deserve special consideration for the assistance and encouragement they provided throughout this project. Linda Hargis provided essential editorial assistance; Laurence Coleman contributed the chapter on readability; James E. Smith stimulated my desire to undertake the project in the first place. Many thanks go to my friend and colleague Ed Gickling and my appreciation to W. Jean Schindler for her professional counsel over the years.

C.H.H.

CONTENTS

1

RECOGNIZING HANDICAPS

The handicapped population

Reading handicaps

The reading curriculum

Topics to consider

1

The handicapped population

CURRICULUM CASUALTIES

With the exception of children who have severe organic disabilities, including vision or hearing problems, the great majority of handicapped children are first identified by their failure to achieve up to grade-level standards during the primary school years. The first assessment of performance is from the regular classroom teacher. The student's performance is measured against the curriculum components of his or her particular grade. Each grade has a set of instructional materials in the basal reader program. Each curricular area has a scope and sequence of skills to be presented over the approximately nine-month school years. So despite, and often with no concession to, substantial learning capabilities of individual students, terms like *learning disabilities* or *educable mental retardation* are applied to as many as 15 percent* of these children in typical

---

*Estimates on occasion exceed 30 percent. See Lilly (1979) for prevalence figures in the various categories.

elementary school populations. In this way, the curriculum itself has been the culprit in labeling or creating handicapping conditions. A majority of these so-called handicapped children are quite normal. They are handicapped only by readiness levels or learning rates that do not synchronize precisely with entry-level skill requirements or the rates of introduction and review making up the curriculum.

These children, who are in fact curriculum casualties or curriculum handicapped, would not have acquired their various labels had the curriculum been adjusted to fit their individual needs, rather than having tried to force the children to achieve in the artificial but clerically simpler sequence of grades, calendar, and materials that comprise reading curricula. We create these handicaps because we do not sensitively adjust the reading curricula to the needs of individual children.

LABELING

There has been considerable interest over the past ten years in the effects of labeling children (Lilly, 1979). The erroneous assumption made in these various researches and commentaries is that the handicapped child's problem arises with the receiving of a diagnostic label from some specialist. What is forgotten here is that classroom teachers first identified these children by their failure to make adequate progress in the curriculum. This failure and its associated frustration are the primary problems of these children.

CURRICULUM RIGIDITY

As early as 1936, Emmett Betts (1936) stated that many reading problems were created "because we do not make practicable adjustments to individual differences. Undoubtedly some types of reading disabilities are caused by requiring a child to engage in reading activities before he is generally ready to participate." The measure of disability Betts used at that time was 15 percent. Ten years later (1946) he attributed the problem to the "lock step" nature of school organization. This procedure was described in terms of the individual classroom and the school system as a whole. Instruction was provided on the assumption that every child was to climb the same curriculum ladder. Objectives were set up in grade levels. Each level represented a rung on the curricular ladder. Children were to take the first step, beginning first grade, at the same chronological age level (usually age 6 by about the end of October). The goal of each teacher was to prepare the class for the next grade. The grade or class was itself broken into units of work through which all children were to proceed. Basal reading programs, as well as programs for other content areas, were designed for these gradations or steps on the assumption that all children are capable of uniform achievement. Children who could not manage to maintain this rate of achievement might be provided with "remedial reading" instruction to help them achieve grade level. Children who could not maintain the pace either repeated the grade or were socially promoted. The same rate of learning progress was required of all children regardless of the intrinsic readiness level or speed of learning of each child.

INDIVIDUAL DIFFERENCES

Much ink has been devoted to dealing with individual differences in reading instruction. In actual practice, however, how frequently do teachers deal with individual differences in reading instruction in their classrooms? How much has attention to individual differences increased since Betts made these critical judgments? In 1978 the author participated in a survey of primary-grade classrooms in urban and rural schools (Gickling, 1979). There it was reaffirmed that the curriculum and grade level of placement dominated teachers' actions in providing reading instruction to children. Despite evidence of the actual level of reading performance, more than 30 percent of the children were not provided with instructional material at that identified level. More than 20 percent of the children were given material that was too difficult for instructional purposes. The teachers misidentified the instructional needs of individual children in the direction of their grade placement rather than actual performance. This was apparent with the most capable or gifted readers, as well. In spite of reading performance several grade levels above actual placement, the greatest concession to any of these children was to provide material one grade level above the students' current grade placement.

Spache (1976) states that primary-grade teachers who are sufficiently flexible can handle pupils who vary six months or so from exact grade placement. In the existing structure, however, a child functioning a year or more below grade placement may present a demand for specialized or individualized instruction that the average teacher does not recognize or meet readily. Spache also points out that 30 percent of students above the primary grades are a year or more below grade-level placement in reading achievement.

Harris and Sipay (1975) claim that 25 percent of American children need reading instruction that differs from regular developmental reading programs. These "slow learners" require materials that proceed at a slower pace.

Jansky and de Hirsch (1972) point out that teachers rated as adequate by principals had a failure rate of 23 percent of their children. Teachers rated as poor, however, showed 49 percent of their children failing. These data certainly suggest that teachers can influence the effectiveness of reading instruction in the classroom, but it is apparent that without a major change in the reading curriculum itself many so-called learning disabled children will continue to be by-products or casualties of the reading curriculum.

Reading handicaps

LEARNING DISABILITIES

The point being emphasized so far is that most children called reading and/or learning disabled are in fact normal, and their primary problem has to do with the inflexibility of reading curricula and materials. There are children with very real learning impairments, however, whose problems are not caused primarily by curricular inadequacies. Some of these children may have one or more problems with attention/distraction or visual or auditory function. These difficulties can be of an extent sufficient to require special treatment or accommodation. Other groups of children may have specific cognitive or linguistic deficits that impair their ability in learning to read. These latter groups of children may have acquired some of the myriad labels to be applied to those with such problems: "minimal brain dysfunction, brain injury, development aphasia, dyslexia, perceptually impaired," to mention only a few. Cruikshank (1971) lists thirty-eight such labels. Despite the large number and variety of labels, these children constitute only a very small proportion of the population known as learning disabled. The vast majority are curriculum casualties.

MENTAL RETARDATION

A variety of categories or labels has been developed to describe various levels of mental retardation (Payne and Mercer, 1975). The categories used here are *borderline* (IQ 68–84), *mild retardation* (IQ 52–67), *moderate retardation* (IQ 36–51), *severe retardation* (IQ 20–35), and *profound retardation* (IQ 20).

The term *mental retardation* is an unfortunate title for the vast majority of the children to whom it is applied. The British term *educationally subnormal* is more accurate and not so likely to imply some physiologically based cognitive defect. The great majority of children called borderline and mildly retarded are completely normal individuals (Hargis, Mercaldo, & Johnson, 1975). Their problem can be expressed in educational terms, as the British label implies. Their level of maturity at any given chronological age and their rate of learning cause even more obvious discrepancies with curricular demands than those revealed by learning disabled children. For the majority of these children the strictures of reading curricula are too great to permit even nearly adequate performance. As a consequence of this apparently defective performance, the unfortunate labels that include the term *retardation* were born.

Borderline retardation   Children in the borderline category, for the most part, benefit from reading-curriculum revision that affects introduction and repetition rates as well as sensitivity to their range of readiness levels. The upper IQ range of this group of children is very frequently included in the learning disabled group (Bryan, 1974).

Mild retardation   The potential for reading achievement within the group of mildly retarded individuals can vary considerably. Virtually all of these children will require specially adapted curriculum and material, however, to achieve their potential.

Moderate retardation Moderately retarded children may attain certain functional reading skills. The cognitive and/or linguistic development of this group usually does not provide the readiness base necessary to acquire this complex skill. As a consequence, these children generally cannot read at the first-grade level. Limited but utilitarian reading skills are attainable if the reading program is systematically structured toward that objective.

HEARING IMPAIRMENT

Two critical factors affect the ability of hearing impaired children to learn to read: the age of onset of the hearing impairment and the degree or extent of the hearing loss.

A child born with a hearing impairment, or one who loses it prior to the acquisition of language, has a potentially serious problem with education and certainly in learning to read. Development of basic language skills is very disrupted; so the fundamental readiness base, mastery of language, will not be intact. The reading program required for these children differs greatly from that provided by standard reading curricula. A deficiency in language requires major changes in material and method.

The interaction of the degree of hearing loss and the age of onset of this disability can produce problems ranging from the most severe (which were just mentioned) to rather mild forms (which may require virtually no special consideration). Hard-of-hearing children, however, constitute a very large though generally overlooked population who are greatly susceptible to reading disabilities.

VISUAL HANDICAPS

The visual handicaps to be considered range from mild to moderate. This category includes children who have sufficient visual acuity and accommodative ability to read regular print.

Research and clinical experience warrant considering here a large group of children frequently overlooked, those whose vision problem may not prevent their learning to read but when coupled with any other negative learning condition may cumulatively cause reading disability. These children include those with marginal refractive difficulty and problems with binocularity.

BEHAVIOR DISORDERS

A basic distinction within the population of behaviorally disordered (emotionally disturbed) children is necessary to provide adequately for reading instruction. The first group so identified has school-related behavior disorders. The behavior of these children is an induced reaction to chronic frustration and failure in school. The direct treatment for these children is the appropriate adjustment in reading curriculum to permit satisfactory instructional progress and avoid failure and its attendant frustration. The behavior disorder or emotional disturbance attributed to this group of children is the manifestation of maladaptive behavior that results from failure and frustration brought on by inappropriate curricula.

The other group of children, probably the smaller of the two groups, has emotional problems causing their learning problems. The range of severity is from mild to profound. The reading problems of these children are the product of their emotional or behavior disorder—not the reverse. The cause and/or the interfering behavior, therefore, must receive priority in the treatment procedures.

SOCIAL-CULTURAL FACTORS

Children from America's diverse social and cultural groups are not necessarily handicapped in regard to learning to read. If a child's culture and dialect or language are sufficiently different from the dominant linguistic form in this country, however, the potential for problems is real. If his or her socioeconomic group is within the poverty level also, problems with health and nutrition or experiential deficits may impair readiness and ability to learn through standard curricula.

The reading curriculum

THE LEAST RESTRICTIVE ENVIRONMENT

Since the passage in 1975 of PL 94-142, the Education for All Handicapped Children Act, major emphasis has been laid on the integration of handicapped children into regular schools and classrooms. For some handicapped children, this integration may be appropriate. Appropriateness was the key consideration of the act's formulation, in fact. If children were to benefit from educational placement in close association with normal peers, it was deemed necessary to formulate an individualized education program, commonly called an IEP. This system bases appropriate placement for each child on the assessment of his or her academic, physical, and social abilities and needs. The assessment information is used to determine the type of personnel and resources needed to meet the set of objectives able to provide the most appropriate education.

George Spache (1976) pointed out how much deviation from grade level in reading the average classroom teacher could manage without special help (no more than six months in the primary grades). The author has participated in research (Gickling, 1979) that evaluated primary-grade classroom teachers' potential for accepting handicapped children in their classrooms. Potential for acceptance was measured by how sensitive to, and how well teachers dealt with, individual differences existing in their classrooms. It was felt that a teacher aware of the actual reading performance of his or her nonhandicapped students, who provided material and instruction at that level, would be the best candidate for accepting handicapped children.

These skills would be fundamental in providing and implementing IEPs. The measures used were teacher judgment of reading-level performance of their own students and level of difficulty of reading material provided for use in reading instruction, and informal assessment of children's reading and their ability to read the materials provided. The tests for word recognition were comprised of work in the basal reader program. Ninety-percent accuracy in reading the words selected from each level was considered an adequate instructional level. If a student achieved this level of accuracy on the material used for instruction, it was felt that an adequate match was being made.

It was found that teachers were not sensitive to the reading-performance level of children either below or above grade level. They did not provide appropriately matched instructional material for those who deviated significantly from grade level. Instructional material and instruction are functions of the grade level of assignment, not the actual reading ability of specific children. The grouping that teachers use in their classes frequently does not include sufficient adjustment in the use of reading materials. Often children are merely grouped according to roughly comparable skills in using the readers available.

CONCESSIONS THAT MUST BE MADE IN THE REGULAR CLASSROOM

If handicapped children are to be accurately placed and managed in the regular classroom, a number of major concessions must be made in the curriculum and materials.

The first is that reading materials provided for each child be matched with their current level of performance. The second has to do with variation in learning rates. Basal reading programs have controls over the introduction of unfamiliar printed words (Hargis, 1974; Herrick, 1961). The usual rate is one new word in 50 to 110 running words. Once the words have been introduced, there are generally accepted provisions for their repetition for purposes of word-recognition mastery (Strickland, 1962). The learning rates of many children, however, fall outside the given rate of word repetition provided by the reading program. More repetition is required to achieve word-recognition mastery than is provided by the available materials. The concession for these children must be to provide supplementary exercises and materials or revised materials that provide for a greater need. This alteration will necessarily affect the length of time required to complete mastery of any specified set of reading terms. All children cannot be expected to complete a given quantity of material in the same calendar period. To impose reading curricula that reflect such expectations only produces casualties in those whose learning rates vary significantly.

ON DEALING WITH INDIVIDUAL DIFFERENCES

There is considerable pressure on teachers and controversy concerning the number of children who read below age- and grade-level standards. The special educator and reading specialist grow to expect large differences in reading ability at each chronological age and grade level. These differences should exist quite naturally. There are some serious problems, however, concerning reading performance that veers from grade-level placement.

The first and largest group is made up of those who are essentially nonreaders, regardless of age or grade placement. These are children who have not benefited from reading instruction at any time because of the disparity between the curriculum provided and their actual learning rate and readiness. It is not uncommon to find students in intermediate grades, junior high, or middle school who still can barely read. Thorough evaluation would separate such children from those whose physical or other problems impede their progress. Most children in this first group are in the normal range of intelligence. The great majority have IQs in the eighties to low nineties. It is predictable that readiness for reading in this group would not occur until seven or eight years of age. The learning rates of these children require 10 to 20 percent greater repetition or duration than in the average child.

These children usually do not survive secondary-education programs. Their lack of reading ability makes an already painful and frustrating educational experience even more intolerable. All too frequently a cycle of school avoidance and truancy leads to the juvenile-offender label. Unfortunately, we find a much greater than expected representation of this group in correctional institutions and in the adult penal system—despite their having had as their learning potential, at the least, functional literacy.* These children have truly become curriculum casualties.

The next group of children is comprised of those who have managed somehow to achieve a reading level close to their

---

*The arbitrary level selected here to represent functional literacy is the fifth grade. For a thoughtful review of the concept of functional literacy, the reader is referred to a paper by Kirsch and Guthrie (1977–78).

potential but still encounter problems in school. This group is exceedingly small in comparison to the previous group. A case illustrating this problem involved a fifteen-year-old tenth-grade girl. The author was called to a rural western high school to evaluate the problems of this teenager who was failing biology, English, algebra, and history. Beginning with an individual intelligence test, the Wechsler Intelligence Scale for Children (WISC), a complete battery of tests was administered to isolate the problem at the root of all the difficulty. The student showed no reading-skill deficiency according to the reading diagnostic test (the Gates-McKillop). The general-achievement test uniformly indicated scores at the seventh-grade level. The results of an informal reading inventory also confirmed a reading level at the seventh grade. The full-scale IQ was 85, which suggested that reading and academic performance at the seventh-grade level was a substantial attainment for this student. Usually students in this IQ range, unfortunately, are well below this reading level. Discussion with the concerned parents of the student revealed why the student had performed so well on the tests. Her parents had tutored her consistently and regularly since she began to experience problems in the first grade. Without this constant extra help and support, the student would likely never have attained such a level of achievement. The parents recognized the limitations on the academic success of their child from their years of patient work with her. They wanted very much to know what they could do to help their child through the frustration and failure she was experiencing in most of her high school courses. Diagnosis revealed that no improvement in reading skill could entirely alleviate the problem. The main problem of this student would seem to have been created by the inflexibility of a curriculum that forced her to read materials and assignments within time limits beyond her ability.

Even when such students are able to make adequate progress, school can remain an extremely difficult, even painful, environment.

Maslow (1970) has provided a very useful hierarchy of basic human needs important for emotionally healthy development. Among these are the needs for safety and affection or belonging. Situations that induce failure and frustration provide for neither of these basic needs and, in fact, erode the child's self-concept and make him question his own value.

There should not be nearly so many nonreaders, regardless of age level, as there are. Nor should there be frustrated and failing children who are making adequate progress, even if it does not meet grade-level standards. As more and more handicapped children are educated in regular education settings, it is sincerely to be hoped that educators will cease to regard individual differences in learning as essentially curable maladies. The two groups of children just discussed could benefit from this observation. Of course, the main benefit would occur if the curriculum were made sufficiently flexible to include the array of developmental levels and learning rates that are a normal part of the population of every chronological age group. Attempts to cure these individual differences only produce casualties. Even the gifted child is likely to be overlooked. When such children perform adequately and easily at their grade-level placement, they are frequently unnoticed. There is seen to be no problem when they are judged by the standard curricular requirements. We are less likely to view gifted children as casualties if they seem to be performing according to the expectations of grade-level placement. But if these gifted children are reading two or more years *below* where they should be, how much less a casualty are they than those who fail to achieve grade level?

MAINTAINING HANDICAPPED CHILDREN IN THE LEAST RESTRICTIVE ENVIRONMENT

Maintaining handicapped children in the regular reading curricula requires a variety of approaches and adjustments, some of which have already been mentioned in rather general terms. A simple administrative action can have the most dramatic effect, making the maintenance problem more manageable and considerably less painful for children. This administrative change requires adjusting the age at which beginning reading instruction begins. Most kindergarten teachers can accurately identify the least mature children in their classes. For these children an extended stay in kindergarten would provide an opportunity to mature. A relatively few months at this age level is a large percentage of a child's life. A few months' extra maturation time can make the difference between success and frustration in beginning reading. Kindergarten, or the readiness period, should be extended before reading instruction begins rather than putting these children in a "no win" situation. Requiring failure to qualify children for assistance is a poor practice.

Extending the period of readiness for beginning reading to as much as age 8 could prevent failure and frustration for 90 percent of the children usually called learning disabled. It would also prevent the application of this label to the majority.

To maintain these children as much as possible in regular reading curricula requires sensitive attention to their varied learning rates. Supplementary help and resources may well be able to provide the extra repetition necessary to achieve mastery of new reading vocabulary and subskills. This work can parallel the basal program, but it necessarily extends the completion time beyond that required for the average student.

THE NATURE OF READING INSTRUCTION

The printed form of the language is still a language process, or communication in print. The communication with which children are familiar should be reflected in the composition of the language they are learning to read.

Language is a communication process, and meaning and comprehension in this sense should be of prime importance. As reading has become more of a subject area in the curriculum, however, it has become reduced to compartmentalized sets of subskills increasingly esoteric and less obviously related to real communication. Reading curricula have become steadily more subcategorized, and reading subskills have proliferated through a process often called "task analysis." As these so-called subskills have grown increasingly abstract, remarkably little agreement has emerged from one reading program to another on which subskills are necessary.

Unfortunately for handicapped children, these subskills have gradually become subject areas in and of themselves—and they have come to dominate reading instructional time. They also seem less directly related to the reading process itself. Their very abstractness may confront a primary weakness in applying them to the learning abilities of the handicapped child (Spache, 1976). As they increasingly dominate reading instructional time, less time is devoted directly to the more concrete reading process. Reading disability is now often viewed as a subskill deficiency even though there is considerable uncertainty as to what the most important subskills are, in which order they should be presented, and the best method of presentation (Spache, 1976; Venezky, 1978).

The author's perspective on reading strongly suggests the need for more direct instructional time spent on reading—that is, instruction in reading as a concrete language process. The reading material used, therefore, must be within the experiential and linguistic thresholds that each child brings to instruction. This consideration as to material composition is basic to conducting direct instruction in reading for handicapped children. One cannot comprehend through listening language that relates unfamiliar experiences, and one certainly cannot read unfamiliar language. Only language conversationally familiar should be used for instruction in beginning reading.

The next consideration, material to be used or prepared, is the instructional load that it places on children. How much new printed information can be introduced? How quickly may it be introduced? How often must it be repeated? These are questions that must be asked for each of the children. All are of fundamental importance in instruction. The comprehension level will fall off if the number of unknowns in printed discourse is too great. If comprehension is too low, the child will soon give up trying. If there are too many unfamiliar printed words, the child cannot use the context effectively to deal with the unfamiliar vocabulary or subskill being introduced. The location or preparation of reading material controlling introduction and repetition rates will require major consideration.

Topics to consider

In a population of normal children, individual variance in readiness for reading is considerably greater than in the curricular concessions made. This creates learning problems, in fact, to be considered in the chapter on readiness for reading.

Some handicapping conditions impose very real impediments to attaining readiness to read in standard curricula. Adjustments and procedures that deal with these problems are also presented.

The importance of differing learning rates has been touched on in this chapter. The effect on the curriculum is yet to be considered. Methods of adjusting the curriculum and preparing reading materials appropriately sensitive to individual differences will be illustrated.

Individual differences and deficits in cognitive development, language, and experiential background influence curriculum and material preparation. These factors will be considered in detail, as will sensory and perceptual problems. Methods of teaching directed to the learning strengths of various handicapped groups will also be presented.

The third chapter of this book deals with assessment. The approaches emphasized are informal methods that are criterion referenced. This form of assessment is stressed in order that it may be more readily and directly used to formulate specific instructional objectives and materials.

REFERENCES

Betts, Emmett Albert. *The prevention and correction of reading difficulties.* Evanston: Row, Peterson, 1936.

Betts, Emmett Albert. *Foundations of reading instruction.* New York: American Book, 1946.

Bryan, Tanis H. Learning disabilities: A new stereotype. *Journal of Learning Disabilities,* 1974, 7 (5), 304–309.

Cruikshank, William M. *Psychology of exceptional children and youth* (3rd ed.) Englewood Cliffs: Prentice-Hall, 1971.

Gickling, Edward E. *Premainstreaming: Regular classroom teacher.* Paper presented at the 57th annual international convention of the Council for Exceptional Children, April 24, 1979.

Hargis, Charles H., *An analysis of the syntactic and figurative structure of popular first grade level basal readers.* Paper presented at the 12th Southeastern Conference on Linguistics, November 1, 1974.

Hargis, Charles H., Mercaldo, David J., & Johnson, H. Wayne. A linguistic and cognitive perspective on retardation. *The Journal of Genetic Psychology,* 1975, *126* (1), 145–154.

Harris, Albert J., & Sipay, Edward R. *How to increase reading ability* (6th ed.). New York: David McKay, 1975.

Herrick, Virgil E. Basal instructional materials in reading. *Development in and through reading: 60th yearbook of the National Society for the Study of Education* (Part 1). Chicago: University of Chicago Press, 1961.

Jansky, Jeannette, & de Hirsch, Katrina. *Preventing reading failure: Prediction, diagnosis, intervention.* New York: Harper & Row, 1972.

Kirsch, Irwin, & Guthrie, John T. The concept and measurement of functional literacy. *Reading Research Quarterly,* 1977–1978, *13* (4), 485–507.

Lilly, M. Stephen. *Children with exceptional needs: A survey of special education.* New York: Holt, Rinehart & Winston, 1979.

Maslow, Abraham H. *Motivation and personality* (2nd ed.). New York: Harper & Row, 1970.

Payne, James S., & Mercer, Cecil D. Definition and prevalence. In James M. Kauffman & James S. Payne (Eds.), *Mental retardation: Introduction and personal perspectives.* Columbus: Charles E. Merrill, 1975.

Schumacher, E. F. *Small is beautiful: Economics as if people mattered.* New York: Harper & Row, 1973.

Spache, George D. *Diagnosing and correcting reading disabilities.* Boston: Allyn & Bacon, 1976.

Strickland, R. G. The language of elementary school children: Its relationship to language of reading textbooks and the quality of reading of selected children. *Bulletin of the School of Education, Indiana University,* 1962, *38* (4).

Venezky, Richard L. Reading acquisition: The occult and the obscure. In Frank B. Murray & John J. Pikulski (Eds.), *The acquisition of reading.* Baltimore: University Park Press, 1978.

2

READINESS FOR READING

General reading readiness

Cognitive readiness

Language readiness

Social development

**Exceptional or extreme variation
in readiness**

**Adjustments in reading-readiness
programs**

2

General reading readiness

MATURITY

A number of frequently noted components constitute reading readiness. Children need a level of cognitive and linguistic maturity that permits them to comprehend and follow the teacher's instructional talk and the language used in the literature of the first grade. They need sufficient social maturity to cooperate and attend within the structures of the first grade. They often require sufficient physical maturity to handle the fine-motor activities associated with beginning reading. More simply, as Harris and Sipay (1975) point out, readiness for reading can be thought of as the general maturity which permits learning to read without undue difficulty.

Since maturation is fundamental to readiness, chronological age is one factor influencing readiness. There are some rather small differences in the rate of development by sex, and in general girls seem to be ready for reading earlier than boys.

Variation in cognitive and linguistic development is extremely important at this age level. A few months of maturation make up a large percentage of the cognitive and linguistic development in a 6-year-old. Interaction of chronological age with cognitive and linguistic development compound the range of readiness levels in any class of kindergarten or first-grade children. Children entering first grade usually are required to reach their sixth birthday some time during the first few months of the school year. Whatever this arbitrary date is, it means that those admitted have about a year of variation in age range. The developmental changes occurring at this age level are rapid, so the difference of a year between the oldest and youngest child in a class is significant. The physical, social, cognitive, and linguistic variation in any class of beginning first-graders is usually readily observable. The differences in readiness to learn to read also become obvious as this instruction begins.

INTELLIGENCE

Although intelligence is probably the most important factor in determining reading readiness, average or even above-average intelligence does not guarantee that adequate achievement will be made in reading. The measurement of intelligence has a number of limitations. There is a variety of reasons why it is difficult to obtain valid results with the instruments available.

Children with severe sensory or motor handicaps pose the greatest problem in assessment. Children who represent social, cultural, or linguistic groups not represented in the test's standardization group are not adequately measured. In these cases, the factors that make the measurement difficult will probably, in and of themselves, have a significant bearing on readiness.

Intelligence tests predict group reading achievement fairly well, as do a number of readiness tests to be discussed in the chapter on assessment. However, specific individual reading achievement levels cannot be predicted with great accuracy by intelligence-test scores, although lower scores are proven indicators of the potential for failure and problems with academic performance.

About 25 percent of American children have IQs below 90. It has been stated that this group requires an adapted reading program (Harris & Sipay, 1975) that accepts their limitations and sets reasonable expectations. The adapted reading program should differ mainly in its slower pace and use of different materials and interests. About 9 percent of the population's IQs fall between 84 (the upper limit of what was called borderline retardation in the first chapter) and 90. The mental-age range for this group of children on entering first grade is about 5.1 to 6.3. This assumes that the chronological age range is from 6.0 to 7.0. Very likely only the older children in the upper IQ range would have little difficulty in beginning reading. The most straightforward and humane way of dealing with the readiness requirements of the children in the IQ range of from 80 to 90 is to extend the readiness period in kindergarten and delay the beginning of reading instruction.

Huey (1908) reports that John Dewey as early as 1898 advocated postponing reading instruction to about the age of eight. This would in all likelihood head off the problems of the less mature child or one with other remediable readiness deficits. It would, however, be inappropriate for the much larger segment of the population who could benefit quite readily from reading instruction over a range of younger age levels.

LANGUAGE

The acquisition of language proceeds rapidly through the years preceding beginning reading instruction. Research, reviewed later in the chapter, indicates as normal considerable variation in the age at which children acquire the essential features of language. As with other traits that vary with maturity, some children will not be ready to read until after the age of 6. A fundamental readiness requirement is, however, that they be able to comprehend the oral directions of the teacher. Also fundamental is the level of language maturity and experience that enables children to understand first-grade reading materials read aloud.

IMPEDIMENTS

Some readiness requirements are best stated in "freedom from" terms. Because of the structure of standard reading programs, a child needs to be free from a number of physical problems that might interfere with readiness or progress. These problems include significant impediments of vision or hearing, health, and nutrition. The central nervous system may have impediments to certain cognitive processes or perceptual and motor functions needed in beginning reading. The social, cultural, or linguistic milieu of the child may prevent his or her relating to the form and structure of the readiness programs.

Cognitive readiness

Some basic thought processes seem to be specific to the human species. These comprise the structure of cognitive development in childhood, following a step-by-step sequence. Piaget has developed a widely known theory of cognitive development. He has provided an outline of sequence and a theoretical explanation (Flavell, 1963). The concept of sequential development is well established in children, handicapped as well as normal, albeit with considerable individual age variation for both. Research studies that test acquisition of individual structures indicate some discrepancy in the identifiable age of completion of these stages (Bryant, 1974; Fogelman, 1970). The level of cognitive development is very important in determining the readiness level of children, however, even if it is difficult to measure with precision. The general outline that Piaget proposes has four periods or levels of cognitive development: first, *sensorimotor* (from 0 to 2 years); second, *preoperations* (from 2 to 7 years); third, *concrete operations* (from 7 to 11 years); fourth, *formal operations* (from 11 to 15 years). The age boundaries are only markers of central tendency. The age of mastering or completion varies considerably in individuals.

Of particular interest in readiness requirements are the cognitive structures that comprise the preoperational period from 2 to 7. A number of the substructures appear related to items in the curriculum. One-to-one correspondence is one such structure, fundamental to development of rational counting. Classifications of increasing complexity are required for vocabulary development. Ordering concrete objects according to increasing or decreasing size, weight, volume, and number requires some ability in seriation. This structure is fundamental to comparison, which is related to the development of certain syntactic structures, rational counting, and later arithmetic operations.

All normal children acquire these structures. Individuals complete the stages at different chronological ages, however, providing further evidence of age variation in readiness for reading. This reaffirms the need for the delay of beginning reading until readiness is achieved or making more flexible the period of reading readiness. The author has found that informal tests that assess development of one-to-one correspondence and comparison or seriation are relatively accurate (in clinical observation) and very easy to administer. The tests will be outlined in the chapter on assessment.

Language readiness

LANGUAGE AND COGNITION

Cognitive growth, especially during the preoperational period of cognitive development, parallels the sequence of development in acquisition of language (Slobin, 1978). In fact, indications are that language is a map of cognitive process (Hargis, Mercaldo, & Johnson, 1975, 1976). Language permits mapping thoughts expressed and received for examination by the recipient of the communication.

COMPREHENSION AND PRODUCTION

Language has two major components in regard to the communication process: comprehension and production. Language must be received and comprehended; it must also be expressed or produced. Reading is an aspect of comprehension. In this case it is the reception and comprehension of a visual form of language. This distinction is important for a number of reasons. Language comprehension precedes and exceeds production in development (Hargis, 1977; McNeill, 1966). Much linguistic research points to a sequential progression that children follow as they master their language (Brown, 1973). Production ability follows comprehension—incrementally and in qualitatively different ways. This sequential development parallels cognitive growth and is often completed at about age 6 or at the end of the preoperational period of development.

The majority of normal children at this age can usually comprehend and enjoy a wide variety of children's literature. As long as the plot or humor is quite concrete, children can follow a rather elaborate sequence of events and keep track of a number of characters. When the same children attempt to describe some recent occurrence or summarize a story or television program, however, their production skills clearly indicate less sophistication. They will likely disarrange the sequence of events, omit important items or characters, and exhibit speech dysfluency (hesitation, repetition, and other forms). This normal discrepancy between comprehension and production is more notable at these early ages. It will persist into adulthood but with a considerable range of differences among individuals. This distinction between comprehension and production is important to keep in mind in determining readiness for reading. The person assessing readiness should not rely excessively on production information to infer readiness. Expressive ability is not likely to match the level of comprehension needed for reading readiness. Fluency is a good indicator of language and general reading readiness. Less fluency or even little apparent production skill, however, does not necessarily mean that a child lacks sufficient comprehension for beginning reading. Comprehension must be assessed directly without relying on production information. Some direct techniques will be discussed in the chapter on assessment.

VARIATION IN DEVELOPMENT

Menyuk (1977) suggests that when children are in the age range of 5 to 7 years they are comprehending and producing utterances adultlike syntactically. Palermo and Molfese (1972) and Chomsky (1969) extend the age for comprehension of the most complex syntactic structure in some children. Mastery of the structure is a basic readiness requirement for reading. The normal development variation in acquisition or mastery of the language is another factor supporting the need for adjusting the age at which reading instruction begins.

As already mentioned, material read to a child must be comprehended. Comprehension is a basic readiness requirement. You cannot read language that you do not comprehend.

Research on the structures used in first-grade materials (Hargis, 1974, 1977) reveals the scope of language structures used. Analysis of the primer and first readers (currently numbers or letters are used in place of this designation) of the most popular basal reading programs revealed lack of control over the introduction of syntax in sentences used. Virtually all structures, including those identified as the most difficult and latest in acquisition, appeared in the readers. The study confirmed that mastery of English syntax is required to meet the basic readiness requirements of beginning reading material.

Analysis of the instructions in the teachers' manuals indicates the same readiness requirements. Samples of teachers' actual instructional talk further confirm the need for mastery of linguistic structure as basic to beginning reading.

Social development

The nature of reading instruction seems to demand substantial attention and cooperation. Regardless of the reading methods or materials, social development seems to parallel cognitive growth. Social development varies, nevertheless, at otherwise equal levels of development—cognitive, linguistic, or intellectual—being much more influenced by experience than the other developmental areas previously mentioned. As a consequence, children who show immaturity in social development are somewhat more likely to benefit from readiness activities specifically directed to their improvement. In some children, however, attention and cooperation levels are not readily improved even through the use of appealing games and activities, and they may persist in parallel play within their chronological-age peer group. These children may be socially on a different developmental timetable and will require patience and time before they can start more highly structured activities.

Exceptional or extreme variation in readiness

The environment—the size of auto seats, length of a bed, height of counters and cabinets—determines whether a tall or short person is exceptional. Wilt Chamberlain is very tall but within normal limits. He is exceptional—even handicapped in certain everyday environments. An adult of four feet, eight inches, may represent an extreme in normal shortness and may also be handicapped in many everyday environments. Many children at the lower end of normal intellectual and cognitive development are handicapped by the school environment. The measuring device is the curriculum. There are, however, children who represent significantly different problems from those accounted for in normal variation. The readiness problems of these children will be considered next.

MENTAL RETARDATION

Intelligence tests can be only fair predictors of readiness for reading and for reading achievement in the general population. In the massive first-grade studies conducted in the 1960s, the correlations between raw scores on the Pintner-Cunningham Primary Test of Mental Ability and subsequent scores on the Stanford Paragraph Meaning Test ranged from .42 to .56. This does not show a very accurate level of prediction of individual levels of reading achievement. Children who are identified at the extreme lower end of the intelligence range, however, will very likely have special problems learning to read.

Moderate retardation   A 6-year-old child who has an IQ of 50 has a mental age of 3.0 and is unlikely to be ready for reading. Not only does the IQ permit calculating mental age; it also provides an index to mental growth. The child with an IQ of 50 will mature mentally at approximately half the rate of a child with an IQ of 100. It must be kept in mind that these measures are estimates. Measurement and other errors limit their precision. But when there are reasonable assurances of validity, the lower IQ scores provide good indication of readiness. The rate of mental growth first described has implications for ultimate levels of cognitive and linguistic development of children who are moderately retarded and lower. This group constitutes only about .1 percent of the population. The rate of mental development for the members of the broad group, interacting with the sequence of cognitive development, affects reading readiness at any age level and the ultimate potential for achievement in cognitive and language-related activities.

The concept of sequential development in the acquisition of cognitive structures is well established and has been applied to the study of retarded children (Farber, 1968; Inhelder, 1968; Kolstoe, 1972; Stephens, 1966; Woodward, 1959). Retarded children will proceed in the normal sequence of development but at a much slower rate, one not sufficient to complete the preoperational level by the time of adolescence. An IQ of approximately 50 is necessary to complete this important cognitive and linguistic developmental milestone (Hargis et al., 1975). At adolescence, children in the IQ ranges below 50 will be frozen, so to speak, at some assessable level within the preoperational or sensorimotor periods of development, depending on the degree of retardation. Woodward (1959) found that if a retarded child could solve a problem related to one cognitive structure, he could solve all the problems below it and problems at the same level. As previously mentioned, the ultimate level of cognitive development is achieved at adolescence. This final level marks with fair accuracy the approximate language level and reading potential of the retarded child. In the IQ ranges below 50, this results in a readiness potential below that required for reading instruction as it is currently defined. Children of this intellectual level are unlikely to attain ability sufficient to read trade books or basal materials even at the first-grade level. The acquisition of any skills that they do attain will not likely be started until the child is at adolescence.

Mild retardation   The IQ range between 52 and 67 at a given chronological age represents considerable diversity and variation in learning rate. These children have the potential to acquire considerable reading skill. The reading achievement levels, however, will likely range through the primary-grade levels. Mildly retarded children can attain essentially normal linguistic development (Mahmoud & Hargis, 1975). They will usually reach readiness for reading, in terms of their language development, when their mental age is about 6 years. Their language will reach normal development in syntax, but vocabulary will be restricted to concrete levels that demonstrate their conceptual development. Figurative use of language will also be very limited. Informal language-comprehension tests provide very useful indexes of readiness for this group. In spite of the diversity of potential, these children do share some common needs and problems. They need reading materials and instruction paced substantially more slowly than that widely available. The readiness period and beginning reading program will necessarily be longer than those provided in standard curricula. The majority of these children are free from the obvious pathological conditions associated with many of the children in the IQ ranges below 52. They evidence their difficulty primarily in slower mental and social growth, usually only readily apparent in school-related settings. This group of children constitutes about 2 percent of the school-age population.

Borderline retardation   The children in the borderline-IQ group (IQ range 68–84) are sometimes called slow learners. About 14 percent of the population falls within this IQ range. All of these children share the potential for functional literacy as the minimum level of reading achievement. Their rates of mental and social maturation place them in conflict with curricular dictates concerning entry and rate of progress.

These children evidence somewhat slower linguistic development. This level of development has a direct bearing on readiness for reading and should be informally measured to determine performance status. The least mature of the group do not acquire the more complex syntactic forms until as late as 9 years of age. Borderline children attain a great deal more abstractness in their lexicons and achieve a greater use of figurative language than those with lower IQs. There will be, however, considerable expected variation of these factors.

LANGUAGE LEARNING DISABILITY

There is no consensus on the terms (Bloom & Lahey, 1978) or the classification of children whose educational or developmental problems are best described in terms of language deficiency. Children who are retarded exhibit language deficits which mirror their cognitive development. Severely hearing impaired children are likely to have major difficulties in language acquisition. Emotionally disturbed children are frequently identified by severe communication problems. Here childhood schizophrenia or psychosis and autism are the usually associated terms. Problems of this severity are likely to have a neurological basis. The neurological disorder most specifically associated with language disability, however, is childhood aphasia.

The language function of some children may be impaired sufficiently to prevent achieving readiness for reading through a normal developmental process, even a process that is considerably delayed. When the language disability is at the basis of the reading deficit, the reading-readiness program will of necessity attend to improvement of this limited behavior. If the language function is not improved to the normal readiness level, reading achievement potential is greatly limited.

Children who are severely emotionally disturbed may have a primary readiness deficit in terms of language disability. Also, those children who have relatively little language involvement may have extreme problems with social development manifest in primary readiness limitation. Withdrawal, indifference, or disruptive behavior requires primary attention and programming through the readiness stage.

HEARING IMPAIRMENTS

When a child has a severe congenital hearing impairment, the effect on language acquisition is dramatically apparent. The hearing mechanism is the primary channel for efficient language acquisition. A hearing impairment prior to beginning of the normal language-acquisition process deprives the deaf child of the basic linguistic data upon which to organize the basic essentials of language competence. This extreme language deficiency is at the core of the readiness needs of the deaf child.

Hearing acuity   Children who lose their hearing some time during the process of acquisition may be limited to the degree of linguistic competence attained to that point. Whatever their language level is, it represents the readiness base a child has to work from. Deaf children will quite likely attain the cognitive level required for readiness through the normal developmental process, though it may be somewhat delayed (Furth, 1966). Nevertheless, language teaching will be the necessary ingredient of the curriculum for deaf children to make up for this deficit.

Children with less severe hearing impairments than profound deafness may suffer from language deficits over a broad range of disability levels. Even mild losses can deprive a child of the quality and richness of language experience available to a normally hearing peer. Such children may be at a disadvantage also in beginning reading programs that provide initial emphasis on letter-sound associations as the basis of the word-identification program. These finer, more abstract associations will create a weak spot in the learning abilities of hearing impaired children. Many of the unvoiced consonants and consonant blends may be indistinguishable from each other or altogether absent from speech-sound perceptions. The readiness requirements of hearing impaired children may include the training of residual hearing in a great many cases. For children with more profound losses, the mode of communication may very well include some form of manual communication. These sign-language systems have a variety of appellations, many of which may fall under the rather vague term *total communication.*

Regardless of the philosophy of instruction, mode of communication, or amount of attention to the use of residual hearing, there is an overriding readiness factor in beginning reading instruction for hearing impaired children: the level of language acquisition that individual children have attained (Hargis, 1970).

Language is comprised of a lexicon (its individual words or vocabulary), syntax (the interrelationships of the words), and figurative structures or devices. These three areas are affected by severe hearing impairment. Children do not develop linguistic competence in figurative structure until the acquisition of syntax is complete (Hargis, 1978). The language assessment to determine reading readiness will need to focus on the level of development of a child's lexicon and syntax. The chapter on assessment will present and illustrate procedures for evaluation in these areas.

Auditory perception   Auditory perception, not to be confused with auditory acuity, is frequently associated with learning disability. Other commonly used terms are *auditory discrimination* and *auditory-sequential memory.* Auditory acuity is measured by audiometric devices and tests that electronically control the pitch and loudness or intensity of the stimulus items. Auditory perception or discrimination abilities are usually measured by a few relatively simple listening procedures. On some tests children may be asked to determine differences among sounds, words, or nonsense words that vary only minimally in sound composition. Some tests require blending a group of sounds to match the name of some illustrated object. On others children may be asked to determine whether words rhyme. Auditory sequential memory is assessed by having children repeat series of digits, syllables, or words.

The results of these tests may be unduly influenced by dialectical differences. Also, apparent deficiencies in the areas assessed here may only be another symptom of a language problem or simple immaturity and not a cause, in and of itself, of a reading problem. Spache (1976) also conjectures, with considerable insight, that difficulties in these areas may be significant if they resemble those skills needed in beginning reading programs that emphasize phonics. The limited correlational strength that the tests do exhibit (mainly at the primary levels), therefore, is probably related to this skill relationship.

It does seem that readiness in terms of auditory perception would best be assessed using a more criterion-referenced approach—that is, by assessing those auditory discrimination skills, quite directly, that are required in the reading program to be used with the child being assessed.

VISUAL IMPAIRMENTS

Just as total blindness precludes the ability to read print, so severe-to-profound vision problems reduce efficiency in learning to read and in reading print. There is a remarkable adaptive power in children, however, to adjust effectively to vision defects. Consequently, research on the relationship between less severe vision problems and reading disabilities has often produced confusing results. Spache (1976) provides a comprehensive review of this research.

Children with vision problems can and do make normal progress in reading. If the child has another problem, however, even one that could normally be overlooked, the cumulative effect may produce a reading disability. This is especially true if the vision problem causes some discomfort.

There are two primary types of visual problems to consider here. Not all of the problems are equally likely to cause reading difficulty. In some cases lesser problems of the same type may be more directly related to reading disability than greater problems of another kind. A child may have more than one vision problem. Some combinations of difficulties are more likely to cause reading problems than others.

The two primary types of visual problems are with acuity or clearness of vision and binocular vision or the coordinated use of both eyes.

Acuity   Reduction in clearness or sharpness of vision can result from a variety of diseases and from injury to the various parts of the eye and its connection to the central nervous system. Harley and Lawrence (1977) review these causes and their visual consequences.

Vision screening to detect all problems in acuity and binocularity should be conducted in kindergarten and continued annually through the elementary grades. Change in vision function is common during these years of rapid growth. The incidence of injury and disease that may affect vision further emphasizes the need for regular vision screening. Vision-screening procedures will be covered in the chapter on assessment. Three common conditions that affect acuity and usually have no organic base are farsightedness *(hyperopia)*, nearsightedness *(myopia)*, and *astigmatism.*

Astigmatism is caused by irregularity in the shape of the eyes' lenses. It is impossible for such eyes to produce an exact image. The images produced will be blurred or distorted. The degree and variation of irregularity of the lens can markedly differ from one to another. Corrective lenses can assist in achieving more adequate focus in these vision problems. Children whose reduced acuity causes problems using conventional readiness materials may have to limit time spent in preparation for reading to permit relative visual comfort.

Myopia is very unlikely to cause difficulty with reading. At the readiness level this condition may create difficulty in coping with visual tasks beyond a few feet distant. The average age range of onset of myopia, however, is from 8 to 12 years. In fact, approximately 80 percent of 5-year-old children are hyperopic. Moreover, at this age they are likely to have more visual accommodative power than at any subsequent age. (Accommodation is the process of adjusting the eyes' lenses to focus clearly on an image. This is a process that requires the effort of muscles around the lens within the structure of the eye.) Most hyperopic children begin to develop better near vision after school starts. For those who remain persistently hyperopic, there is potential for difficulty. Close work that extends for periods beyond their ability to accommodate comfortably can contribute to a dislike for near-vision activities and can produce more distracted off-task time. Excessive accommodation can cause headache, eye pain, and nausea. These children will prefer, and readiness activities should capitalize on, this good distance vision. Convex lenses of proper strength can make close visual tasks more acceptable.

Hyperopia is quite likely to be overlooked by the most current vision-screening procedures. The Snellen Test, or variations thereof, is the most commonly used such device. The instrument tests only distance acuity. As a consequence, myopic children are identified and hyperopic children appear to have normal vision. If hyperopia is overlooked as a problem for the child, failure in reading is likely.

Because of the great tendency to hyperopia in most children, it is probably wise not to overemphasize fine, near-point work. Regardless of the type of acuity problem, near-distance work should be of the large-print type with clear, distinct images and illustrations. This makes accommodation easier for the hyperopic child and reduces the level of fine discrimination required of others.

Binocularity   Normal vision requires the coordinated simultaneous use of both eyes. Sets of muscles control the movement of each eye in its respective orbit. The movement of each eye must be coordinated and directed so that vision from both eyes can be fused to form a clear image. For visual activities from about twenty feet and beyond, the lines of vision for the two eyes are parallel. From about twenty feet in, the eyes must converge increasingly as the distance decreases. In normal vision with normal muscle balance, this can be done without extra effort up to the reading distance of about nine to sixteen inches, depending on the age of the individual. If there is muscle imbalance, this convergence may require abnormal effort, which can in turn cause fatigue when the reading activity extends beyond the period of easy convergence.

If the separate images perceived in each eye cannot be coordinated and fused, double vision *(diplopia)* may result. A certain amount of deficiency in binocular control can be managed through muscular effort. Double vision does occur, however, when fatigue accumulates after sustained reading. If the deficiency is great, one of the eyes may psychologically suppress the image to the brain to avoid the confusion of double vision.

The eyes must efficiently accommodate and converge according to the changing vision distance and circumstances. Impediments in the function of either eye at the reading distance are particularly important to identify. Some children who have substantially poorer acuity in one eye may resultantly have some difficulty in binocular vision. They do, in fact, have a significantly greater incidence of reading disability.

There are several types of muscle balance problems. The milder forms are placed under the general heading of *heterophoria*. Within this classification are three subcategories descriptive of the direction of the muscle imbalance. *Esophoria* is the tendency of the eye to converge or pull toward the nose. Of all "phorias" this seems to be the most troublesome for children. *Exophoria* is the tendency for the eye to pull away from the nose. The term *hyperphoria* indicates the tendency for one eye to deviate either above or below the horizontal plane which should be common to both eyes in normal vision.

When the problem is more severe and manifests itself visibly, *tropia* replaces *phoria* in technical terminology. The term *heterotropia* or *strabismus* indicates manifest deviation in muscle balance. *Esotropia,* also called "cross-eye," occurs when the eye is turned inward. With *exotropia,* or "wall-eye" the eye turns outward.

If there is an excessive difference in visual acuity in one eye when there is also a muscle imbalance, the term *amblyopia* may be used. One additional vision problem that involves muscular control is called *nystagmus*. In this case there is a rhythmic involuntary movement of the eyes.

When mild and severe binocular vision problems are compared as to their effect on readiness for reading and reading achievement, the results may seem unexpected. Children with more severe binocular problems are likely to suppress the vision in one eye at near points and read fairly effectively with the other eye. Children with lesser problems may be plagued with varieties of discomfort and pain associated with the continued exertion of coordination.

When there is a tendency for one eye to leave the point of balanced vision, then a child may receive confusing information. As the child's eyes move down a line of print and make a return sweep to the next line, the eyes must maintain accommodation and convergence. There are numerous opportunities for losing one or the other and finding a different placement in each eye. There is an even greater likelihood of difficulty with reading when *hyperopia* exists along with fusion problems.

Many children have mild vision problems difficult to identify with screening instruments. Their accommodative ability often allows them to perform within acceptable limits for the short duration of vision-screening tests. Even when the children are identified as having mild problems by a screening procedure, subsequent referral to a vision specialist may not be productive. Many marginal problems, especially binocular problems, may be called "overreferrals" by these specialists, who may be unaware of the visual demands of beginning reading instruction. The fact that a child can comfortably fuse his vision at no closer than twenty-five inches may be nothing more than interesting to an ophthalmologist, but a child required to do seat work for extended periods of time at a closer distance may associate the considerable discomfort with a dislike for reading.

Children with various forms of vision problems may benefit from glasses, eye exercises, surgery, or combinations of these. When the vision conditions change under these treatments, it is likely that some adjustment will be needed in the instructional format. Even though vision may be markedly improved, the child may still require shorter reading assignments, frequent rest periods, more distance work, and large-print materials that permit easier accommodation or fusion. In some children these adjustments may be necessary only toward the end of the school day as fatigue develops.

Visual perception   Even when a child's visual acuity and binocular vision are normal, there may be immature visual perception. Younger children pay attention to some of the main characteristics of visual stimuli, sufficient to identify or discriminate, but may not attend to finer details, such as distinguishing features of letters and words. As a consequence, they make many more errors even in matching letters or words (Harris & Sipay, 1975; Pick, 1978). Visual discrimination may be related to so-called reversal errors. The perception error may involve the orientation of letters, as in *b* and *d, p* and *q,* or *m* and *w.* It can involve orientation of letters in words, as in reversing *saw* and *was* or *on* and *no.* This kind of error declines with age and reading experience (Harley & Lawrence, 1977). Orientation makes very little difference in the visual discrimination of a preschool-age child. A car is still a car regardless of the direction it takes. A key is still a key, whatever way it is held. But a child learns that there is a great deal of difference between *b* and *d* or *w* and *m.* The research related to the developmental sequence in attaining visual skills related to letterlike figures indicates about 80-percent mastery by age 6.

The perception of these and other specific distinguishing features is related to readiness for reading. The best single predictor of first-grade reading achievement is the ability to recognize the letters of the alphabet prior to beginning reading instruction (Bond & Dykstra, 1967; Muehl & DiNello, 1976).

A variety of visual-perception tests and training programs directed to the improvement of those vision skills supposedly related to reading have been developed. The research concerning the correlation of these tests and training programs with subsequent reading achievement shows no clearly promising relationship (Buckland & Barlow, 1973; Hammill & Bartel, 1978; Keogh, 1974; Park, 1978–79). From the author's perspective the greatest benefit can be obtained from direct instruction in identification of letters and words, rather than on the perception of shapes and forms that will assumedly relate later to the ability to recognize letters and words.

The fact that maturity is involved in visual perceptual ability indicates a developmental consideration to be made for less visually mature children. Indeed, children who score lower on tests of visual perception also score lower on tests of reading readiness. Even in cases where the visual-perception problem may be caused by pathology involving the central nervous system, direct instruction seems to be the most efficient teaching approach. The format of instruction may be structured more highly to permit careful visual discrimination of letters and words according to specific distinguishing features or orientations. Problems with visual acuity and binocular vision can interfere with visual-perception maturation. Thorough vision screening ought to take priority over visual-perceptual assessment, in determining treatment and curricular adjustments.

Adjustments in reading-readiness programs

GENERAL

There are many different reading-readiness programs and tests. There are many more supposed components of readiness contained within these tests and programs than could possibly be taught if they were all included in one curriculum.

The author has included some general readiness considerations as a relatively simple but helpful list of items that can directly facilitate the beginning of reading instruction. Emphasis is laid on individual variation in development. Adequate maturation in terms of perceptual, linguistic, cognitive, and social development are essential for learning these reading-readiness components. Also required is sufficient perceptual maturation to utilize the basic format of the readiness program. The chapter on assessment provides inventories and checklists to evaluate readiness in these terms.

Normal variation in developmental rate points to extending the length of the readiness period as a necessary concession. Expanding the enriched experiences of preschool curricula for those children who may be deprived in this regard seems beneficial also. Extension of the readiness period or delaying reading instruction for many children may permit maturation of perceptual, cognitive, linguistic, and social functions resulting in more normal achievement in reading instruction.

Readiness activities should be direct, simple, and as concretely related to reading itself as possible. They should capitalize on relative strength in associative and rote learning processes whenever there is the opportunity.

The primary readiness activities should evolve from reading to the children in a variety of formats. This begins the earliest association between language in its auditory form to language in its visual form. Reading from books whose language is within the communication threshold of the child should be an extended daily activity. Daily reading of signs, labels, and captions should influence the curricula and materials in the room.

Reading to the children is gradually extended to include large story charts, experience charts, and "big books." With these activities, attention is directed from the temporal order of spoken language to the added dimensions of left-to-right and top-to-bottom sequence in printed form. Children can begin to identify the two-dimensional placement and boundaries for the spoken word as each is directly and concretely related to its visual counterpart.

The children should begin learning to identify both uppercase and lowercase manuscript forms of letters at about this time.* Writing activities, including writing their own names, is a helpful activity if there is no motor disability. The teacher can compose experience charts, and the children can recognize the constituent letters and left-to-right sequence of letter placement within words. Children will gradually perceive an increasing number of distinguishing features of words, especially the most common structure words.

Copying of short experience stories is a simple, helpful integration of language arts activities at this level. This also helps call attention to the boundaries of sentences, capital letters, and ending punctuation. Later these familiar experience stories can become the first regular independent oral-reading activity.

---

*The predictive relationship between the ability to identify letters and later reading achievement was mentioned earlier. There is an interesting, but the author feels unenlightening, controversy on the value of teaching them as a readiness activity. Chisholm and Knafle (1978) review the research and offer an experiment of their own. Research on this topic had been so far removed from direct instruction in reading as to make it of little value.

Word selection in popular basal reading programs appears to be somewhat divergent and arbitrary. Some words appear with great frequency because they have great utility in the language. They are the structure words that make up a large percentage of all print and speech. The Dolch list of 220 basic sight words contains such words. They appear with a high degree of frequency and repetition in all basal readers. A variety of word lists may provide a helpful basis for planning readiness experiences. Some of these will be discussed later. If the child has sufficient ability to benefit later from a basal reading program, the vocabulary of which it is comprised should be used in the readiness experiences. The children should become familiar with the sound and meaning of all words that they will be expected to read. This is a fundamental readiness requirement.

An additional consideration in the approach used to teach sight words to handicapped children is currently not a part of regular reading curricula: the imagery level of words. This determines to a great degree the level of difficulty of learning to recognize the printed form of words (Hargis, 1978b; Hargis & Gickling, 1978). Imagery or concreteness of words is defined as the level to which a mental image of their referent may be formed. Some nouns such as *table, horse,* or *boy* are very concrete and have a high imagery level. Other nouns such as *end, year,* and *mile* have a low imagery level. Children at kindergarten-age level and retarded children at the same mental-age levels learn to recognize nouns having high imagery much more easily than those having low imagery. Lower-imagery nouns require more repetition and use in concrete contexts to assist in their learning.

Research on structure words indicates clearly that they are much more difficult to learn than high-imagery nouns. Structure words are those that serve primarily syntactic functions in sentences—like *the, that, of, and, there, when.* It is obvious that these have low imagery. All the structure words are included on the Dolch list and other primary-grade lists. They appear with great frequency in reading material at the primary level, as they necessarily do in all discourse. Their apparent simplicity and commonness belie the great difficulty involved in learning to recognize them at sight. Too frequently these words are taught from lists and in isolation on cards, an approach frequently frustrating. They should be taught in phrases or sentences containing high-imagery words to significantly enhance ease of learning.

The lower the imagery level of words, the more their presentation must be mediated with high-imagery content. Only high-imagery nouns lend themselves to teaching from cards or lists.

Children should next begin to learn to use context to help predict unfamiliar printed words. Initially these activities will be in oral context, provided by the teacher, and a given unfamiliar (or relatively unfamiliar) printed word. Pictures that provide some context are useful also. As the child develops a repertoire of words recognized by sight, activities can be structured using those in context to help call to mind the spoken counterpart of the unfamiliar printed word.

For some children, instruction in letter-sound associations may be possible and helpful. Initially this should be limited to the sounds of consonant letters at the beginning of words. This knowledge may then be coupled with the use of context to encourage using context with initial consonant sounds to predict or call to mind unfamiliar printed words. These activities extend beyond readiness into beginning reading instruction, however.

ADAPTIONS

The social development of the child demands the first consideration. Readiness activities require attentiveness and cooperation. These may necessarily be the focus of attention for extended periods. Simple games and activities that enlist and develop attentiveness and cooperation may be necessary prerequisites to the activities outlined above. Techniques of encouraging these attributes may have to continue into the readiness period as the only major adaption.

The level of linguistic development will also be a major consideration. Hearing impaired children may have most other developmental-readiness prerequisites. This may also be true of children with specific language-learning disabilities. Instructional communication, the language of the stories, and experience charts all have to be adjusted to fall within the language level of each child. Such adjustment can create very technical problems that require the teacher to have considerable knowledge of linguistic development. More attention will be given this problem in the section on teaching methods. A scope-and-sequence chart on the acquisition of English is also provided so that the developmental level of the child can be plotted and this threshold of communication identified.

Children with milder hearing impairments may require only favorable adjustment of their acoustic environment. Placement near the teacher to allow more effective use of hearing aids and visual cues is one way of doing this. Children with more severe hearing impairments might benefit from the current generation of FM radio amplification systems, which would require that only the teacher wear a rather small, convenient transmitter microphone for contact with the child's hearing aid receiver.

The auditory perception of the various speech sounds should be assessed in all of these children. It permits the teacher to evaluate those sounds likely to pose difficulty in forming letter-to-sound associations and those that might be difficult to recognize in words that contain them.

Visually handicapped children require consideration primarily in terms of visual format. Some children qualify for materials and resource assistance if they are designated partially sighted.

Good illumination without glare, large print, sensitive balance of distance and close work, and the duration of each of these activities are primary considerations. The American Printing House for the Blind furnishes a list of commercially available materials for use with low-vision children. These materials, however, are suitable for children with the entire range of vision problems.

REFERENCES

Bloom, Lois, & Lahey, Margaret. *Language development and language disorders.* New York: John Wiley, 1978.

Bond, Guy L., & Dykstra, Robert. The cooperative research program in first-grade reading instruction. *Reading Research Quarterly,* 1967, *2*(4).

Brown, Roger. *A first language: The early stages.* Cambridge: Harvard University Press, 1973.

Bryant, Peter. *Perception and understanding in young children: An experimental approach.* London: Methuen, 1974.

Buckland, Pearl, & Balow, Bruce. Effect of visual perceptual training on reading achievement. *Exceptional Children,* 1973, *39*(4), 299–304.

Chisholm, Diane, & Knafle, June D. Letter-name knowledge as a prerequisite to learning to read. *Reading Improvement,* 1978, *15*(1), 2–7.

Chomsky, Carol. *The acquisition of syntax of children from 5 to 10.* Cambridge: Massachusetts Institute of Technology, 1969.

Farber, B. *Mental retardation: Its social context and social consequences.* New York: Houghton Mifflin, 1968.

Flavell, J. *The developmental psychology of Jean Piaget.* Princeton: Van Nostrand, 1963.

Fogelman, K. R. *Piagetian tests for the primary school.* London: National Foundation for Educational Research in England and Wales, 1970.

Furth, Hans G. *Thinking without language.* New York: Free Press, 1966.

Hammill, Donald D., & Bartel, Nettie R. *Teaching children with learning and behavior problems* (2nd ed.). Boston: Allyn & Bacon, 1978.

Hargis, Charles H. The relationship of available instructional reading materials to deficiency in reading achievement. *American Annals of the Deaf,* 1970, *115*, 27–29.

Hargis, Charles H. *An analysis of the syntactic and figurative structure of popular first grade level basal readers.* Paper presented at the 12th meeting of the Southeastern Conference on Linguistics, Washington, D.C. 1974.

Hargis, Charles H. *The syntax of conservation.* Paper presented at the 16th meeting of the Southeastern Conference on Linguistics, Atlanta, November 1976.

Hargis, Charles H. *English syntax: An outline for clinicians and teachers of language handicapped children.* Springfield: Charles C Thomas, 1977.

Hargis, Charles H. *Guidelines for the preparation of reading and language materials for hearing impaired children.* Paper presented at the National Convention of the Alexander Graham Bell Association for the Deaf, St. Louis, June 25, 1978. (a)

Hargis, Charles H. *Word recognition development as a function of imagery level.* Paper presented at the summer meeting of the Linguistic Society of America, Champaign-Urbana, University of Illinois, July 28, 1978. (b)

Hargis, Charles H., & Gickling, Edward E. The function of imagery in word recognition development. *The Reading Teacher,* 1978, *31*(8), 870–874.

Hargis, Charles H., Mercaldo, David J., & Johnson, H. Wayne. A linguistic and cognitive perspective on retardation. *Journal of Genetic Psychology,* 1975, *126,* 145–154.

Harley, Randall K. & Lawrence, Allen G. *Visual impairments in the schools.* Springfield: Charles C Thomas, 1977.

Harris, Albert J., & Sipay, Edward R. *How to increase reading ability* (6th ed.). New York: David McKay, 1975.

Huey, Edmond Burke. *The psychology and pedagogy of reading.* New York: Macmillan, 1908.

Inhelder, B. *The diagnosis of reasoning in the mentally retarded.* New York: Stein & Day, 1968.

Keogh, B. K. Optometric vision training programs for children with learning disabilities: Review of issues and research. *Journal of Learning Disabilities,* 1974, *7,* 216–231.

Kolstoe, Oliver P. *Mental retardation: An educational viewpoint.* New York: Holt, Rinehart & Winston, 1972.

Mahmoud, Cathy, & Hargis, Charles H. *The acquisition of ask/tell constructions in the language of normal, retarded and gifted children.* Paper presented at the 14th meeting of the Southeastern Conference of Linguistics, Atlanta, November 1975.

McNeill, D. Developmental psycholinguistics. In F. Smith & G. A. Miller (Eds.), *The genesis of language.* Cambridge: Massachusetts Institute of Technology, 1966.

Menyuk, Paula. *Language and maturation.* Cambridge: Massachusetts Institute of Technology, 1977.

Muehl, Sigman, & DiNello, Mario C. Early first-grade skills related to subsequent reading performance: A seven year followup study. *Journal of Reading Behavior,* 1976, *8,* 67–81.

Palermo, David S., & Molfese, Dennis L. Language acquisition from five onward. *Psychology Bulletin, 78*(6), 1972.

Park, Rosemarie. Performance on geometric figure copying tests as predictors of types of reading errors in decoding. *Reading Research Quarterly,* 1978–1979, *14,* 100–118.

Pick, Anne D. Perception in the acquisition of reading. In Frank B. Murray & John J. Pikulski (Eds.), *The acquisition of reading.* Baltimore: University Park Press, 1978.

Slobin, Dan. Cognitive prerequisites for the development of grammar. In Lois Bloom (Ed.), *Readings in language development.* New York: John Wiley, 1978.

Spache, George D. *Diagnosing and correcting reading disabilities.* Boston: Allyn & Bacon, 1976.

Stephens, W. B. Piaget and Inhelder: Application of theory and diagnostic techniques to the area of mental retardation. *Education and Training of the Mentally Retarded,* 1966, *2,* 75–86.

Woodward, M. The behavior of idiots interpreted by Piaget's theory of sensori-motor development. *British Journal of Educational Psychology,* 1959, *29,* 60–71.

3

ASSESSMENT

Purposes of assessment

Terminology used in assessment

Essentials of assessment

Some issues in reading assessment

Reading assessment

Parallel language and reading programs

3

Purposes of assessment

Several important purposes for assessment or testing relate to the teaching of reading. The first purpose is to avoid failure in reading instruction. Are the children ready to begin reading instruction or able to enter the next instructional level? The second purpose is to identify children who are having problems. Failure itself, unfortunately, is most often the indication of a problem. There are children who are making much less than optimal progress, however, who manage to meet grade-level standards. Without appropriate assessment, these children might be overlooked. The third purpose of assessment is to identify the causes of reading problems. These include organic causes, such as vision and hearing problems, and curricular difficulties. These causes, which require a variety of assessment devices, may be controlled or eliminated. The fourth purpose of assessment is the testing needed for actual teaching. The information obtained from this form of assessment can help set short-term, specific, immediate objectives for everyday reading instruction. In other words, the basic information for instructional decisions is derived from this form of assessment. The fifth purpose of assessment is for accountability. The tests used here are of the standardized or norm-referenced reading-achievement type. With these test results the reading-performance levels of individual children or groups of children can be compared to those in the general population. Performance change-over time can also be determined to evaluate the effectiveness of a teacher, a teaching method, or some new materials.

There is a bewildering variety of tests and test procedures available and used in connection with reading for handicapped children. Terminology associated with assessment sometimes adds to the bewilderment. In order to describe supposed essentials and nonessentials of testing, the author will briefly define some of this terminology—albeit subjectively in some instances. These definitions will also clarify further how current assessment procedures fit this book's position on the five basic purposes of assessment.

Terminology used in assessment

VALIDITY

The validity of the assessment devices that can be used to meet the five stated objectives must be directly related to those objectives. Procedures not so related will serve no practical purpose. Validity must be specific to the purposes of tests. The test results should provide the necessary information to fulfill the purposes of assessment. Salvia and Ysseldyke (1978) correctly assert that "to evaluate a test's validity, test users must have a clear understanding of what is to be measured. The definition of what is to be measured precedes the decision about how the measuring is to be done."

Three main types of validity are generally discussed in regard to assessment (Wallace & Larsen, 1978). The first of these is *content validity*. This refers to how well the test measures the subject-matter content and behaviors under consideration. In order to have content validity, a test must be comprised of a sufficient number of items from the topic (i.e., skill, subject area, level of development, etc.). The test, with a sufficient representation of such items, should then prove the presence or absence of development in the area being assessed.

The second form of validity is called *criterion-related validity* (Salvia & Ysseldyke, 1978; Wallace & Larsen, 1978). The degree of accuracy the assessment device provides in estimating a person's current (*concurrent validity*) or projected (*predictive validity*) performance indicates its level of criterion-related validity. The concurrent criterion-related validity of a test is usually determined by comparing it with an accepted established instrument measuring the behavior in question. Standardized reading tests frequently report in terms of other tests of the same type (the *criterion measures*). The major assumption here is that the criterion measure is itself valid in the same sense. A major shortcoming of many reading tests is their similarity to such criterion measures but dissimilarity to the criteria represented in the ultimate criterion measure, the reading curriculum. In other words, the test should relate with precision to what is being taught, not just to another test. Research by Jenkins and Pany (1978) shows that not all standardized reading tests representatively sample different reading curricula. Significant biases appear to exist suggesting that student achievement in a particular curriculum may not be reflected in achievement-test scores.

For maximum validity, both content and concurrent, teachers should have curriculum-based tests—those that sample words and skills presented on the curriculum in actual use.

Predictive validity requires a valid criterion measure. How well does a measure of reading readiness (aptitude for learning to read) predict later success in reading? Reading-readiness test items may not be made up of the future criterion measure, reading itself. The items may instead judge a number of skills (more or less subjectively) as necessary before beginning reading instruction. Once reading instruction is in progress, subsequent reading achievement can be predicted more accurately because the criterion measure (reading) is actually a part of the criterion being predicted.

Content and criterion-related validity are not easily separable. They are interdependent, in fact, in a valid test.

The third type of validity is called *construct validity*. This is a more abstract quality than the other types and so is frequently very difficult to determine. Constructs are abstractions or ideas that may be used to explain a behavior (Wallace & Larsen, 1978). They include such psychological notions as aptitude, perception, intelligence, or creativity.

The construct validity of a test is usually evaluated through indirect evidence or inference (Salvia & Ysseldyke, 1978). Validity might be established in several ways. For example, if a test of visual perception is to diagnose reading problems, it should discriminate between children with and without reading problems. Test scores on such constructs may have a correlation with reading achievement. So do IQ, family income, and chronological age, however, and they are not necessarily part of the reading process or causally related to reading deficiency. Tests measuring constructs such as perception are often used to determine causes of reading difficulty. The problem in using such tests to diagnose reading problems is in the tenuous nature of some constructs and the fact that some, such as perception, might form the basis of the educational treatment.

RELIABILITY

Reliable tests give consistent results. They are made up of well-constructed, unambiguous items. There should be little error, based on quality of the test's construction, in the results obtained. Reliable tests are dependable. Teachers tend to overevaluate the importance of a reliable test, however. Test manuals may indicate high-reliability coefficients (1.00 indicates absolute reliability; 0.00 indicates zero reliability). High reliability does not guarantee *validity* for intended use, however. Validity and reliability are occasionally confused because the coefficients used for both are the same (from 0.00 to 1.00), and there is a certain necessary relationship between the two. Reliability does not insure validity, but it is a necessary condition for it.

Reliability becomes an important consideration for teachers constructing informal or classroom curriculum-related tests because these tests are used in most of their teaching. Unless care is taken in the formulation of tests to reduce error caused by poor test items, inaccurate assessment or poor diagnostic information will be the result.

NORM-REFERENCED TESTING

Most published tests are norm referenced. This means that they have been given to groups representing any number of populations. These may be assembled by age, grade level, sex, school district, or region, for example. In this way, depending on the type of norms furnished with a test, one individual can be compared to the norm or a group's performance can be compared with normative group performance.

Such tests may be used in a variety of beneficial ways in reading. They may assess some aptitude, evaluate a program, or measure accountability. Usually, however, they are not particularly helpful in formulating specific instructional objectives—that is, unless the items contained in the test correspond very closely to those that make up the reading curriculum. Usually norm-referenced tests can sample only a few behaviors or components of a curriculum and so have limited instructional use.

CRITERION-REFERENCED TESTING

Criterion-referenced tests differ from norm-referenced tests in that they are designed to evaluate an individual's level of performance or mastery of specific instruction objectives. Criterion-referenced tests are designed to answer specific questions, rather than to make comparisons. A criterion-referenced test item might ask the question, "Can a given child spell the word *anthrax* or recognize the word *pig*?" Mastery of these specific items is indicated by the correct spelling or reading of these words. Such tests are helpful in identifying where instruction should begin and what specifically should be taught. The results also show when the student has completed or mastered the instructional objective specified in the test. Criterion-referenced test items are often linked to specific instructional objectives and follow the curricular sequence.

The adequate use of criterion-referenced tests assumes that a completely individualized curriculum has been adopted. If so, instructional decisions for individual children will be based on these test results, and individuals may take as much time as necessary to attain mastery of the objectives.

Criterion-referenced tests in reading often assess a variety of subskills assumed to be constituents of the more comprehensive ability of reading. Herein rest some of the greatest difficulties. When there are sets of assumed subskills, as Prescott (1971) and Tuinman (1978) point out, there is little value in criterion-referenced measurement without a definite hierarchy of such skills. Also, there must be validity in the assumption that mastery of one skill is essential for mastery of another in this hierarchy of complexity. Research on the hierarchy of reading subskills and evaluation of such research, however, has done little to confirm the notion that such hierarchies can be specified with precision (Bourque, 1980; Filp, 1975; Prescott, 1971; Stennett, Smythe, & Hardy, 1975; Walmsley, 1978–79). Reading achievement may be delayed pending mastery of those subskills. Even though the readiness relationship of one skill to the subsequent one is not established, children may be required to master the lower-order skills before going on to the next level.

How such objectives are formulated is remarkably subjective. Tuinman (1978) points out that whether they work for a test company or are teachers serving on a summer test construction team, test constructors basically have license to add objectives and formulate new tests endlessly. This has resulted in test proliferation and sometimes makes testing a general nuisance. There is a need for a carefully prepared set of objectives based on a scientifically prepared hierarchy of valid reading subskills. Only when such objectives are available can this type of criterion-referenced testing be really valid or useful.

Objectives and items referenced to them on tests have what might be called "face validity." In Anastasi's (1961) words, they "look valid" to people who use them. Too often the development of such subskill objectives comes to constitute the curriculum at the expense of a more broadly defined communication-process reading skill. Children achieving these subskill objectives may give the impression of "reading" achievement, though operationally they are making little progress in reading. Levels of mastery or standards of performance are frequently emphasized components in criterion-referenced testing. This is perhaps its most controversial and imprecise aspect (Glass, 1978). The word *criterion* itself is often confused with a standard or mastery level, or a cut-off score, instead of more accurately with the behavior linked to the test. What constitutes mastery or minimum competence is a very subjective notion, and requirements for a "criterion of mastery" often range from 70 percent to 98 percent of items correct on criterion-referenced tests. Glass suggests that the only sensible interpretation of data from such assessment procedures should be the observation of change and rate of change in performance, and that setting performance standards on tests by any known method may well be a waste of time.

Criterion-referenced tests should be given not merely to establish a cut-off or level of mastery but to determine specifically what is known and what is not known. In this way specific individual instructional decisions may be made.

In spite of the controversial nature of standards of performance for criterion-referenced tests, several important and utilitarian standards can be accepted. The first has to do with determining simply which curricular items in reading are known or mastered and which are not. The next is using this information to structure reading activities that are attention maintaining, an important standard for use in assessing comprehension of instructional-level reading materials. Such use of information usually requires setting a standard of at least 70-percent success. This subject will receive more attention in the sections on informal tests and reading assessment and in subsequent chapters.

TASK ANALYSIS

The process of analyzing complex skills and dividing them into component subskills to be mastered is called task analysis. Many criterion-referenced tests are based on such analyses. Johnson and Kress (1971) recognize two types of criterion-referenced tests in reading.

One type determines whether an individual can follow a set of directions dependent on reading. Can a shop student assemble a carburetor, for example, or can an individual complete an income tax form? Sight recognition of a list of printed words would represent another such test. These tests measure overall reading skill.

The other type of criterion-referenced test measures *progress toward* mastery of a complex skill or ability. Here criterion-referenced tests are used more diagnostically. Suppose that during oral reading a child is not able to identify a number of words in his third-grade-level reader. A teacher may analyze each of these words in terms of their letter-sound associations or other structural characteristics. A test can then be constructed that will require the use of these word-analysis techniques. The teacher can then ascertain which of these word-analysis skills has not been mastered and where the apparent impediment to identifying the words in the reading selection is. The teacher then can determine how far from attaining mastery of these subskills the child is. Further task analysis of the steps leading to mastery of the subskill will require development of a criterion-referenced test to determine what constitutes mastery of each of these steps. Theoretically it is possible to break any task down to irreducibly small units.

Any of the broader objectives or skills presented can be analyzed this way to formulate specific objectives. Criterion-referenced tests can thus be prepared to monitor progress, placing a child more accurately on the learning "ladder" of subskills to be climbed to reach mastery of the more complex objective. As with establishing hierarchies of subskills, the big problem with task analysis in reading is that what constitutes reading subskills, including many of the word-analysis or decoding subskills, has not been verified as essential. This is true both in terms of sequencing and interrelatedness.

If such subskills are not verified or verifiable as a part of a major skill, they probably should not be made objectives. Certainly if a child is able to acquire, or already demonstrates, mastery of the complex skill, there seems little reason to add subskills to a list of objectives for that child.

Task analysis can produce an inordinate number of objectives. In reading it is possible to identify an amazing variety of subskills. Often they seem to become increasingly abstract (syllabication rules, r-controlled vowels and g-plus-vowel rules) instead of simpler and more manageable.

In assessment, simpler, more encompassing skills should be tested first to eliminate minute and only tenuously appropriate steps. In this way progress to the next level of instruction may proceed without impediment. If a child demonstrates skill in the larger objective, one need not teach a supposed subskill simply because it was missed on a test.

This rule of simplicity should be followed in task analysis. If a supposed subskill seems more complex than the skill of which it is an assumed constituent, the subskill should not be an objective for teaching. A more direct approach is warranted.

INFORMAL ASSESSMENT

Informal assessment usually refers to teacher-made tests. One of the most widely used informal assessment procedures is the informal reading inventory. This procedure was first described by Betts (1946). Its primary use is to identify the level of difficulty in reading selections in terms of any given child's reading ability. Betts described three reading levels: the independent or recreational level, the instructional level, and the frustration level. The *instructional level* is the level of reading difficulty appropriate for guided reading instruction. The *independent or recreational level* is the level at which the child can read without teaching assistance. The *frustration level* begins where the child's reading comprehension drops off and attention may not be easily maintained without signs of tension. The levels of difficulty for each of these reading levels is shown in the following table.

Independent or recreational level	Instructional level	Frustration level
fewer than 2% unknown words	2–4% unknown words	more than 4% unknown words
90% or better comprehension	75% or better comprehension	50% and below comprehension

This type of informal assessment is an important criterion-referenced testing procedure. The level of performance is clearly specified, and the selections can have direct relevance to the curriculum if the reading selections that constitute the test are those that the child is using. The child's behavior (the attainment of reading skill on the reading material being used) can most adequately be evaluated by this method. Also the suitability of reading materials for use with any child can best be determined. Selections of from 100 to 150 words are taken from those materials to be evaluated. The child reads the passage orally, the teacher records the errors, and then the child answers the comprehension questions.

As simple as the procedure sounds, a number of difficulties are associated with its use (Spache, 1976b; Wallace & Larsen, 1978). Too often it is used as a standardized test to obtain grade-level scores, rather than to fit specific material to specific children. A detailed discussion of the informal-reading inventories is presented further on in the chapter.

Teacher-made tests are often used to test parts of the reading curriculum if no other test is available. These can be a most effective means of testing the specific objectives formulated for specific children. Wallace and Larsen (1978) view this precision of informal-assessment techniques (in pinpointing specific skill strengths and weaknesses) a distinct advantage of this approach.

SCREENING

Screening tests are used, or should be, to avoid placing a child in a failure situation. They should also be used to discover which children are apparently making less progress in reading than they could potentially achieve. Vision, hearing, and readiness tests should routinely be administered for the former reason. Various types of group intelligence measures as well as norm-referenced achievement tests can be used for the latter purpose. As the name implies, screening instruments should be used to refer children for further evaluation so that intervention can be planned with sufficient detail.

Screening instruments may lack precision. Inaccuracy in the direction of over-referral from such instruments, however, is preferable to under-referral. Screening tests may be used effectively to narrow down the location of reading difficulty or level of achievement. This permits more efficient use of diagnostic or more detailed criterion-referenced tests.

DIAGNOSIS

Educational diagnosis usually refers to the assessment procedures used to identify the specific needs of students with learning problems. Traditionally it has been associated with the identification of the etiology of the problem, the classification of the handicapping condition, or the labeling of children.

The current notion of diagnosis makes it a guide to the instructional process. It is considered a part of a model of teaching variously called diagnostic-prescriptive, -corrective, or -remedial. In this approach to teaching, assessment is carefully articulated with the instruction being provided.

Two approaches to diagnosis and to diagnostic-prescriptive methods are associated with reading instruction for handicapped children (Haring & Bateman, 1977; Salvia & Ysseldyke, 1978). The first of these is the process- or ability-training model, and the second is the task-analysis model.

In the *process-training model,* the focus of diagnosis is usually on the identification of perceptual, psycholinguistic, or psychomotor ability deficits, assumed to be the cause of some learning difficulty. The treatment or prescription will be designed either to remediate or to bypass the deficit in whichever process it is found.

In the *task-analysis model,* when a child fails in reading, assessment is used to identify the weakness in skill development that has caused the problem. The treatment or prescription is designed to remediate the weakness.

Advocates of the process-training approach assume that there is a valid construct underlying their theoretical position. There is, however, little evidence to support this assumption. Advocates of the task-analysis approach assume that there are valid hierarchies of subskills in reading that can be analyzed and arranged sequentially. This is likely too grand an assumption.

Both approaches claim that strengths and weaknesses are assessed. In fact, however, the focus of diagnosis and the subsequent intervention emphasize weakness or skill deficiency. There are no stated formulas or systematic approaches to balancing the measurement of weakness and strength and then programming them equitably through the prescription.

The term *diagnosis* in education implies the identification of a problem, but it is critical to identify what children know or what skills they have. This information is necessary to prepare instructional materials and activities that maintain attention and induce success. The author has too often fallen into the diagnostic trap of identifying varieties of "deficiencies," planning a variety of activities meant to address them, only to find that these activities were frustrating and unproductive. This happened because the work was comprised largely of items that the child did not know or had not mastered. Success must be programmed relating unknowns to knowns. Assessment, therefore, must focus on what children know.

SENSORY ASSESSMENT

The terms *screening* and *diagnosis* can be appropriately applied to vision and hearing assessment in the schools. The tests used in screening should identify those children who may have a vision or hearing problem that might contribute to reading difficulty. The instruments and procedures used in vision and hearing assessment should be quite sensitive to the various sensory functions associated with reading. They should be sensitive to the point of over-referral so that the fewest possible number of children will be missed in the screening process. Unfortunately little attention is paid to the visual functioning of students who experience reading difficulties (Spache, 1976b). It is also an unfortunate fact that only a few states require any sort of hearing screening in the schools (Hargis, 1976a).

Vision screening should include tests of visual acuity for both near and distant points. They should also assess the coordinated function of both eyes in this area.

Hearing screening should assess auditory acuity in representative frequencies critical to the discrimination of spoken language. The usual sequence of childhood health problems and the normal physiological changes that occur during the primary grades make an annual program of hearing and vision screening very important.

AUDITORY AND VISUAL PERCEPTION

Auditory and visual acuity are not to be confused with auditory and visual perception. As Strauss and Lehtinen (1947) point out, perception is a mental function that lies between thought and the sensory functions of sight and hearing. It is the step between sensation and the highest form of cognitive function.

Perceptual and perceptual-motor tests have a history of use as diagnostic instruments for identifying brain injury. There was an increase in use of the instruments to diagnose learning disabilities up until the early 1970s. At about this time the cumulative research evidence showed that most tests of perception were unreliable and that training in perceptual skill areas provided no significant benefits in any areas of academic achievement (Arter & Jenkins, 1979; Hammill & Bartel, 1978; Salvia & Ysseldyke, 1978; Seaton, 1977; Wallace & Larsen, 1978). The author shares the view of Frank Smith (1978), who states simply that if a child has enough auditory skill to have learned spoken language and enough visual acuity to distinguish a pin from a paper clip, he has sufficient perceptual abilities to learn to read. Though his analogy seems somewhat casual, it suggests the most straightforward way of assessing auditory and visual perception as they relate to learning to read. Significant auditory perceptual problems will impair language learning and communication. This can be most usefully assessed through language-comprehension tests. Visual perception can most usefully be assessed by determining if a child can visually identify or discriminate among small common objects or shapes that have visual discrimination demands similar to those of letters and words.

DISCREPANCIES

The discrepancy between achievement and aptitude has for a long time been a measure associated with learning disabilities and remedial reading. Comparing a student's academic aptitude with achievement is necessary to determine who will benefit from special remedial help. Remedial instruction is required for dealing with discrepancies. If poor academic achievement represents actual aptitude, a student does not require remedial intervention. There is no discrepancy gap to close.

There has been a wide variety of methods for comparing aptitude with achievement. As is pointed out in an article on achievement-aptitude discrepancies (Hanna, Dyck, & Holen, 1979), however, attempts to make this seemingly simple comparison are frequently complicated.

To identify children with learning disabilities, comparisons between aptitude and achievement should be made on standard instruments or instruments with the same norm groups. The discrepancy in reading most likely to arise has to do with the relevance of the aptitude measure. Aptitude measures should be as relevant as possible to the area of achievement under consideration. Certainly a verbal measure is more relevant to reading achievement than a nonverbal aptitude measure. For the teacher, or for screening purposes, listening comprehension of graded reading passages is probably adequate. If a child is reading instructionally at a grade level substantially below that at which at least 75-percent comprehension is attained from listening, some discrepancy is present. This is also a more valid approach to determining discrepancies in the formulation of instructional objectives.

CASE HISTORY

Knowledge of students' development and background may well provide insight into their learning problems.

Some information may have obvious relevance to the form of remedial action in the classroom. Information on language spoken in the home, for example, could directly influence the curriculum. How much sleep the child gets or what he has to eat for breakfast may affect his behavior in school. Excessive stress, which may well affect school performance, can result if a child must face daily threats or abuse from a bully or a gang.

Information from a child's past in family and community as well as attention to the child's current status in these regards should be of constant interest or concern. Health and nutritional information may be similarly enlightening. Growling empty stomachs are seldom conducive to attention even under ideal teaching conditions. The children who routinely breakfast on cola and potato chips are as likely to benefit from a nutritional intervention as from an instructional one.

Essentials of assessment

In the face of the multitude of tests available and promoted, it can be difficult to maintain focus and simplicity in the approach to reading assessment.

The essentials of assessment, in the author's view, are related to the five purposes covered earlier in the chapter. They make it possible to focus better and to limit the scope of assessment.

AVOIDING FAILURE

The time to prevent a child's failure in reading is before reading instruction starts. We seem to rush to start reading instruction, then once it is begun make every effort to force children to achieve grade-level standards. The inevitable result of these practices is failure for too large a percentage of children.

Measurement of readiness for beginning reading is vitally important. Equally important is that information gained concerning lack of readiness be acted upon. A delay of instruction, some compensatory programming, or a prolongation of the readiness period from a few months to even a year or two should be institutionalized options of every reading curriculum. Failure and its attendant stress and frustration are to be avoided.

Reading-readiness tests have long been criticized for their imprecise prediction of reading achievement. The predictive validity of popular tests of reading readiness (the correlation between test score and reading achievement at the end of first grade) ranges from about .50 to .70. Correlation coefficients of this size are substantial in terms of predictions for groups of children. Granted, such coefficients do not permit accurate prediction of reading achievement for individual students, but these tests do predict failure in specific children with considerable accuracy. The most important use of readiness tests is to locate preschoolers or kindergartners likely to fail, not to predict specific achievement levels.

Standardized reading-readiness tests should accurately identify 80 percent of the children who are not ready. In order to be effective, a standardized reading-readiness test should have a reported reliability coefficient of about .90 or better. When using such standardized instruments, the results should be moderated by teacher judgment. The tests effectively predict potential failures. These children should be carefully observed and evaluated. Some children fail because of factors not related to the abilities sampled by such tests. For these children, teacher judgment and information on background and family may be the only means of identifying potential difficulties.

Some popular reading-readiness tests that may be used with good results are Gates-MacGinitie Reading Skills Test,* Harrison-Stroud Reading Readiness Profiles, MacMillan Reading Readiness Test, Metropolitan Readiness Tests, Clymer-Barrett Pre-reading Battery, and Murphy-Durrell Reading Readiness Analysis. These tests have the advantages of easy group administration, high reliability, and predictive validity. Harris and Sipay (1975) further recommend the Monroe Reading Aptitude Tests. Parts of this instrument have the limitation of individual administration, which makes time a problem in screening. Walker Readiness Test for Disadvantaged Preschool Children is individually administered and takes about ten minutes per child. (It was standardized for use with almost twelve thousand Head Start and day care center children.)

Predictive validity and reliability are important factors in selecting reading-readiness tests, but there are other considerations as well. Not the least of these are ease and speed of administration. Group tests can be used in screening and are less time consuming than individual tests. For a group of students with special needs clearly outside the norm, the standardized tests may not be so accurate in determining readiness as a more specialized instrument. Standardized tests are fairly accurate in finding the high-risk children but do not supply information concerning readiness for reading instruction in the deficit area. If a child is identified through screening as having a readiness deficit in the area of language, for example, an instrument specific to this area of assessment will be needed. With it the teacher can determine when the child has attained the necessary entry-level language ability.

Low scores on readiness tests should direct the teacher to other screening procedures. If vision and hearing screening are not generally required, they should be made available at least for those children who show a readiness deficit.

Many schools use group intelligence tests. The predictive validity in terms of reading achievement is often comparable to

---

*Lists of the mentioned tests are in Appendix A.

that of acceptable reading-readiness tests. They can be used efficiently in screening in much the same way as the reading-readiness tests. Harris and Sipay find the following group acceptable in a reading-readiness function: Pintner-Cunningham Primary Test, Otis-Lennon Mental Ability Test, Primary I, SRA Primary Mental Abilities, California Test of Mental Maturity, Pre-Primary Battery, and Kuhlman-Anderson Measure of Academic Potential.

Some children with severe hearing impairments may have been identified before starting school. Regardless of how they have been identified, any of the children with significant hearing impairment should receive further language assessment. As was mentioned in Chapter 2, these children may have their reading-readiness problems and requirements best defined in terms of their level of language attainment. Hearing impairment can be very disruptive to normal language development in terms of both vocabulary and syntax. A suspected or confirmed hearing impairment warrants detailed language assessment.

Children with a learning disability in language (regardless of cause), those with a meager background of experience, or others from a different cultural and/or linguistic background may have language-readiness deficiencies similar to, if somewhat less severe than, the hearing impaired.

The language requirements of all popular basic reading programs assume comprehension mastery of their constituent vocabularies and all English syntax (Hargis 1974, 1977). Nearly all readiness tests and the aforementioned group intelligence tests have vocabulary subtests. Any indication of a verbal deficit in readiness warrants more detailed assessment.

The Peabody Picture Vocabulary Test (PPVT) is one that can be easily administered by a teacher to obtain a good estimate of the vocabulary component of a child's level of language functioning. Norms on the PPVT are based on ages from 2 up.

In the area of syntax assessment, the Test for Auditory Comprehension of Language is appropriate for readiness determination. Norms are available for ages 3-11 to 6-11. The Northwestern Syntax Screening Test is also potentially helpful. It has norms for ages 3-11 to 7-11. Though these instruments are for screening purposes, they will provide readiness information in regard to this specific language area.

The Test of Language Development has both vocabulary and syntax among its subtests. It incorporates the essential features of the two previously mentioned syntax tests. The test has language ages and scaled scores for children aged 4-0 and 8-11.

The most comprehensive syntax test developed for use with younger, profoundly deaf children (about age 4 and older) is the curriculum-referenced test in use at the Tennessee School for the Deaf. This test of comprehension of syntactic structure is used for the placement of children in the scope and sequence of the language-development curriculum. This test has representative items from all the major syntactic structures arranged in sequence from beginning levels to mastery. The mastery level indicates sufficient language readiness skill for using standard reading materials for instruction. This test was developed and is used only at the Tennessee School for the Deaf curriculum for language teaching. No standardization information is available.

The Test of Syntactic Ability is a comprehensive measure of syntax acquisition that can be used, and has been nationally standardized, with deaf children of age 10 and older. The standardization data from the test are a testimonial to the severe language-readiness deficit of the congenitally deaf. Syntactic structures that must be mastered before beginning regular reading materials are still lacking in most deaf children of age 10 and older.

Reading instruction may begin when children who are severely language handicapped are otherwise cognitively ready, but the reading instruction and materials must incorporate controls over whichever linguistic structures these children may be lacking. This requires carefully criterion-referenced assessment, the criterion being the scope and sequence of normal language acquisition in comprehension terms. As the language-development program proceeds, the reading which is carefully articulated with it proceeds as well. When children demonstrate mastery over the previously missing language structures, readiness is established, and at some level entry to regular reading materials is possible.

In order to avoid failure, children moving from one grade or level of instruction to the next must have their readiness for the next level established. Here criterion-referenced tests are appropriate. These tests are referenced carefully to the curriculum. Samples of the scope and sequence of the reading instructional materials form the basis of assessment. The tests can verify readiness for the next level of instruction by testing students using material they have covered or will encounter. If the material is sequential and/or related, as in a basal reading program, satisfactory performance on the instructional material preceding may be sufficient evidence of readiness for the next level.

Listening comprehension can be used to estimate readiness for the next level of instruction. This may be especially helpful in terms of language readiness. A selection or story from the next level of instruction is read to the student, and comprehension is measured to establish language readiness. In this otherwise appealingly simple assessment procedure, formulating unreliable comprehension questions is the greatest hazard.

The Diagnostic Reading Scales reading-assessment device is apparently the only standardized test in which evidence of reliability and predictive validity for listening comprehension are reported. The scales contain reading selections that are well graded in difficulty, each with comprehension questions. The selections may be presented orally to test listening comprehension. Insofar as these graded selections, or for that matter any graded selections so used, represent the reading-difficulty levels in the actual curriculum, they can be helpful.

It is important to remember that standardized reading tests are usually not sufficiently correlated with specific reading programs to warrant their use as readiness determinants for promotion of individual children. Specific criterion-referenced measurement, in which the criterion is the curriculum in actual use, is essential to avoidance of failure.

Cognitive/linguistic development may be informally assessed through measures of some cognitive structure described by Piaget. Preoperational cognitive development is probably related to readiness for reading. Murray (1978) notes the relation of specific operational features to reading comprehension. He further states that operational thought may be a sufficient, if not necessary, condition for reading.

Informal measures of specific operational structures can be used as readiness measures. Following directions that contain some of the elements of conservation, such as seriation or transitivity, can give a very good indication of both cognitive and language readiness (Hargis, 1976b). Language is assessed in that certain sentence forms must be used to elicit judgments or actions that are indicative of components of operational thought. Conditional and comparative subordinate clauses, and certain coordinating conjunctions, such as "but," are essential linguistic components.

Verbal directions such as the following contain some such sentence structures and can elicit responses at the late preoperational level.

If the cow is bigger than the horse, (then) put the pig in the box.

If it is the biggest animal, (then) put the horse in the truck.

The avoidance of failure should be a primary function of assessment. This book attempts to keep the number of assessment procedures to a minimum. Often informal measures will be necessary. These frequently are of the criterion-referenced (curriculum-referenced) type. When informal measurement is necessary, problems of test reliability arise.

FINDING PROBLEMS

It is unfortunate that it so often takes a child's failure to confirm the existence of a problem. Failure in reading instruction should not be the primary instrument of identification. Children never should be required to fail before appropriate instructional measures are taken.

Failure can occur in two ways. The more obvious way is when a child falls behind the ongoing level of instruction in the classroom. The inability to do the required work stands out and is frequently accompanied by additional distracting problems. This failure may be characterized by the discrepancy between grade or curriculum requirements and the level of functional reading ability of the child. The second type of failure occurs when a child does not measure up to his or her potential for achievement. This aptitude and achievement discrepancy was discussed earlier in the chapter. If a student has a reading achievement potential above the grade level of placement but is functioning well only at that grade level, there is a discrepancy. There may be no attendant stress or other failure-related behavior because instructional demands do not exceed the child's reading level. For this reason it is doubly likely to go unnoticed. Some would not label this type of discrepancy as a "learning disability" if it occurred in gifted children.

Even among those failing to achieve grade-level standards, there are frequent cases of aptitude-achievement discrepancy. Failure begets failure in reading instruction, so children are likely to fall further and further behind their achievement potential. Bateman (1965) noted the significance of discrepancy in providing special or remedial services. If a child is achieving up to an accurately established achievement potential, and instructional demands are matched to this level, appropriate educational services are probably being provided.

Information gained from reading-achievement measurement should be tempered by information on potential. Some major difficulties to overcome are measured in terms of this discrepancy. Certainly the very existence of a reading deficiency is most fundamentally determined by an aptitude-achievement discrepancy.

A definite problem exists if a student is not progressing as well as capability permits. A measure of potential is required to ascertain the existence of a problem (discrepancy).

The measure of potential or aptitude should be as relevant as possible to reading achievement. Verbal measures are more relevant to the measure of reading potential than nonverbal measures are. In children who have some linguistic disadvantage, as in the case of hearing impaired children or children for whom English is a second language, however, nonverbal measures may be a necessary compromise. The nonverbal or performance halves of the Wechsler Scales (WPPSI, WISC-R, WAIS) have been frequently used with hearing impaired children. Also used are the Arthur adaption of the Lieter International Performance Scale, The Nebraska Test of Learning Aptitude, Goodenough-Harris Drawing Test, Columbia Mental Maturity Scale, and the Raven Progressive Matrices. Use of most of these tests requires some special training. Moreover, adequate administration of tests to hearing impaired children in particular requires experience with this group.

Even though there is the constant probability of underestimating potential, group intelligence-test information may be sufficient if tempered by teacher judgment. The Slosson Intelligence Test is a verbal-oriented individual test that does not require special training to administer. If there are questions concerning the results of a group test, a teacher may follow up with an instrument like this in order to obtain a fairer estimate of a child's potential. Other individual tests may require specially trained personnel. The Wechsler or the Stanford-Binet tests might well be considered, especially if there is a possibility that a child's potential has been underestimated. Teacher judgment and the child's background need to remain a moderating influence on the information obtained from these tests as well.

The most relevant aptitude measure of all is quite likely to be a measure of listening-comprehension level. A standardized measure of listening comprehension was previously discussed in conjunction with readiness. The instrument containing it is the Diagnostic Reading Scales. Each of the graded reading selections is matched with considerable precision to the reading level of each grade. The reliability of the comprehension questions is established. The discrepancy, if any, can be determined by using the test for establishing both the instructional reading level and the listening comprehension level of a child.

Informal tests of reading level and listening comprehension are potentially the most relevant. In this instance, selections are taken from each of the grade levels of reading materials being used by that particular student. The procedure followed in preparing this test is the one outlined for informal reading inventories. The instrument is administered as an informal reading inventory, and the highest instructional reading level is established. From this level up, the reading selections are read aloud by the examiner, and the level of comprehension through listening is determined. The listening-capacity level is the highest level at which the student attains 70-percent comprehension. The informal approach has the advantage of being most criterion referenced. It is directly related to the reading instructional materials to be used. The relevance of the assessment information is thereby insured. Problems in measuring comprehension and formulating comprehension questions pose the greatest difficulty in this informal procedure. These problems and proposed solutions will be discussed in later sections.

FINDING CAUSES OF READING PROBLEMS

Once a reading problem is identified, its cause should be determined. In many instances the cause of a problem is the result of a mismatch between the level of reading instruction and the current reading ability of a child. A number of problems, however, do not have roots in the school's curriculum and instructional methods. These problems may have as their source causes to be found within the child or his environment. They may be eliminated outside the educational framework if they are identified.

Teacher judgment in the observation of the child's health is particularly important. The child's environment out of school may be the source of a difficulty. Here again, teacher observation and judgment will be the necessary diagnostic tools. Conditions related to health and nutrition must be handled through the child's home or through medical referral. Some vision and hearing problems can be alleviated directly through opthalmological/optometric or otological/audiological service. Medication, glasses, or hearing aids may suffice, and the curriculum for the child may be very little affected.

Others, however, may require alterations in the instruction format. Those more severely handicapped, especially the hearing impaired, may require major revisions in their curriculum. At any rate, identification is necessary in all of these instances.

Vision screening As Spache (1976b) points out, vision screening in most schools is still overemphasizing the importance of visual acuity at far point. The Snellen Chart, developed in 1862, is still the most widely used screening instrument, although it only measures acuity at twenty feet. Near-distance vision activity, however, most of which is at less than twenty inches, makes up an exceedingly large portion of the visual requirements of reading. The Snellen test provides no indication of near-distance acuity or binocular function (the effective simultaneous use of both eyes at a reading distance). Both of these should be tested.

The popularity of the Snellen test as a screening procedure is at least in part related to the medical emphasis on the measurement of distance visual acuity and to the legal classification system for the determination of impaired vision (20/70 to 20/200 in the better eye) and blindness (greater than 20/200 in the better eye).

Prevailing practices in vision screening, as well as the primary definitions for visual impairment, have prevented the majority of children who have binocular and other near-distance vision problems from being identified or served. Many children whose vision problems affect near-distance function in reading could benefit from some of the devices and methods used with low-vision children.

Spache (1976a) limits his recommendations for vision screening procedures and instruments to four. These are the Keystone Visual Survey Tests, the Ortho-Rater, the Professional Vision Tester, and the Titmus Biopter. A complete reference to these will be found in Appendix A. Spache recommends the use of his own test (Spache Binocular Reading Test) to supplement each of the others. This test, which can be inserted in any stereoscope, measures the relative binocular participation of both eyes in a sustained reading activity. It is an important additional test to use if there is any indication of a binocular problem. The Keystone Tests of Binocular Skills is also a sustained reading test.

The greatest criticism of these instruments is their tendency to over-refer. The Ortho-Rater may be the least prone to do this. All of the instruments are accurate in identifying most children with difficulties in the important visual functions. Far better the tendency to over-referral than to miss 60 percent of the children who need attention. Over-referral, of course, means that a child with no vision problem, according to the definition of the term, is referred for help unnecessarily to a professional. If the professional's definition does not completely concur with the evaluation of the problems noted by the screening procedure, this discrepancy in definition will constitute much of the scope of over-referrals. Reliability of the screening procedure itself will account for the remainder.

Regardless of the level of assistance provided when a referral is made to some professional, the teacher should be apprised of the problem and should be prepared to act accordingly.

Spache lists a variety of informal tests that may be helpful in the absence of the recommended screening instruments. They may also be used to confirm the results from one of the recommended screening procedures, especially if the results seemed ambiguous or equivocal. The first group of four are to test binocular function.

Skeffington String Test. A two-to-three-foot string is knotted sixteen inches from one end. Without blocking the vision from either eye, the examiner or the subject holds this end of the string on the bridge of the nose and the other end directly in front of the subject. The subject is asked to look at the knot and tell how many strings are seen. The subject should see two strings forming a *V* at the knot. Children may have to show how the string appears to them with their hands. If the subject sees two strings crossing before the knot, overconvergence *(esophoria)* is indicated. If the strings cross behind the knot, underconvergence *(exophoria)* is indicated. Seeing only one string indicates suppression. If one string and knot appear higher than the other, a vertical imbalance *(hyperphoria)* is indicated.

Cover Test. The subject focuses on a shiny object or small light held at arm's length directly in front, level with the eyes. A card covers one eye, then is quickly removed. The examiner notes if the covered eye shifts position. This test is repeated for the other eye. Both eyes should be checked several times.

Pursuits Test. The examiner moves a shiny object or light in an arc with a radius of about sixteen to eighteen inches from the subject's eyes. The object is moved smoothly up and down in a vertical arc, from left to right in a horizontal arc, and in repeated diagonal arcs. The object can be smoothly rotated in any of these planes also. The eyes should move smoothly with the movement and light reflected in both eyes continuously.

Binocular Test. The subject holds up a finger at arm's length in the direction of a small target object at some distance beyond. The subject is directed to look past the finger to the more distant object. The subject should see two fingers. Have the subject change focus to the fingers. He should then see two of the more distant targets.

The next two tests are for accommodation-convergence.

Pencil Test. Move a vertically held pencil in a horizontal plane toward the subject's nose. Have the subject tell you at what point two pencils can be seen. Watch for sudden divergence of one eye. Repeat the test several times. If the subject sees two pencils or one eye diverging before the pencil reaches a point about five inches from the nose, a problem is indicated.

Point-to-Point Test. Have the subject jump the eyes from a point of focus on an object at near distance (fourteen to eighteen inches) to a point of focus across the room upon a signal. The subject should identify a well-known word at a distant point of focus. Uncover the word as a signal is given. The subject should say the word without hesitation. The test can be reversed so that the change to a near point can be tested.

Spache points out that a number of vision studies have shown that planned observation by teachers can aid considerably in the detection of children with problems. The following checklist of symptoms has been validated by comparison with professional examination:

> reddened eyes or eyelids
> encrusted eyelids or sties
> tearing
> burning or itching eyes with sustained work
> headaches with sustained close work
> nausea with sustained close work
> dizziness with sustained close work
> blurring of print with sustained reading
> one eye drifting in or out at times
> squint, closure, or covering of one eye
> head tilting while reading or writing
> constant blink while reading
> book held in an unusual position
> frequent errors in copying from chalkboard to paper
> early fatigue and avoidance of close work
> excessive left-to-right head movements while reading
> forward strain to see distant objects

Hearing screening   Screening for hearing acuity should be a normal annual assessment procedure through the primary grades. Portable pure-tone audiometers are the instruments normally used in schools for hearing screening. They must be used individually. At one time a number of group hearing tests were used for hearing screening. They have been largely replaced with pure-tone audiometers because of their superior reliability.

A number of acceptable pure-tone audiometers are available for screening purposes. Those that have been manufactured in the United States since 1970 conform to the specifications of the American National Standards Institute (ANSI). They may be considered basically identical in respect to their minimum screening-test capabilities. These instruments can accurately screen for problems in hearing acuity, given adequately quiet test conditions and a modest amount of training for the tester. A list of some of these audiometers is included in Appendix A.

These instruments are good indicators of the existence of a hearing problem. Two procedures can be used with these instruments to detect hearing problems. The pure-tone screening test usually entails checking each of the frequencies—500, 1000, 2000, and 6000 Hz at twenty-five decibels, and 4000 Hz at thirty decibels. A tone at each of these frequencies at the indicated levels of loudness is presented, to discover if the subject can respond. This is done for both ears. If a child fails to hear any of the tones in one or both ears, the test is repeated. The child who fails the second screening procedure may then be given a pure-tone threshold test. Here the threshold of hearing sensitivities may be determined. This means that the loudness in decibels of the faintest sounds that can just be perceived is identified. The procedure is more lengthy than for screening and demands a quiet test area. The criteria for failure is the same as for the screening procedure. Referral for audiological or medical services is warranted if there is evidence of reduced hearing at any of the tested frequencies. A hearing loss of as little as twenty-five decibels can definitely have implications in causing reading difficulty.

If annual hearing screening is not required for all children, it should be available at least for children who show some discrepancy in readiness or achievement. The results of any individual test of intelligence administered to any child should be accompanied by hearing screening results. If not, the intelligence-test results should not become a part of a child's permanent records or be used in placement. If there is evidence of significant hearing impairment, the validity of intelligence-test results must immediately be called into question.

The frequency of illness and infections of the middle ear at the primary-grade levels makes teacher observation a necessary adjunct to hearing screening. A child with chronic cold symptoms should be watched carefully and medical referral made if involvement of the middle ear is evident. If a child complains of an earache, especially accompanied by a cold, a referral is warranted. Indications of drainage from the ears suggests that the medical referral is long overdue.

TESTING FOR TEACHING

Public Law 94-142 requires that each handicapped child receiving special education and related services have an individualized education program (IEP). The IEP document is to include the child's present level of educational performance, a statement of annual goals, short-term objectives, and appropriate criteria for determining whether instructional objectives are being achieved. These, among other requirements, are directly related to assessment for reading instruction.

Testing for teaching reading requires several types of assessment to fulfill actual instructional needs as well as the legal requirements of the IEP. Basically, to fulfill the requirements of the IEP, the annual assessment procedures must include several dimensions. Assessment must provide information concerning a child's present level of educational performance. Here, both norm-referenced and curriculum-referenced reading achievement tests can be used. Norm-referenced tests may be used to identify a child's reading skill according to norms appropriate for him. The child's age, socioeconomic, and cultural background should be considered. Beyond having appropriate normative information, the assessment devices should be adapted for use with children who have sensory or physical disabilities. Probably the best example of a norm-referenced achievement test for use with a group of handicapped children is the special edition of the Stanford Achievement Test, which was adapted for hearing impaired children. This form, available through the Office of Demographic Studies at Gallaudet College, has undergone extensive normative study with a representative population of hearing impaired children in the United States.

Present level of reading ability can be determined more realistically relative to other, similar children if this normative information and/or adaptions are available. The kind of information gained from these tests is necessary to evaluate the productivity of the instructional process better.

Curriculum-referenced tests should be used to identify the child's current level of functioning within the reading curriculum in use. A starting place or readiness level is most accurately established through this form of assessment.

More comprehensive results and reading skill levels can be obtained from this use of norm-referenced and curriculum-referenced testing. These results can be used in formulating annual goals and short-term objectives. An appropriate measure of reading potential is also necessary if reasonable attainable goals and objectives are to be prepared for all students.

The IEP provision in the law is open to wide interpretation and is an area of controversy. It represents, however, at least in general terms, what is generally preferred practice. And as Royer and Schumer (1976) report, teachers' predictions (objectives and goals) based on careful assessment of elementary-aged children in remedial reading programs, showed that children made significantly greater gains.

Besides these general assessment devices, there must be routine direct evaluation based on instruction and materials in daily use. Evaluation is a major component of the instructional process itself. This evaluation is detailed curriculum-referenced measurement.

The essentials of testing for teaching must be determined in large part by the curriculum. Test content must reflect what is being taught or the test is not useful for making instructional decisions. As Howell, Kaplan, and O'Connell (1979) point out, if a teacher uses a test designed to cover the content of the concepts and skills that have been presented to the learner, the content validity will be high. If another measure is used, however, the correlation between the materials presented and the test items may not be so high. The results of tests deficient in content validity may conflict with the observed performance in the classroom.

Occasionally teachers or school psychologists administer diagnostic tests to children with apparent reading difficulty. The motivation for using such tests can be quite varied (habit, training, availability, popularity, etc.). The tests themselves may have no relevance to the child's curriculum. Deficiencies in skills, processes, or aptitudes are invariably identified, but often the deficiency has little relation to what is going on in reading instruction. Identification of the deficiency prompts the development of ancillary remedial curricula to deal with any supposed deficit. Sometimes these parallel or replace the instructional program in progress. Often the intervention, based on noncurriculum-referenced tests, only diverts or fragments instruction and reduces the opportunity for a more focused reading program and for time actively engaged in reading.

Measures of comprehensive skills (as opposed to measures of subskills) in reading achievement can verify actual reading improvement. This can validate, with individual children, the use of a reading program. Tests of word recognition and of reading connected discourse (paragraph meaning, graded paragraphs or selections) can serve this function. These are components of many standardized tests and in some cases constitute the basic test form. Other components of standardized tests made up of word-identification subskills are much less likely to have content validity when correlated with specific reading curricula. They also are not per se (as is frequently intimated and sometimes boldly asserted) a part of the reading process. If they were, no congenitally deaf child would ever learn to read. A variety of reading subskills forms a large part of virtually all reading programs available today. These subskills are presented in different orders and with different emphases. These are not reflected by norm-referenced tests—that is, unless one is prepared for each and every curriculum. The learner's progress in acquiring the subskills in these programs must be assessed by curriculum-referenced tests. You must test what you are teaching. Even if one assesses what is being taught, however, it is possible to obscure the results by using a procedure that is not curriculum referenced. Such a questionable practice, used to assess word-identification skill, is the nonsense-word or syllable approach (Walmsley, 1978–79). The "phonic" generalization being assessed is incorporated in a nonsense word assumedly to determine more accurately its mastery. Poor performance on real words, however, cannot be inferred from poor performance on nonsense syllables.

Over the years the author has observed the dichotomy between word-identification programs and reading achievement in special classes. One may recognize these teacher comments: "He knows his sounds, but he can't read any of the words," or "He knows all those words, but he doesn't know his sounds yet." As Walmsley (1978–79) states, "the fact of a test being criterion-referenced does not legitimize the test's objectives." Even good readers may do poorly on certain tests of phonic generalizations, but to recommend remedial instruction on such obviously trivial deficits would be ridiculous. That recommendation may well be made, however, for a poor reader who misses the same items.

Teachers tend to confuse word identification or subskill teaching with reading itself. Each should be assessed separately. The exception to this is with the severely hearing impaired for whom subskills should not be assessed at all; nor should they be a significant part of their reading curriculum. With mentally retarded children only the most utilitarian word-identification skills should be assessed, and even then their deficit should not be considered an obstacle to reading progress if learning is taking place (as evidenced by broader reading measures).

Reading curricula are often designed to fit test results. This is a basic tenet of diagnostic prescriptive teaching. However, a subskill deficit in word identification on some diagnostic test does not necessarily mean that more and more emphasis should be placed on teaching those subskills. This is especially true if actual reading ability is increasing. One should not let supposed subskills dominate either assessment or the reading curriculum.

Measures of actual reading from the reading materials being used are the most important gauges of progress in reading and the most telling guides to formulating specific instructional objectives. Two types of informal assessment are most helpful.

One is word-recognition assessment. These tests should be based on the words being introduced in the child's reading materials or program. The other is the assessment of silent and oral (if appropriate) reading of selections from the child's reading materials. These two test types should be used for determining placement level for the child, checking achievement after teaching, and the evaluation and preparation of reading materials for use with specific children.

The word-recognition tests are especially useful for children who have made very little progress in reading or who are at the beginning stages of reading. Identifying those words that a child knows is the most important aspect of assessment with vocabulary at this level.

Children whose reading problems are defined in terms of language difference or deficiency may need additional assessment in the areas of syntax and idiomatic and figurative structure. You cannot read language forms that you have not heard or mastered.

When a deficiency in syntax is involved, a syntax-sensitive reading program is necessary. Assessment places the child in a particular position in the scope and sequence of syntactic development, and reading materials sensitive to that level must be provided. Identification of knowns is critical here as well. Identification of known vocabulary and syntactic structures should be the focus of assessment. This is necessary for identifying a threshold of communication within which a child can read attentively and with comprehension.

Besides the hearing impaired, culturally diverse children and those for whom English is not the primary language are most likely to have difficulty with figurative or idiomatic structure (Adkins, 1970; Burns, 1980; Hargis, 1970, 1974). These elements occur with increasing frequency to over three per page by third-grade level in popular basal materials (Hargis, 1978). There are screening tests of figurative-language comprehension (Gochnour, 1976; Horne, 1967; Pollio, 1979), but the most relevant procedure for assessment is to select the idiomatic and figurative structures that appear in the child's reading material.

These forms of assessment can permit a child to be placed in a reading program if, in fact, there is one that fits his developmental needs in terms of known vocabulary syntax and nonliteral usage. This assessment can provide the information needed to evaluate prospective reading material or can serve as the basis for the preparation of new reading material.

The problem with noncurriculum-referenced "diagnostic reading tests" should be reemphasized. A great many are available. These tests invariably identify some deficiency, often having little relation to what is going on in reading instruction. The identification may prompt development of ancillary remedial curricula to deal with the supposed deficit(s). Sometimes these parallel, sometimes replace, instruction. Often they divert or fragment its focus and reduce the opportunity for time actively engaged in reading.

TEACHING AND TESTING

Failure and its attendant behaviors result from the use of reading instructional material that is too difficult. On the other hand, these same behaviors can be the cause of reading difficulty and failure even if the material is at an appropriate instructional level. In the latter case the focus of instruction must emphasize control of the interfering behavior. In the former it should be sufficient to adjust the reading curriculum to meet the child's instructional-level needs. This approach is preferable.

The first step in assessment is to find out how much reading ability the student has and then prepare the reading program to fit within that skill level. The material should maintain attention. (Chapter 4 is devoted to the subject of instructional level.)

The second stage of assessment can then occur. This is the observation of students working at an appropriate instructional reading level. The off-task behaviors that remain after sufficient opportunity to get used to working at this level are then the focus of assessment. The persisting residual off-task behaviors very likely themselves contribute to the learning problem and require intervention specific to them. In other words, if a child is continually inattentive or distracted from reading activities within his ability requirements, the problem of attention, distraction, or any other off-task behaviors must be specifically dealt with. Ample opportunity must be provided to observe the child after the reading material has been structured to meet his needs. Children who have experienced nothing but failure and frustration for years have developed a repertoire of off-task behaviors. Such students need sufficient opportunity to adjust to reading material that is not failure inducing and permits attention maintenance. Two weeks should be sufficient time. If there is residual off-task behavior after this time, the behavior itself may well be the primary cause of the reading difficulty.

Remedial curriculum construction and intervention can most accurately be based on the observation of residual behaviors. Only in this way can one be certain of dealing with a cause or a symptom. Through teaching and testing a teacher is able to observe the repetition rate required for individual children. Often, in basal reading programs, there seems to be inconsistent, or no more than token, repetition of some words once they have been introduced. With many handicapped students, however, adequate repetition for mastery is very important.

Much of the work in identification of reading material or its preparation for handicapped children must be based on the continued observation and testing that occurs during teaching. The preparation of reading material is necessary as long as the student's instructional level and need for repetition lie outside that provided by available published material.

Accountability and program evaluation are a part of the teaching and testing process. Students' progress must be assessed against acceptable standardized measures of reading achievement and appropriate curriculum-referenced reading measures. It is important to measure progress within the curriculum, but the curriculum itself may require validation, even if only with respect to a single child. It will be necessary to use tests valid in content that represent an acceptably broad view of reading. You cannot always use your own tests. Accountability may suffer.

Some issues in reading assessment

STRENGTHS AND WEAKNESSES

It seems generally accepted that both the strengths or skills and weaknesses or deficits of handicapped children should be assessed. This notion needs more detailed consideration than the rather cursory attention it usually receives.

The first consideration has to do with what weaknesses or deficits are. Some people, who are advocates of process- or aptitude-deficit views of reading disability, test for strengths and weaknesses in the areas of perceptual or "psycholinguistic" processes.

Others, such as Haring and Bateman (1977) or Carnine and Silbert (1979), hold a rather strict view of reading as composed of a hierarchy of word-identification subskills. Holders of this view emphasize the assessment of subskills, and deficits are defined in terms of subskills.

The questions that must be raised concern the validity of considering each a deficit or impediment to learning to read. Does its deficit affect readiness or reading performance? When is the deficit, indicated through some test, invalid or only trivial information? Suppose a child has learned to understand spoken language but is still a nonreader. The child demonstrates readiness for some level of reading instruction in a test of listening comprehension. Then process testing indicates that the child has some auditory perceptual deficit. These results are contradictory. The listening-comprehension test indicates auditory perceptual ability sufficient to learn the language and to read, so information concerning the deficit in auditory perception is trivial. The same analogy can be drawn for the child who can pass near-point tests of visual function and can make Smith's distinction between the pin and the paper clip. Here also, if there were evidence of a deficit in visual perception, it would be trivial.

In the case of the view of reading subskills as deficits, the same questions must be posed. Does the deficit of a subskill relate to deficiency in reading achievement? Clearly when good readers have such deficits the validity in regard to the specific subskill can be called into question and the fact of its deficit is trivial.

When children can recognize words containing the very subskills (various letter-sound associations or structural components) in which they have deficits, the importance of the subskill in learning to read these words must be regarded as less than compelling. Nevertheless, gaining independence in identifying unfamiliar printed words (words unfamiliar only in print) through the use of valid word-identification subskills is desirable. The questions remaining for later consideration concern which of the subskills should be considered and how much emphasis should be placed on them. For some children subskill deficit is to be expected. Severely hearing impaired children cannot decode. They cannot use these skills to call to mind the familiar spoken counterpart of an unfamiliar printed word. There *is* no familiar spoken counterpart!

Decoding approaches are intellectual processes. Emphasis on them may be emphasis on a child's learning weakness. As Spache (1976a) points out, pupils with lesser mental ability learn phonic rules only with difficulty and may not apply the generalizations as aids to word identification when reading. In many cases slower or retarded students who show mastery of certain isolated subskills cannot identify words that demonstrate them. The fact that any subskill appears on a test does not automatically validate its importance for specific children. Also, the fact that a child misses it on a test does not mean that it will be a cause of his reading difficulty. Too many objectives and too many curricular items are included in a child's reading program simply because they were missed on some test.

Reading subskills should be selected from what the child can readily learn and how well he can transfer this learning to the independent identification of words. These decisions can only be made through teaching and observation.

The second consideration concerning strengths and weaknesses is whether they are considered equally in assessment. Deficits have become the center of emphasis. In fact, we seem to have a mind set for finding deficits real or imagined. I believe the direction in emphasis should shift. It is critically important to identify whatever reading ability or capability a child has. Sometimes this is difficult to find, but it is the starting place necessary for structuring reading materials and activities. Knowing what words a child knows is necessary to prepare or identify reading materials that fall within his instructional reading level. Structuring the ratio of knowns to unknowns in any reading activity is the essence of providing individualized instruction and determining whether a child can remain on task or will fail. Knowns must dominate the ratio of knowns to unknowns in reading instructional material and so must receive proportionally greater emphasis in assessment.

EMPHASIS IN ASSESSMENT

The emphasis in assessment on what a child knows permits one to prepare or identify reading material at appropriate levels of instruction. Curriculum-referenced vocabulary tests are fundamental to materials preparation and identification. Word-recognition tests both in and out of context are necessary because each condition provides its own results and information. Tests of comprehension and rate of reading-connected discourse are of equal importance. Much available reading material is not constructed with specific learner's needs in mind. Assessment information from children should provide the guide to the materials' evaluation or adaption.

The assessment of word-identification skills and programming should not constitute the reading curriculum. It must be related to developmental progress in increased fluency in reading as a language process. This progress should not be interpreted to emphasize deficits in word identification. The tests that are used sometimes have the effect of dictating the form of the curriculum. The test comes first; then curricular items are prepared that are directed at remediating deficits identified by the test. Here the test has provided the definition of reading, and it dictates the structure of the curriculum. Avoid this trap.

Reading assessment

Assessment during reading instruction should be used directly and frequently, as a structured part of each lesson plan. Informal curriculum-referenced tests constitute the primary type for such assessment.

Reading is fundamentally a visual language-comprehension process. Most reading, as in reading a story or following a set of printed directions, involves dealing with connected discourse. Signs and labels also provide constant single-word or phrase reading opportunities, however. Reading-assessment procedures should be sensitive to these communication functions of reading. Often assessment procedures seem to diverge in form from real reading situations. Insofar as they depart, they lose content validity for practical application. Isolating or fragmenting letters or syllables from words to test letter-sound associations is an example. Another is the assessment of word-identification skills by using nonsense syllables. As was pointed out by Walmsley (1978–79), poor performance on these tests does not indicate poor performance on real words.

In this section the informal assessment techniques stressed relate to actual reading behavior or performance. The areas of assessment cover word recognition, connected discourse, and word-identification skills.

INFORMAL READING INVENTORIES

The use of what has come to be called the informal reading inventory (IRI) evolved from the work of Emmett Betts and his associates on levels of reading difficulty. The basic description of the independent, instructional, and the frustration reading levels was outlined briefly earlier in the chapter. Betts (1946) described a variety of behaviors, including levels of comprehension and oral-reading errors, associated with three levels of difficulty. The primary motive for describing the three levels of difficulty was to determine whether or not the reading material given a child was of an appropriate level of difficulty for its intended purposes. The descriptive guidelines provided a practical way of determining the reading difficulty or readability of a specific book for a specific child, still the most relevant and practical application of this informal measurement procedure. Lovitt and Hansen (1976) have demonstrated effectiveness both for placing (direct use) and maintaining (frequent use) learning disabled children in appropriate reading levels.

There are a number of problems and criticisms concerning the use of the informal reading-inventory approach. Spache (1976b) has outlined them with considerable detail. Many of these criticisms accrue from inappropriate use of the method, although some are inherent in the nature of the procedure.

It is ironic that several criticisms of the IRI concern a use for which it was not intended. It has little practical importance in determining what reading grade level a child has attained. This is like using the IRI as an achievement test. Standardized instruments that contain graded paragraphs do this job more accurately. The Gilmore Oral Reading Tests, the Gray Oral Reading Tests, the Diagnostic Reading Scales are examples.

There is no assurance that the sample selections taken from each reading level from a basal reading series accurately reflect the average readability for that grade. Basal readers vary widely both within and between series, in terms of reading level at any designated grade level (Spache, 1976b).

The indirect use of the IRI is a questionable extension of identifying grade-level achievement. In this case, a teacher administers an IRI, identifies the instructional reading level, then places the child in a book that has the same designated grade level. Admittedly this placement is much better than chance, but, as was pointed out previously, it is also very likely that the selection in the IRI and the book selected differ in terms of difficulty. The only accurate use of the procedure is direct. Here, a selection can be taken from the books available for use with the child. The child can then be placed in the specific book of appropriate instructional-level skill. Teachers should make their informal reading inventories from reading material that they have available for use with their children. Only then can they insure the direct measurement of instructional reading level in terms of material intended for the child's use.

Measurement of comprehension is fundamental in determining the instructional reading level. The preparation of ten to twenty comprehension questions for each selection in the IRI is usually recommended. The questions ideally should measure such things as recall of detail, evaluation, inference, and interpretation.

Another major criticism of the IRI is the problem of formulating such questions. This can be done only in the most subjective way. Not all passages lend themselves equally to the formulation of the same kinds of questions. Experience suggests that reliable results can be obtained by using questions that are formulated directly from sentences in the selection and require a yes or no response. Consistency in difficulty of comprehension questions and maximum reliability among all the selections can be maintained in this manner. This procedure is recommended because of the remarkable difficulty frequently encountered in trying to formulate questions of various types. Without the yes/no format, the questions often are more obscure or more difficult than what they are supposedly interrogating. Interrater judgments of item consistency are only readily handled by the yes/no format. The concerns as to the reliable evaluation of comprehension can be alleviated by insuring that there are an adequate number of questions. Twenty seems to be sufficient.

At about the third-grade level the Cloze procedure (a full description of this technique is in the chapter on readability) can be used to measure comprehension. In this method, instead of comprehension questions a typed copy of the selection is prepared in which every fifth word is deleted. A standard-size blank sufficiently large to write in a word is left in the place of each deletion. The child reads the passage and writes in the words thought to be missing. Only exact word replacement, unambiguous misspellings accepted, are scored as correct. Thirty-eight- to 44-percent exact word replacement corresponds to about the 75-percent comprehension level. This is a valid procedure for assessing comprehension. The problem of formulating questions is eliminated completely. The Cloze-treated passage should be 250 words in length so that fifty blanks and responses can be used. Spache (1976b) recommends that every tenth word be deleted—a 500-word passage to obtain fifty responses.

The IRI procedure usually requires oral reading to check word identification or recognition. After the oral reading the comprehension questions are asked. If the Cloze procedure is to be used also to test comprehension, two forms of the passage will be needed. The Cloze-treated form will necessarily be given first and the comprehension measure taken. Then the untreated passage can be administered to check word identification.

Research on the ability of teachers to identify and record oral reading errors during testing shows that many so-called errors are missed entirely. Adequate reliable scoring using any scoring criteria in many instances requires the use of a tape recorder so that portions can be repeated enough times to identify and record all errors accurately. The IRI approach has received considerable criticism concerning scoring of oral-reading errors. One problem has been the variety of scoring procedures recommended, but even within a scoring procedure, the lack of interrater reliability in scoring oral reading errors has been widely noted (Pflaum, 1979).

It has also been suggested that oral-reading errors from the IRI be used for determining problems in word-identification skills. The number and variety of errors obtained on an IRI, however, are probably insufficient for adequate evaluation. The IRI is of limited value in diagnosing such problems. Assessment in word-identification skills is better approached through more systematic direct means. Items that test the various skills that are part of the curriculum better serve this purpose.

For purposes of identifying material for use with a child, two types of word-recognition errors are the most significant. Since unknown and unfamiliar printed words most directly contribute to reading difficulty in children with no congenital hearing impairment, errors that point them out are very important. Oral-reading errors indicating unfamiliar and unknown words, together with a reliable measure of comprehension, make informal assessment very helpful in evaluating reading material. Errors of gross mispronunciation (not dialect variants as seen for some), substitutions, hesitations, and refusals (aided after five seconds) are the principal indicators of unknown and unfamiliar words and should be recorded during oral reading. These words should be noted on the examiner's copy of the reading sample. After the oral reading is completed, the examiner should isolate each of the words (with the exception of refusals) and test them. The words could be printed on cards for this testing, but the simplest way is to go back to the student's copy and point to each of the words in question. The student can be asked what each word is. The number unknown is tabulated. Words tested in isolation are more likely to be missed than words in context (Allington & McGill-Franzen, 1980; Goodman, 1965). The examiner, however, can verify whether the words are unfamiliar or unknown by the response to the word in isolation. This verification is necessary because the added demands placed on the child by "at first sight" oral reading, especially the challenging material at the instructional reading level, frequently cause dysfluency that can be mistaken for problems with unfamiliar words.

Betts (1946) points out that "vocabulary load is one of the most formidable barriers to reading." The percentage of words that can be unknown in a passage at the instructional level seems quite small (2–4 percent). Relatively few new words have considerable impact on level of comprehension, however. Thorndike (1934) quite conservatively stated that the student should encounter no more than one new word in two hundred, in supplementary reading activities.

The author's research indicates that the vocabulary load in the range of 2–4 percent permits adequate on-task behavior and less demand on teacher time. A comprehension level at 70–75 percent is also a necessary condition for on-task maintenance. Comprehension usually drops rapidly, as does on-task time, when vocabulary load passes 4 percent.

The assessment of errors that indicates vocabulary load has been stressed. Attention to these alone can simplify the scoring of an IRI. Information on vocabulary provides important information on placing the child in the right reading material. There are procedures for evaluating various kinds of errors, however, the most popular approach to this type of error (miscue) analysis being that of Goodman and Burke (1972) in their *Reading miscue inventory*. As Hood (1978) points out in her evaluation of the procedure, it has important implications for researchers and clinicians but limited use for most classroom situations because of the large time requirements for administering and scoring. In addition, the miscue-analysis procedure does not provide information concerning reading level. Its most important contribution might be in developing teacher sensitivity to error quality to be used in any oral reading situation.

The informal reading inventory is the most important procedure for direct measurement in reading. It allows material to be selected by its direct use in the inventory. Progress can be monitored and a child maintained at an instructional reading level by frequent continued use of the material in the informal-inventory procedure.

Many children may not have sufficient reading ability to read any connected discourse at an instructional level. Simple word recognition may be as far as assessment can go with these children. Word-recognition tests can be used as a pretest or screening procedure to indicate the best level at which to start. As mentioned previously, words tested in isolation produce more errors than the same ones in context. Seventy-five to 85 percent accuracy in word recognition is roughly equivalent to the instructional reading level obtained by reading connected discourse.

The few words recognized by some constitute the basis for preparation of reading material instructionally appropriate. If words are selected from a basal series, the remaining unknown terms from the next reading level can be taught until the children can read that book at an instructional level.

Virtually all guidelines for grading oral reading contain, in addition to a variety of recommendations concerning error types, recommendations for noting other behaviors while reading. Among these are poor phrasing, ignoring punctuation, monotonous voice, inappropriate pitch or volume, frequent repeating, lip movement, using finger to keep place, losing place, tension, and word-by-word reading. Some of these behaviors may be the result of the test situation. Others result from at-sight oral reading of rather challenging material. Pointing and losing place may also be related to vision problems. Word-by-word reading or word calling can be the result of overemphasis on phonics with little use of context. These behaviors should be noted in regard to the context in which the reading is done, as well as the difficulty level of the passage.

One important class of behavior, the off-task variety, should be observed during reading instruction. If the child is constantly looking into space, out of his seat at any chance, frequently distracted by virtually anything, the difficulty level of the reading task should be evaluated and necessary adjustments made.

At beginning reading levels, certain words pose extra difficulty in word-recognition assessment. These are the most common of all, the structure words, part of virtually all sentences. They include articles, prepositions, conjunctions, auxiliary verbs, subordinating conjunctions, and words similar. They look simple because they are so common and familiar, but they are quite abstract in the sense that they have no concrete referent. In fact, they can alone label nothing and as a consequence are comprehensible only in conjunction with other words. These are a part of beginning-reading materials and word lists. They are frequently tested in isolation and very often missed. The special problem that occurs when assessing these words from lists such as the Dolch list is that a prescription for teaching is based on the words missed during testing. The remedial program then emphasizes the teaching of these words—frequently in isolation, the least meaningful way. Some, whose remedial programs have been structured this way, after literally years (three years, in one instance) still only know a small percentage of the Dolch words. Children tend to require more trials to master these words than any of the other primary words (Hargis & Gickling, 1980). They are more readily learned in association with other, more concrete words in appropriate contextual arrangements, and this is the way that they should be presented.

ASSESSMENT OF WORD-IDENTIFICATION SKILLS

The term *word-identification skill* is simply one that the author has grown accustomed to using. Other terms used include *decoding skill, word-analysis skill, word-attack skill, phonic skill,* and *phonetic skill,* to name some fairly common ones. Each of these general terms harbors subclassifications that also have a variety of titles. Some common ones are *letter-sound associations, grapheme-phoneme associations, structural-analysis skills, auditory blending,* and *syllabication.* These are also comprised of a variety of more specific subsets of subskills. Not only do the names vary somewhat, but various reading programs do not introduce the same skills or the same skill in the same sequence. Ekwall (1976) has compiled a scope-and-sequence chart for teaching word-identification skills based upon the analysis of five popular basal reading programs. It certainly has to be considered extensive. Gray (1960) treated word-analysis skills rather exhaustively in his book *On their own in reading.* He presented a lengthy body of word-identification skills. It takes about a three-credit-hour course for a quarter term in a teacher-training program to learn them: the sheer number of word-identification skills makes one think that only a proficient reader could learn them.

Reading experts have a variety of beliefs concerning which general reading skills are important. A good many mention auditory discrimination as a very-early-readiness or beginning-reading skill. Carnine and Silbert (1979) go so far as to say that it is directly related to decoding in reading; and as auditory skills do not require knowledge of letter-sound correspondences, instruction in blending sounds into words can begin in lesson one. But Bourque's (1980) study of hierarchies places auditory discrimination in a much later position.

Some programs stress vowels as the most useful subskill and present them early. But research on vowel-sound placement in the hierarchy of subskills places them later than initial consonants and often after final consonants.

In the author's opinion, there are some important considerations for subskill testing. Only those subskills you are teaching should be tested. Almost all reading approaches have a scope and sequence of subskills that are presented over their course of study. Most also have accompanying skill tests. Do not test against exhaustive lists of subskills that have been compiled to be all-inclusive. The fact that a child misses some assumed subskill does not mean that work in reading should focus on that supposed deficit. Actual reading should continue.

A rather crude hierarchy of subskills is emerging from today's research. It may be only a hierarchy of difficulty, not sequenced stages of readiness for subsequent levels. However, these do provide a key to making word-analysis skills more teachable and learnable. As these guidelines emerge they should be used in both curriculum and test construction.

Word-identification subskills are assessed in numerous ways. The common approach that uses nonsense words or syllables has already been criticized. Walmsley (1978–79) pointed out that frequency of occurrence of a word in oral and written expression influenced the ease and accuracy of its pronunciation in his tests. Test constructors must control for frequency of occurrence of words when attempting to assess subskills. If not, subjects' performance on the test may be ambiguous or uninterpretable.

In subskill test construction several considerations must influence preparation and/or interpretation. Is the skill tested in isolation or in context? This consideration has several levels. On many tests letter-sound associations are assessed by asking the child to pronounce letters in isolation from words. Children normally hear words, not fragmented sounds. The placement of certain letter-sound associations in nonsense syllables is the next level. Here, the letter-sound association is isolated from meaningful context of a real word. The next level is the isolated presentation of real words. Here, the context of the word is available, but the sentence context is not. Sentence or discourse context seems to be particularly important in providing clues to the vowel sounds in words.

These levels of isolation or use of context are related to understanding. Tests close to actual language use are more comprehensible and will stimulate more accurate response. Another factor is the frequency of occurrence of words interacting with the level of imagery the words have. All of these things must be considered in constructing or interpreting word-identification skill tests.

The manner of administration or test format can also influence the results. In some tests a child is given oral stimuli and is to make sound-to-letter association from a limited number of printed choices. In other tests the letters are the stimuli, and the child is to make a letter-to-sound association. In this case there are many fewer limits on choices. For primary-age children sound-symbol associations are easier to recognize than symbol-sound associations (Hardy, Smythe, Stennett, & Wilson, 1972). The most important considerations to make here are those that contribute to maintaining the consistency of format or keeping the direction of testing in mind when interpreting results.

Most reading programs require knowledge of both upper-case and lowercase letters. Some use the letter names, but a few use letter sounds. Given lists of both uppercase and lowercase letters, the child is to respond with the name or sound of each. Some teaching and testing formats use letter groupings that have clearly distinguishing features. This reduces the level of difficulty to match a developing skill level.

Letter-sound associations should be tested in real words. The type of procedure advocated by McKee (1966) represents the most simple and direct form of assessment. In general the assessment procedure should include initial and final consonants, initial consonant blends, vowels, ending consonant blends, common inflected forms or endings, and syllables. This sequence follows roughly the hierarchy of difficulty of each of the subskills.

The format for this assessment procedure is represented by the following examples. To make a test on initial consonants, print a row of words for each association to be checked. The following example is for *w:*

   w: drove   dove   wove   rove

All of the words in each row should be exactly alike except for the beginning consonant, and the printed form of each word should be new to the child. In each row the child is to mark the word beginning with the same sound that the teacher provides. So, in testing the initial *w* sound, the examiner says, "Draw a line under the word that begins with the same sound as is in *weed* and *west.*"

To make a test on final consonants, print a row of words for each association to be checked. The following example is for *b.*

   b: cud   cup   cub   cuff

Here the words in each row should be alike except for the ending sound. Say to the child, "Draw a line under the word that ends with the same sound that you hear at the end of *crib* and *rub.*"

Tests of initial and final consonant blends should follow the same format as the previous two examples. The following are for initial *spr-* and final *-dge* respectively:

   spr-: stain   train   sprain   drain

   -dge: risk   rink   rid   ridge

For the first item say, "Draw a line under the word that begins with the same sound as *sprout* and *sprinkle.*" For the second item say, "Draw a line under the word that ends with the same sound as ends *fudge* and *dodge.*"

Tests of vowels require a row of words that sound alike except for the vowel being checked. The following example is for the short *e:*

   e: spike   speck   spook   spoke

Two approaches can be used here. The simpler one is to say, "Draw a line under the word that you think is *speck.*" The more difficult approach is to say, "Draw a line under the word that has the same vowel sound that you hear in *pest* and *hem.*"

To test common syllables, print rows of words for each association to be tested.

The following are examples for *-tion* and *com-:*

-tion: attendant   attended   attentive   attention

com-: compute   cemented   candid   control

For the first row say, "Draw a line under the word that ends with the same sound as is in *action* and *mention*." For the second row say, "Draw a line under the word that begins with the same sound as begins *compare* and *compact*."

The format is consistent and can be learned readily. Mastery of the word-identification skill in question can be checked reliably after this format is learned. Though these procedures test words in isolation, the sound-to-symbol direction of the test makes up for some of the missing context of discourse. The use of context in word-identification skill should be checked as well. Given an incomplete sentence orally, a child can select from a multiple choice of words that vary according to the sound-symbol association being checked. Use of context itself is an extremely important factor in word identification and efficient reading.

Parallel language and reading programs

For any child whose reading problem can be defined in terms of a language disorder, the reading program must incorporate adjustments for the particular area of deficiency. Assessment procedures have to provide information concerning these deficits. A major purpose of assessment is the identification of reading material that is instructionally appropriate. A child can encounter only so many new linguistic elements in reading discourse before comprehension falls off and attention cannot be maintained.

The use of informal procedures to identify unfamiliar and unknown words so that instructional level material can be developed was discussed earlier. For children with disorders in language comprehension, linguistic elements, as well as the printed form of words, may be unfamiliar or unknown. The primary area of concern is syntax. Receptive mastery of syntax is a readiness requirement for normal-achievement entry in beginning reading. If the children are deficient in the acquisition of syntax but are otherwise cognitively ready for reading instruction, reading materials within their level of language development should be provided. Their reading material must control unknown syntactic structures as well as vocabulary. To identify the instructional level and prepare instructional-level materials, language handicapped children must be tested against the scope and sequence of syntactic structure to determine which are known and may then be used freely. The ratio of knowns to unknowns must be maintained according to instructional-level requirements. New vocabulary, as was previously stated, should be limited to the range of 2–4 percent for the instructional level. New syntactic structures should receive roughly twice the difficulty weight as new vocabulary (Hargis, 1978). Syntactic structures usually encompass more than one word, and though the number of words does vary considerably, the double weighting appears to be an adequate standard. Like new words, syntactic structures can gradually be introduced in reading. They should be introduced following the sequence of normal development. The scope and sequence of acquisition of syntactic structure should provide the basic guidelines for assessment and programming for language handicapped children. Appendix B has a scope-and-sequence chart for the syntax of English sentences. The notation for each structure in the scope-and-sequence chart is symbolic, so sentences containing examples of each structure are also provided for more concrete illustration.

Parallel language and reading programs must be conducted until such time as the language handicapped child has completed the receptive mastery of the scope of syntactic structures. Then a merger with regular reading materials, which lack control over the introduction of syntactic forms, can be made.

REFERENCES

Adkins, P. G. Relevancy in children's language. *The Reading Teacher,* 1970, *24,* 7–11.

Allington, Richard L., & McGill-Franzen, Anne. Word identification errors in isolation and in context: Apples *vs.* oranges. *The Reading Teacher,* 1980, *33,* 795–800.

Anastasi, Ann. *Psychological testing* (2nd ed.). New York: Macmillan, 1961.

Arter, Judith A., & Jenkins, Joseph R. Differential diagnosis—prescriptive teaching: A critical appraisal. *Review of Educational Research,* 1979, *49,* 517–555.

Bateman, B. An educator's view of a diagnostic approach to learning disorders. In J. Hellmuth, *Learning disorders* (Vol. 1). Seattle: Special Child, 1965.

Betts, Emmett A. *Foundations of reading instruction.* New York: American Book, 1946.

Bourque, Mary L. Specification and validation of reading skills hierarchies. *Reading Research Quarterly,* 1980, *15,* 237–267.

Burns, Paul C. *It really isn't raining cats and dogs—Figurative language.* Paper presented at the 25th annual convention of the International Reading Association, St. Louis, May 6, 1980.

Carnine, Douglas, & Silbert, Jerry. *Direct instruction reading.* Columbus: Charles E. Merrill, 1979.

Ekwall, E. E. *Diagnosis and remediation of the disabled reader.* Boston: Allyn & Bacon, 1976.

Filp, Johanna. Relationship among reading subskills: A hierarchical hypothesis. *Journal of Reading Behavior,* 1975, *7,* 229–240.

Glass, Gene V. Standards and criteria. *Journal of Educational Measurement,* 1978, *15,* 237–261.

Gochnour, Elizabeth A. *Gochnour idiom screening test.* New Orleans: Gock House, 1976.

Goodman, Kenneth S. A linguistic study of cues and miscues in reading. *Elementary English,* 1965, *42,* 639–643.

Goodman, Yetta M., & Burke, Carolyn L. *Reading miscue inventory.* New York: Macmillan, 1972.

Gray, William S. *On their own in reading.* Chicago: Scott, Foresman, 1960.

Hammill, Donald D., & Bartel, Nettie R. *Teaching children with learning and behavior problems* (2nd ed.). Boston: Allyn & Bacon, 1978.

Hanna, Gerald S., Dyck, Norma J., & Holen, Michael C. Objective analysis of achievement—Aptitude discrepancies in LD classification. *Learning Disabilities Quarterly,* 1979, *2,* 32–38.

Hardy, Madeline, Smythe, P. C., Stennett, R. G., & Wilson, H. R. Developmental patterns in elemental reading skills: Phoneme-grapheme and grapheme-phoneme correspondence. *Journal of Educational Psychology,* 1972, *63,* 433–436.

Hargis, Charles H. The relationship of available instructional reading materials to deficiency in reading achievement. *American Annals of the Deaf,* 1970, *115,* 27–29.

Hargis, Charles H. *An analysis of the syntactic and figurative structure of popular first grade level basal readers.* Paper presented at the 12th meeting of the Southeastern Conference on Linguistics, Washington, D.C., 1974.

Hargis, Charles H. Comprehensive planning for hearing impaired children: A report from an ad hoc committee of the Division for Children with Communication Disorders, Council for Exceptional Children, March, 1976. (a)

Hargis, Charles H. *The syntax of conservation.* Paper presented at the 16th meeting of the Southeastern Conference on Linguistics, Atlanta, November, 1976. (b)

Hargis, Charles H. *English syntax: An outline for clinicians and teachers of language handicapped children.* Springfield: Charles C Thomas, 1977.

Hargis, Charles H. *Guidelines for the preparation of reading and language materials for hearing impaired children.* Paper presented at the national convention of the Alexander Graham Bell Association, St. Louis, June 25, 1978.

Hargis, Charles H., & Gickling, E. E. *Word recognition development as a function of imagery level and syntactic classification.* Paper presented at the 6th regional conference of the International Reading Association, Norfolk, Va., Nov. 14, 1980.

Haring, Norris, & Bateman, Barbara. *Teaching the learning disabled child.* Englewood Cliffs: Prentice-Hall, 1977.

Harris, Albert J., & Sipay, Edward R. *How to increase reading ability* (6th ed.). New York: David McKay, 1975.

Hood, Joyce. Is miscue analysis practical for teachers? *The Reading Teacher,* 1978, *32,* 260–266.

Horne, R. N. A study of figurative language in sixth grade children. *Dissertation Abstracts,* 1967, *27,* 3367A.

Howell, Kenneth W., Kaplan, Joseph S., & O'Connell, Christine Y. *Evaluating exceptional children: A task analysis approach.* Columbus: Charles E. Merrill, 1979.

Jenkins, Joseph R., & Pany, Darlene. Standardized achievement tests: How useful for special education? *Exceptional Children,* 1978, *44,* 448–453.

Johnson, Marjorie S., & Kress, Roy. Task analysis for criterion-referenced tests. *The Reading Teacher,* 1971, *24,* 353–359.

Lovitt, Thomas C., & Hansen, Cheryl L. Round one—Placing the child in the right reader. *Journal of Learning Disabilities,* 1976, *9,* 347–353.

McKee, Paul. *Reading: A program of instruction for the elementary school.* Boston: Houghton Mifflin, 1966.

Murray, Frank B. Implications of Piaget's theory for reading instruction. In S. Jay Samuels (Ed.), *What research has to say about reading instruction.* Newark, Del.: International Reading Association, 1978.

Pflaum, Susanna W. Diagnosis of oral reading. *The Reading Teacher,* 1979, *33,* 278–284.

Pollio, Marilyn. A test of metaphoric comprehension and some preliminary developmental data. *Child Language,* 1979, *6,* 111–120.

Prescott, George. Criterion-referenced test interpretation in reading. *The Reading Teacher,* 1971, *24,* 347–354.

Royer, James M., & Schumer, Harry. Reading achievement gains as a function of teacher predictions. *The Journal of Educational Research,* 1976, *69,* 232–235.

Salvia, John, & Ysseldyke, James E. *Assessment in special and remedial education.* Boston: Houghton Mifflin, 1978.

Seaton, Hal W. The effects of a visual perception training program on reading achievement. *Journal of Reading Behavior,* 1977, *9,* 188–192.

Smith, Frank. *Reading Without Nonsense.* New York: Teachers College Press, 1978.

Spache, George D. *Diagnosing and correcting reading disabilities.* Boston: Allyn & Bacon, 1976. (a)

Spache, George D. *Investigating the issues of reading disabilities.* Boston: Allyn & Bacon, 1976. (b)

Stennett, R. G., Smythe, P. C., & Hardy, Madeline. Hierarchical organization of reading subskills: Statistical approaches. *Journal of Reading Behavior,* 1975, *7,* 223–228.

Strauss, A., & Lehtenen, L. *Psychopathology and education of the brain injured child.* New York: Grune & Stratton, 1947.

Thorndike, E. L. Improving the ability to read. *Teachers College Record,* 1934, *36,* 229–241.

Tuinman, J. Jaap. Criterion referenced measurement in a norm referenced context. In S. Jay Samuels (Ed.), *What research has to say about reading instruction.* Newark, Del.: International Reading Association, 1978.

Wallace, Gerald, & Larsen, Stephen C. *Educational assessment of learning problems: Testing for teaching.* Boston: Allyn & Bacon, 1978.

Walmsley, Sean A. The criterion referenced measurement of an early reading behavior. *Reading Research Quarterly,* 1978–79, *14,* 574–604.

CHAPTER **4**

INSTRUCTIONAL LEVELS AND RATES

Reading levels

Factors influencing reading level

Variation in learning rates

Adapting instructional materials

4

Reading levels

Emmett A. Betts is generally credited with presenting the notion of three reading levels, considered previously in the chapter on assessment. They were detailed in his book *Foundations of reading instruction* (1946). The levels are fundamentally important ideas for conceptually relating the sequence of assessment, planning, and implementing for any child regardless of handicap. The differential factors in defining these reading levels for various groups of children are considered in this chapter.

INSTRUCTIONAL, INDEPENDENT, AND FRUSTRATION READING LEVELS

A child's success or failure is most often a function of the match between his reading-ability level and the reading level of the material being used. Reading levels that induce frustration and failure are nonproductive so should be avoided. Two levels should receive careful consideration and should be structured into every child's reading activities. The level of difficulty in reading material depends upon how much of it is unknown or unfamiliar to each child. The ratio of knowns to unknowns in printed discourse determines the level of difficulty. For the instructional reading level, Betts suggested that the unknown component of the ratio could be in the range of 2–4 percent. This level of difficulty is appropriate for instructional purposes. Newly introduced vocabulary should occupy the unknown segment, 2–4 percent. As the words are mastered and become part of the child's instant word-recognition vocabulary, new words can be introduced, but the percentage of new and unfamiliar words should be held to 2–4 percent. This percentage range may seem rather small; in fact, however, unknown words in these numbers can produce reading passages of considerable challenge.

In order to illustrate the effect of instructional-level difficulty for skilled, mature readers, some passages have been specially prepared. The following selection contains about 4-percent unknown or unfamiliar words. This, of course, is true only if the harder words are outside your reading vocabulary.

1

The fear of famine was becoming widespread, and the old man had been uncertain that he could maintain his position of authority in the village. However, the fortuitous events of the previous night gave him just the opportunity that he needed. He could now argue forcefully that he was the *propitiator* of the *Yahwehs.* How else could the people explain the sudden appearance the night before of the vast number of *widgeons?**

This level of difficulty is considered within the instructionally appropriate range. It is only appropriate, of course, if the teacher is prepared to help the child cope with the unfamiliar components in the selection. In the above example it was necessary to use rather unusual or obscure words to increase the likelihood of their being unfamiliar to the audience for whom this book was intended. In the instance of wholly unfamiliar words, the teacher must provide some definition or experience

---

*Explanatory passages for each example are in Appendix C.

with the words before exposing the child to the selection. If not, the new words should be placed in a context strong enough to assist the child in arriving at an appropriate meaning. For words unfamiliar only in print, the teacher should provide sufficient introduction to the printed form in association with their spoken counterparts to aid in their identification in the reading selection. If the child has sufficient skill in independent word identification, this, combined with the story's context, may be sufficient to permit the student to cope with the new words. At any rate, even a very skilled, mature reader may need some additional support to read at these rather challenging levels.

The next selection is written with about 8 percent of the words hard or unfamiliar.

2

The work had been especially fatiguing that season. The *muzhiks* once again trudged silently home through the humid lingering heat of the day. A few had lined up to get a *revivifying potation* from a *colporteur* who was apparently stingy with his dole. One young *muzhik* who felt cheated argued belligerently. But for the appearance of an *intercessor*, some violence might have erupted. Heat and *lassitude* further slowed the tempo of emotion, and the *dilatory* march home resumed.

The challenge in this passage should be more pronounced (depending on how many and how unfamiliar the words are and on how effective the known part is in contributing contextual support to the maintenance of comprehension). Any reading more difficult than the instructional level is considered at frustration level. Not only does it produce frustration and failure in the child, but it requires an inordinate amount of demand on teacher time to introduce, clarify, and support, if the student is to be maintained on task. Demand on teacher time is often far too great to permit using this material efficiently in reading instruction.

The comprehension level of about 75 percent has been estimated as appropriate for instructional-level reading activities. Indeed this level of comprehension does seem to be associated with adequate on-task behavior and freedom from tension when reading. In the following passage about 2 percent of the words are unfamiliar. Context will almost carry the meaning to unknown words. It can be seen, though, that it does not take many new words to be disconcerting.

3

Joe pulled the covers tightly over his head. He wished that he had left the light on in the hall. He was sure now that what he had thought was a pile of dirty clothes in the corner of the room was in fact a *golliwog*. Possibly, he thought, if he remained completely still until morning, the thing might miss him. At that moment, when he was just beginning to feel somewhat secure, he heard a soft creaking noise. This must be an *orgillon*. He wished then that he had taken the flashlight to bed with him. Jeff had told him that if you shone a light on an *orgillon* it would go away.

Betts (1946) called the "basal" level what has also been called the "independent" or "recreational" level:

> . . . the highest level at which an individual can read and satisfy all the criteria for desirable reading behavior in silent- and oral-reading situations. Information on basal reading level is essential for directing extensive reading activities because the readability of materials should be at or near that level. In short, the basal reading level approximates the level at which "free," supplementary, independent, or extensive reading can be done successfully. (445–446)

At the basal level minimum comprehension should be 90 percent with fewer than 2 percent of the words unknown. At this reading level a child needs no help or prereading instruction from the teacher. Recreational reading can best be done at this level. Even though the interest pull of some types of material can be very strong for some children, the continuous struggle with too-difficult material can squelch such interest.

At this independent level reading as a fluent language process can be accomplished—that is, of course, if sufficient opportunity for reading at this level and sufficient access to such material are available. If a topic or area of interest can be found within this independent level, reading can be established as a recreational activity. In this way, reading becomes a self-reinforcing activity. The volume of reading will increase sufficiently to add many words to a child's instant word-recognition vocabulary, and reading can become an increasingly fluent form of receptive language.

The frustration level that Betts described can be most clearly defined by comparing it to the minimum requirements for the instructional level. For a child who encounters more than 4-percent unknown words and comprehends less than 70 percent, the ability to remain engaged in a reading activity is curtailed. The difficulty of the material will simply not permit attention maintenance with comprehension.

ENGAGED TIME

The most important attribute of both the independent or basal level and the instructional level is their time engaged in reading. Research on academically engaged time—that is, time actually spent on task (in this case in reading)—shows the direct correlation between amount of time so spent and achievement (Gickling & Armstrong, 1978; Rosenshine & Berliner, 1978). Of primary importance is that reading material be provided for such engaged time, if adequate progress in reading is to be made. Unfortunately often those children failing in reading and needing such time are provided with reading matter that is at frustration level and does not permit the child to stay on task.

Independent and instructional-level reading activities permit and maximize time engaged in reading. Time so engaged is directly related to achievement.

INTEREST AND MOTIVATION

There is much to be said for and about motivation and interest related to reading materials, but these cannot substitute for the correct reading level. As already mentioned, motivation and interest can help overcome ambiguity and stress induced by difficult material, but in the longer term difficult reading material can squelch both motivation and interest.

INFORMAL AND CORRELATIONAL APPROACHES

Especially at the primary grade levels, care must be taken in identifying independent and instructional reading levels.

Informal procedures for their identification were illustrated in the chapter on assessment. It is important to recognize, in identifying these reading levels in children, that these informal criterion-referenced procedures are the most robust. Too often correlational rather than direct approaches to identifying the independent and instructional reading levels are used. If standardized tests that yield a grade-level equivalent are to be used to find books of the same stated reading level, there is likely to be a mismatch of book-grade level and child-reading level. In both examples, the lower the reading ability of the child the less accurate these correlational procedures are likely to be. The error of measurement associated with these tests and that associated with identifying the grade of books by readability formulas can compound inaccuracy in matching student with reading material. This should be considered in using these correlational approaches in more than general ways. The direct measurement of a particular child's performance with specific reading material is necessary to determine its suitability for independent and instructional uses.

Correlational approaches to book selection can be used more effectively with those children who can read at advanced levels. Children who can read at high levels may in fact demonstrate the ability to read instructionally over more than one level of difficulty. Such children are better able to overcome the problem of actual variation in reading difficulty of basal readers from their stated difficulty level. Spache (1976) checked the readability of twenty popular basal reading series. In the first grade the preprimer, the primer, and first reader were checked. A reader from each of the other grades from second through sixth were analyzed. Spache found that among the twenty series the range of difficulty was more than a full grade level between the easiest and hardest at the first grade, about two years' difference among readers at the second, third, and fourth grades, and about a year and a half at the fifth and sixth grades. In other words, the publisher's designated reading grade level for a book is no guarantee of precision.

Though readability formulas are not precise, they can provide an objective measure of reading materials on traits that they evaluate. These traits are often vocabulary and sentence length. At any rate they are good comparative measures of the same traits, if the relative difficulty of various reading materials is to be evaluated. Their use can improve the precision of placement, using correlational approaches, by making it possible to evaluate more accurately the relative difficulty level of proposed reading materials.

Factors influencing reading level

Certain factors influence the level of reading difficulty for all children. Other factors contribute prominently to difficulty with certain groups of children. Each of these primary factors will be considered separately.

WORDS UNKNOWN ONLY IN PRINT

Beginning reading material should meet one readiness standard: that the language presented in the written discourse be familiar to children if spoken or read to them. Words being introduced in beginning reading materials should be unfamiliar only in print. (Deaf children are exceptions to this standard in that for them there may be no familiar "spoken" counterpart of the unfamiliar printed word. More will be said about this later.)

A primary objective of most reading programs is to provide the child with sufficient "decoding" skill to identify the familiar spoken counterparts of the unfamiliar printed words. If the child has never heard the word spoken, obviously, its unfamiliar printed form cannot be decoded in this way. The context of the passage and the sentence in which a word unfamiliar only in print is contained can help clarify the familiar spoken form of the word. If the passage is at an instructional level, the context is sufficiently strong for identification of 38 to 42 percent of the words deleted in the Cloze procedure. This is true with the mildly retarded as well as the nonretarded (Hargis, 1972). Additional word-identification skills can further reduce the uncertainty about the word. Unfamiliar words successfully identified are often read with some hesitation in an informal reading inventory or other oral-reading activity. Even words to which word-identification skills do not readily apply should become increasingly familiar through continued exposure.

These words may also be among those scored as hesitancies when giving an informal reading inventory.

For all children, with the exception of those having severe hearing impairment, the vocabulary load in beginning reading instruction should be comprised of the normal listening vocabulary of the children.

UNFAMILIAR VOCABULARY

Words unfamiliar in both written and spoken form pose more difficulty in teaching. For any child whose reading difficulty is definable in terms of language difference or deficiency, the problem is compounded. In the case of deaf children, most of whom require a reading program that parallels and is integrated with the language-teaching curriculum, this unfamiliar vocabulary should be introduced systematically within the instructional rates.

There are two overriding considerations in dealing with unfamiliar words. The first has to do with experience. Does the word represent something within the child's experience? If it does, the difficulty posed by the word is considerably lessened. The story's context is normally helpful in predicting meaning for such words—that is, if the story is within the instructional level for the person reading it. In the examples provided earlier, such expressions were placed in the stories to illustrate their effect on comprehension. In those examples, the most obscure available synonyms were substituted for common words. Even though the words look intimidating at times, they do not pose nearly the problem that terms with referents completely outside one's experience do. In these cases, no synonyms are available, and definitions are likely to be couched in terms equally unfamiliar. Consider the following example about gas arc welding:

4

Helium was the first gas to be used as a shielding gas in the gas arc welding process. However, the gas is costly, and it has some arc resistance. This gas was used extensively during World War II to weld aluminum.

Argon gas is also used in the gas welding process. Argon is heavier and diffuses more slowly than helium.

Therefore, about one-third the volume of argon compared to helium is needed. Even though argon is more expensive per cubic foot than helium, helium is lighter and diffuses more rapidly. So less argon is used. Argon gives a stable arc and is less sensitive to arc length than helium. Consequently, it provides a smooth arc.

Carbon dioxide is less expensive than the other gases. It is extremely sensitive to arc length.

If the reader has experience related to this field, of course, the challenge of the material is considerably lessened. Although the vocabulary load is likely within the instructional range, the presentation of such material requires equipment, demonstration, or pictures.

It is very difficult to present totally unfamiliar words without associated experience. If the words have utility in terms of their frequency of appearance in the reading material encountered, the associated experience must be provided as a part of the reading instruction.

The hierarchy of difficulty needs to be recognized in dealing with vocabulary in beginning reading material. Easiest in the hierarchy are words unfamiliar only in print. Next easiest are words unfamiliar in spoken form but related to the child's experience. Most difficult are words conveying ideas or concepts outside the child's experience. Wherever possible, beginning reading materials should be comprised of words unfamiliar only in print. These can be introduced efficiently if the instructional level is used as a guideline for material selection or preparation. Words more generally unfamiliar require parallel language-teaching activities. After primary reading levels are passed, new words are more often drawn from the latter two categories. Learning to cope with meaning difficulties in these words then becomes the major objective for all children who are able to achieve that point.

UNFAMILIAR SYNTAX

On the average, children have completed comprehension mastery of syntax by age six. For most nonhandicapped children, therefore, there need be little control over the use of any of the different syntactic forms that comprise English. This lack of control is an actual fact. Analysis of the primers and first readers of popular basal reader series confirms that there are no controls over the use of syntactic structures (Hargis, 1974). All forms used make no provision for systematic introduction or repetition. It is precisely this kind of control, however, that is necessary for children who, for reasons of their handicaps or rate of development, have not acquired this basic readiness requirement.

The impact of a strange syntactic structure on comprehension in the following example illustrates a new (synthetically created) non-English syntactic form used twice:

5

Mary wanted a new bike for her birthday. She understood how impractical a bike would be for her. She lived with her parents on the fifteenth floor of a tall apartment building. Not only would it be difficult to get the bike up and down the elevators and out through the lobby; it would be difficult to get the bike to *vleem*. They could see from their apartment the park. Also, there were almost no sidewalks, and the street traffic around the building seemed heavy all the time. At least she knew how to ride a bike. She had learned at *vleet* lived in a house in a quiet suburb, her cousin's. It seemed as though bikes were everywhere out there. Oh well, she would try to be happy with the skates that she was sure her parents had already bought for her.

A new form of relative clause structure was used in this selection. It required that different relative pronouns serve as the unusual words. This selection is within the instructional level provided that everything else is familiar.

Research on the effect of syntactic structures (Hargis, 1978a) suggests that a new syntactic form can contribute even more difficulty than a new word does. It is usual for a syntactic structure to encompass a group of words and to be introduced by, or incorporate a variety of, structure words like relative pronouns, subordinating conjunctions, coordinating conjunctions, and others. So it seems reasonable that they be expected to have a wider impact than on the sentence in which they occur.

The following selection repeats the use of two new non-English syntactic structures:

6

The old cows some of were not producing milk enough to pay for their keep. The farmer remembered their big production days and thought of how much they had contributed to his and his family's present prosperity. *The old cows each of* had produced more than 150 thousand *lbs.* of milk since they came into production. *Vleed they produced the calves* made up *the herd the rest of most of.* These old cows seemed like old friends. He just couldn't bring himself to haul them to the slaughter house to become *hamburger a bunch of just. The ideas most of he* had didn't seem good enough. *Vleed he could think of the only thing* was to put off any decision for one more season.

A new determiner form was used, and the relative clause form introduced in the previous selection was repeated in this one. There were seven occurrences of the two new forms—two for the relative clause and five for the determiner. For most readers this selection is quite frustrating.

In the evaluation of readability using readability formulas, hard words are counted only once even though they appear again and with various inflectional changes. The contribution to difficulty is not so great when words are repeated as when all of them are new and different. This is true of a syntactic structure as well, when that structure does not also include a different structure word.

Beyond the need to control the number or percentage of syntactic forms being introduced is the need to select appropriate syntactic forms to introduce. The acquisition of syntax follows a developmental sequence. A chart illustrating the scope and sequence of the acquisition process is provided in Appendix A. This chart serves as a guide for the selection of the next developmentally appropriate syntactic structures. These controls and procedures are necessary to prepare instructionally appropriate material until the child has completed the developmental process. Only then may the syntactic controls be removed.

Syntactic structures are maps of cognitive structure. Without the development of the cognitive structure, it is not possible to teach a child to comprehend its syntactic map. With hearing impaired children the basic cognitive development underlying syntactic development proceeds in the normal developmental sequence. This means that the teaching of syntax can proceed unimpaired through language and reading instruction. For children with a cognitive deficit (such as those having moderate or greater retardation) at the basis of the linguistic deficiency, the controls may have to be permanent. Material containing syntactic forms beyond their level of development is not comprehensible to them. The reading material must continue to be especially prepared to be within their threshold of communication, or no reading can occur.

UNFAMILIAR FIGURATIVE AND IDIOMATIC STRUCTURES

Nonliteral language is in common daily use by ordinary speakers and listeners. It occurs in virtually all linguistic contexts, frequently in basal readers. An analysis of eight popular basal reading programs revealed that idiomatic and figurative structures appear at the rate of 1.5 per page in the second grade and 2.03 per page at third-grade level. For children who cannot deal with nonliteral use of language, this rate of appearance is a formidable obstacle to comprehension. Even though the vocabulary that comprises the figurative expression may be familiar, error and puzzlement are inevitable. Consider these examples of primary-level figurative structure:

> Earth is a merry-go-round spaceship that turns and turns. (*With skies and wings,* Lexington, Mass., Ginn, 1973, p. 180)

> So he took off his clothes and dived into the stream and swam around inside the song the water was singing. (*How it is nowadays,* Lexington, Mass., Ginn, 1973, p. 288)

Most figurative structures encompass more than one word. Probably as a consequence, they appear to contribute even more to reading difficulty for each occurrence than does the occurrence of a new word (Hargis, 1978a).

The terms *frozen* and *novel* have been used to distinguish idioms from figurative structure (Barlow, Kerlin, & Pollio, 1971). Idioms or frozen structures are in common use. They spring from new figurative structures that have come into popular usage. Sometimes slang expressions in current use represent some novel form that has become popularized. If slang remains in the language, it too will become just a cliché or idiomatic form. Figurative structure, or novel figurative structure, is as the word *novel* denotes, new or unique.

Figurative and idiomatic structures include a substantial variety of words, phrases, and sentences that differ from literal use. In samples from the primary basal readers, the author was able to identify the following figurative types:

simile	personification	onomatopoeia
metaphor	metonymy (synecdoche)	anthimeria
hyperbole	pun	litotes
periphrasis	rhetorical question	oxymoron

Idiomatic structure is produced by many of the same figurative devices as above. These are popularized in use and have been added to our language, however—often first as slang. A few examples of idioms from the primary readers follow.

in an uproar	time running out
sunk	a sitting duck
in the same boat	break the silence
safe and sound	fish out
lose his breath	drew up at the curb

The longer the idiom is in popular use the more likely its figurative origins are to be obscured. When this is the case, these idioms must be treated like any new vocabulary item.

The foregoing examples of idioms only suggest the wide variety that routinely occurs. Idiomatic structures are often culture specific. Therefore, children from various cultural backgrounds are likely to arrive at erroneous literal interpretations or to be utterly confused in their attempts to deal with them.

There is no control over the introduction or repetition of idiomatic and figurative structure in basal readers (Hargis,

1974). The problem with comprehension of figurative structure has been noted by Adkins (1970), Dechant (1970), Robertson (1973), and Burns (1980). Little (1981) noted the significant additional difficulty that children with mild learning handicaps have in coping with it. The severe problem that hearing impaired children have with figurative structure has long been recognized.

The ability to deal with novel figurative structure requires comprehension mastery of syntax and of the literal form of the vocabulary of which it is composed. This provides a necessary, but not sufficient, readiness base for the comprehension of figurative structure. The next step in the acquisition of comprehension of figurative structure is to deal with the systematic violation of some of the syntactic restrictions already mastered. In order to illustrate the systematic violation of syntactic rules, it is necessary to have some notion of how the rules work. In regard to figurative structure, the most common syntactic rules have to do with the selectional restrictions between nouns and verbs and other lexical items that may co-occur in sentences. For example, we expect sentences like these:

The radish grew in a small pot.
The rock struck the dog.

In these sentences the noun subjects have appropriate verbs. Here the selectional requirements are met. In the following sentences the selectional restrictions have been violated.

The radish sneezed.
The rock talked to the dog.

The verb *sneeze* requires an animate noun for a subject, and the verb *talk* requires a human noun for a subject. The purposeless violation of these selectional restrictions makes these sentences nonsensical.

When there is purpose in the violation, however, we get figurative structure. Consider the following two examples of the purposeful violation of the same selectional restrictions:

It had been so cold and wet that even the radishes sneezed.
It had been so hot and dry that even the rocks talked about moving.

These examples were both hyperbole and personification. In the following examples only personification is involved.

> The moon climbed over the mountain.
> New concepts wait patiently for discovery.

For the purpose of studying figurative usage, nouns should be considered according to whichever of their features exert selectional influences. Such features concern whether or not a noun has one or the other of certain polar-feature pairs. Examples of the most important of such polar pairs are abstract (concrete), living (nonliving), animate (nonanimate), and human (nonhuman). All nouns have one or the other of each of these features. The previous sentence examples show how these features exert selectional influence with verbs. In some metaphors, nouns with different features are linked:

> Peter is the rock the church is built on.
> Joe is a little monkey.

In the first sentence *Peter* and *rock* are linked; their features are not compatible. In the second sentence *Joe* and *monkey* violate the same restriction, giving Joe a monkey's characteristics.

Noun features exert influence on a variety of other sentence components when these influences are purposely manipulated. The results are many forms of novel figurative utterances. The important consideration here is that the child be able to handle concrete, literal uses of the restrictions before these are manipulated to deal with figurative meaning. Figurative devices produce indirect, abstract expression. The ability to cope with figurative structure requires normal cognitive development. Retarded children have limited ability to deal independently with novel figurative language. Common idioms can be mastered through a rote associative approach. In all cases, however, the introduction should be controlled. They do contribute greatly to reading difficulty and are a primary problem in the available instructional reading material.

Variation in learning rates

Introduction of a new word or structure in reading is certainly no guarantee that it has been learned. Generally it is assumed that a new word must be repeated to become sufficiently familiar for instant recognition. There are apparently provisions for the gradual introduction of new words in basal reading programs. Herrick (1961) found that the introduction rate in the readers he studied was one new word in 50 to a low of one in 110 running words. This control exists, though there hardly seems to be a consensus on its details. Strickland (1963), in a study of the language of basal readers, found no control over the introduction or repetition of syntactic forms in basal readers, but (interestingly) she assumed that there were generally accepted controls over the introduction and repetition of new words.

Gates (1931) concluded that individuals differed considerably in the rate at which they developed familiarity with printed words encountered in reading material. His studies of children in different IQ groups showed a marked correlation between IQ and number of repetitions necessary to acquire a reading vocabulary. He reported findings for children in the chronological age range of 6.1 to 7.5 at the beginning of the school term. As a result of these studies, Gates recommended an average minimum number of systematic repetitions in printed material as needed for mastery at various IQ levels. Fifty-five repetitions were the recommended average for children in the IQ range of 60 to 69. Increasingly fewer repetitions were needed in each higher IQ group until only twenty repetitions were recommended for those children in the range of 120 to 129. In spite of these recommendations, research suggests that, beyond the absence of uniformity in introduction rate, there are exceedingly wide variations in provisions for repetition both between and within reading programs. In examining selected words from readers at the primary-grade levels, we have found a range of repetition of from one to fifty-seven within the same book. The higher repetition rates are somewhat misleading in that they are for structure words like *this* and *are,* of such high utility that they must comprise a large part of all discourse. In these cases, the higher repetition is brought about by the great need to use certain words frequently. Only twelve words—*a, and, I, in, is, it, of, the, that, to, was,* and *he*—constitute 25 percent of all printed discourse. Remarkably few words constitute the necessary bulk of words that must occur. About sixty-eight words constitute 50 percent of all printed discourse. These words occur with extremely high natural frequency without formal provision for repetition. Except for these words, however, there is great variation in the rate of repetition. The range of repetition for words not on the Dolch list was frequently from as few as once to as many as forty-nine times in a book in which they appeared. There also appears to be no consistency about where the word is repeated. It may be in the next sentence or not until the following chapter.

Obviously this variation in the provision for repetition is not a critical deficiency for a majority of children. For many children, however, this constitutes a considerable shortcoming. It can contribute to the difficulty in finding available published material suitably matched to the potential learning rate of many handicapped and of other children handicapped only in terms of the learning requirements of the available material.

Learning requirements also differ according to certain word characteristics. There are no apparent efforts to differentiate between words on the basis of these characteristics. The characteristics that affect the teaching/learning requirements of words have to do with imagery levels. This factor has received some previous consideration. A mental picture of the referent for concrete nouns can be readily formed. This concrete characteristic indicates a high imagery level. It is not so easy to form a clear mental image of abstract nouns. Research on imagery level (Hargis, 1978b; Hargis & Gickling, 1978; Hargis & Gickling, 1980) indicate that high-imagery nouns require less repetition for children to master. Structure words and low-imagery nouns require more repetition.

The contextual placement of certain words is also important in considering how much repetition is needed. Sentence context has a demonstrated facilitating effect on the verbal learning of retarded children (Jensen & Rohwer, 1963a, 1963b; Payne, Polloway, Smith, & Payne, 1977). Learning of structure words and low-imagery words greatly benefits from introduction and repetition in meaningful contexts. Repetition of these words in isolation is much less effective.

It is perhaps fortunate that much repetition of the structure words of our language occurs quite naturally because certain terms comprise parts of most sentences. If the sentence has meaning for the child, the context is helpful in facilitating the learning of the structure words. If structure words are coupled with low-imagery nouns or occur in sentences or discourse outside the child's experience, the repetition that occurs is likely to be limited in effectiveness. If the repetition of words occurs in a figurative or idiomatic structure, the impact of the repetition may also be limited.

Often the author has observed that a large portion of remedial effort with children who have severely limited reading ability has been directed to teaching so-called "sight words," usually the Dolch List. Frequently the effort is on teaching the work in isolation, often with flash cards or as a part of various games. The results are disappointing. There are no high-imagery nouns on the Dolch list, and there are only about sixteen on the first 10 percent of those in *3000 instant words* (Sakiey & Fry, 1979). Presenting the words in isolation does seem to be the most simple, direct method of teaching these words; but the learning rate, even with great amounts of repetition, is very disappointing. There is no precedent in any language or reading situation for reading structure words that occur with high frequency in isolation. One never sees a sign or a label with single words like *were, the, this, of,* or *with.* Learning these words can be greatly facilitated by insuring that their repetition occurs in meaningful discourse. Experience stories offer a beneficial medium for providing repetition for words that appear frequently, like the Dolch words. The common structure words and pronouns inevitably are repeated. It may, however, be difficult to provide systematic repetition of new words that appear less often.

Words within the child's experience are meaningful. Comprehension stands out as a factor in influencing learning rate or ease of learning and retention of sight words (Brescia & Braun, 1977; Wittrock, 1978). Pictures also can provide understandable context to increase learning rate and retention (Lesgold, De Good, & Levin, 1977).

The introduction and repetition of new words in most reading programs is apparently adequate for most children. In terms of the needs of groups of handicapped children and, unfortunately, many nonhandicapped children, however, these introductions are haphazard and inadequate. The imagery level of a type of word must be considered. The context in which words are introduced must have meaning. Control over the format of repetition for either a structure or form word is also necessary. Structure words require placement in meaningful syntactic contexts. High-imagery nouns that convey meaning to the child make the most appropriate contextual components of a phrase or sentence. Pictures clearly illustrating story context have a similar facilitating effect. Adequate additional provisions for repetition in a sufficiently appropriate context must be made for many handicapped children. The needed rate of repetition may well vary from child to child, but it is certainly most efficiently provided in appropriate contexts and in meaningful material.

There are no controls at all for either the introduction or repetition of syntactic structures or idiomatic structures. This creates a problem that teachers must currently deal with through various adjustments and adaptions. Details of managing these problems are considered in the chapter on preparation and selection of reading materials.

Adapting instructional materials

With many children who have experienced great difficulty in learning to read for an extended period, it is very difficult to find material with a format appropriate to age but sufficiently simple in terms of the ratio of knowns to unknowns being introduced. Also, it is one thing to identify material appropriate at an instructional level and still another to maintain instruction there, when the learning rates of children vary significantly from the rather vague and often haphazard provisions for repetition provided by various published programs. If the necessary assessment procedures to identify appropriate reading material reveal that the child cannot read available material at an instructional level, it becomes necessary to prepare some additional material. This can be transitional material that provides controls over introduction and repetition, the necessary intermediate steps leading the child to the point of reading the regular available material. The attainment of this objective does not mean that the child can maintain normal progress in that reading program. If the repetition requirement needed to meet a student's learning rate is not met, the material very quickly becomes frustrating. The newly introduced words remain unfamiliar longer and may not be mastered. The load of words remaining unfamiliar accumulates and approaches, then surpasses, the child's threshold of comprehension and ability to stay on task. In order to maintain the child in the regular reading program, it may be necessary to provide additional material that parallels the regular program. The purpose is to provide the necessary additional repetition and reduce the introduction rate to within the child's instructional-level threshold.

Individualized instructional reading material can permit two necessary components of student behavior: comprehension and engaged or on-task behaviors. Individualized instruction is thought of in many ways, but its critical components concern the ratio of knowns to unknowns in reading and drill activities. On-task or engaged time is heavily dependent upon the structure of reading material. Instructional-level materials permit on-task behavior. Frustration-level materials, on the other hand, encourage off-task behavior. Time spent actively engaged in reading is the necessary ingredient in reading as a language process.

When children do not have appropriate instructional-level material to engage time, other behaviors appear. Obviously, a child not engaged in the instructional activity must be doing something else. A child unable to engage in meaningful classwork or peer interaction develops inappropriate behavior. This behavior can take a variety of forms—from refusal to work or temper outbursts to physical or mental withdrawal. A negative attitude toward reading will result in avoidance. Frustration-level materials do not permit sustained attention and give rise to such labels as "poor attention span" or "attentional deficit."

Appropriate rates for introduction and repetition are the foundation of individualized instruction, critical factors in permitting on-task or engaged time in reading. The ability to read itself seems to be an excellent reinforcer. It can only be reinforcing, however, if the child experiences a high rate of success and comprehension while engaging in reading activities. Appropriately structured instructional and independent reading activities carry intrinsically the most generally reinforcing constituent. Success, as Skinner (1972) points out, is enough reinforcement for most people. Material designed to facilitate correct response produces enough frequent success.

Task completion is a much more readily attainable objective when reading activity is at an instructional level. Hewitt (1980) emphasizes the motivation supplied by successful task completion. Successes at all levels, during reading and by completing reading activities, are the highly motivating results of providing material that satisfies individual instructional needs.

In the chapter on assessment, we discussed a basic procedure for identifying children with learning disabilities caused by factors other than the reading curriculum. This assessment procedure involves identifying the instructional reading level of learning disabled children, then observing their behavior over an extended period while maintaining instruction at this level. Residual off-task behaviors, even after an extended period using appropriately individualized instructional material, are primary evidence that the cause of the learning difficulty must be dealt with specifically. Whatever remedial action is taken, however, does not lessen the need to prepare appropriate instructional-level reading activities for the children. It is counterproductive to attempt to change off-task behavior when the task itself does not permit attention maintenance.

The persisting off-task behaviors need to be observed and base-line data concerning on-task time recorded. If a child's attention maintenance does not extend to the length of the normally assigned work period, which may be from twenty to fifty minutes, the work should be shortened so that task completion is possible within the current range of the child's capacity to attend. The child needs to feel the reinforcement provided by task completion. Consistent experiences of task completion can gradually extend the work period. If necessary, tangible reinforcement can be added to increase duration.

The attention problem of some children may be the result of distraction. Sensitivity to distraction must initially be handled by adjusting the environment to reduce the level of distraction to within the child's current threshold of toleration. Quiet areas, study carrels, or booths may provide an environment sufficiently free from distraction to promote task completion. After this point, the toleration may gradually be increased toward more reasonable levels of distraction.

REFERENCES

Adkins, P. G. Relevancy in children's language. *Reading Teacher*, 1970, *24*, 7–11.

Barlow, J. H., Kerlin, J. R., & Pollio, H. R. *Training manual for identifying figurative language* (Tech. Rep. No. 1). Knoxville: Metaphor Research Group, University of Tennessee, 1971.

Betts, Emmet A. *Foundations of reading instruction.* New York: American Book, 1946.

Brescia, Shelagh M., & Braun, Carl. Associative verbal encoding and sight vocabulary acquisition and retention. *Journal of Reading Behavior*, 1977, *9*, 259–267.

Burns, Paul C. *It really isn't raining cats and dogs—figurative language.* Paper presented at the 25th annual convention of the International Reading Association, St. Louis, May 6, 1980.

Dechant, Emerald V. *Improving the teaching of reading.* Englewood Cliffs: Prentice-Hill, 1970.

Gates, Arthur I. *Interest and ability in reading.* New York: Macmillan, 1931.

Gickling, Edward E., & Armstrong, David L. Levels of instructional difficulty as related to on-task behavior, task completion, and comprehension. *Journal of Learning Disabilities*, 1978, *11*, 559–566.

Hargis, Charles H. A comparison of retarded and nonretarded children on the ability to use context in reading. *American Journal of Mental Deficiency*, 1972, *76*, 726–728.

Hargis, Charles H. *An analysis of the syntactic and figurative structure of popular first-grade level basal readers.* Paper presented at the 12th meeting of the Southeastern Conference on Linguistics, Washington, D.C., November 1974.

Hargis, Charles H. *Guidelines for the preparation of reading and language materials for hearing impaired children.* Paper presented at the Alexander Graham Bell Association for the Deaf national convention, St. Louis, June 25, 1978. (a)

Hargis, Charles H. *Word recognition development as a function of imagery level.* Paper presented at the summer meeting of the Linguistic Society of America, Champaign-Urbana, University of Illinois, July 28, 1978. (b)

Hargis, Charles H., & Gickling, Edward E. The function of imagery in word recognition development. *The Reading Teacher*, 1978, *31*, 570–574.

Hargis, Charles H., & Gickling, Edward E. *Word recognition development as a function of imagery level and syntactic classification.* Paper presented at the 6th southeastern regional conference of the International Reading Association, Norfolk, Va., November 14, 1980.

Herrick, Virgil E. Basal instructional materials in reading. *Development in and through reading: 60th yearbook of the National Society of the Study of Education* (Part 1). Chicago: University of Chicago Press, 1961.

Hewitt, Frank M., & Taylor, Frank D. *The emotionally disturbed child in the classroom: The orchestration of success* (2nd ed.). Boston: Allyn & Bacon, 1980.

Jensen, A. R., & Rohwer, W. D. The effect of mental mediation on the learning and retention of paired associates by retarded adults. *American Journal of Mental Deficiency,* 1963, *68,* 80–84. (a)

Jensen, A. R., & Rohwer, W. D. Verbal mediation in paired associates and serial learning. *Journal of Verbal Learning and Verbal Behavior,* 1963, *1,* 346–352. (b)

Lesgold, Alan M., De Good, Hildrene, & Levin, Joel R. Pictures and young children's prose learning: A supplementary report. *Journal of Reading Behavior,* 1977, *9,* 353–360.

Little, Karen. *The effect of figurative language on the reading comprehension of mildly educationally handicapped children.* Unpublished master's thesis, University of Tennessee, 1981.

Payne, James S., Polloway, Edward A., Smith, James E., Jr., & Payne, Ruth Ann. *Strategies for teaching the mentally retarded.* Columbus: Charles E. Merrill, 1977.

Robertson, Jean E. Figurative language. *Instructor,* 1973, *13,* 50–51.

Rosenshine, Barak V., & Berliner, David C. Academic engaged time. *British Journal of Teacher Education,* 1978, *4,* 3–16.

Sakiey, Elizabeth, & Fry, Edward: *3000 instant words.* Highland Park, N.J.: Dreier, 1979.

Skinner, B. F. Teaching: The arrangement of contingencies under which something is taught. In N. G. Haring & A. H. Hayden (Eds.), *Improvement of instruction.* Seattle: Special Child, 1972.

Spache, George D. *Investigating the issues of reading disabilities.* Boston: Allyn & Bacon, 1976.

Strickland, R. G. The language of elementary school children: Its relationship to language of reading textbooks and the quality of reading of selected children. *Bulletin of the School of Education, Indiana University,* 1962, *38,* 101–103.

Wittrock, M. C. The cognitive movement in instruction. *Educational Researcher,* 1978, *8,* 5–11.

5

METHODS OF
TEACHING READING

Instructional levels

Skills teaching

Oral reading

Sight words

Approaches to beginning reading

**Adaptions for children
with sensory impairments**

5

Instructional levels

As Smith (1978) points out, what a child needs most in learning to read is reading itself. Time engaged in reading is essential to developing reading ability. When reading programs fragment the material into minute sets of readiness skills, word-identification skills, and isolated sight words, the essential ingredient is slighted. Increasingly we seem to assume that reading instruction is composed of a myriad of such constituents as these, and unfortunately, the more disabled the reader, the more fractionated the reading program becomes. This is always at the expense of the essential ingredient—meaningful reading. The child with reading difficulty actually needs the reverse—more time engaged in reading and less on "component skills."

Setting aside time for actual reading is essential, but equally important is the kind of material that is made available for the students to read. The availability of material at an appropriate instructional and independent level for each student is necessary to make time engaged in reading possible and to maximize time spent in reading. There are some procedures for maintaining a child in reading without careful attention to materials selection. These procedures should only be viewed as transitional or temporary, however. They can be helpful, but they are not substitutes for the selection of instructional-level material. These procedures are discussed further on in the chapter.

The regular use of instructional-level reading material provides exercise in independent reading: reading as a receptive language process at a level that can be meaningful.

Instructional-level material can permit a student to read within a large classroom with children having a variety of reading levels. Without instructional-level materials to engage a child in reading, someone must be present to intervene each time the child has difficulty. As intervention increases, moreover, the time engaged in reading is lessened and becomes increasingly less like a normal receptive language activity. The material is only comprehensible as long as a teacher or tutor is stationed by the child's side to provide information on the overload of unknown components.

The demand on teacher time extends beyond just the need to provide missing information and to deal with a variety of off-task behaviors that are the result of the student's inability to attend.

Teachers must choose when and how the demands on their time will be met. Will they be met with the preparation and selection of appropriate materials or by their acting as tutors, helping children to conform to the available material and to stay on task? Instructional-level material can be self-engaging. Because the child needs much less help at the instructional level, he need not compare himself unfavorably to students who seem to require less help.

Instructional-level materials serve several critical motivational functions. One just mentioned is the feeling of competence gained through the ability to read more independently. Also of primary importance is the avoidance of failure. The frustration and apprehension about reading that results from failure is anathema to progress. By definition and structure, instructional-level reading materials insure success. The reinforcement provided by success in reading is essential and in most cases, especially with children who have experienced reading difficulty, sufficient. The reward is reading itself. On the other hand, without instructional-level material, reading may be a punishing activity, for which the students feel apprehension and which they want to avoid. Children who are afraid of failing to read are not likely to learn to read (Smith, 1978), and certainly no one who *is* failing at reading can learn to read.

Adequate comprehension is necessary to indicate that the material read is sufficiently meaningful. Hocevar and Hocevar (1978) found that when the content of reading material was meaningfully related to recent cognitive experiences, beginning readers read with 25 percent fewer errors. Meaningful material maximizes the use of context, probably the most important component of learning to read. At the instructional level, sufficient known, understandable context can help predict the unknown and unfamiliar words. Such prediction or risk taking, as Smith (1975, 1978) states, is necessary for learning to read. A child must feel enough confidence to risk making an error. The teacher certainly should provide an atmosphere that fosters such prediction, and the material itself should be structured to encourage accurate prediction as enhanced by adequately strong context. As material becomes more difficult than the instructional level, prediction becomes more like random guessing, and errors that interfere with comprehension remain uncorrected. Success at prediction is intrinsically reinforcing, and instructional-level material optimizes this success. A child may make an error in prediction, but the error is much more likely to be a sensible substitution that does not interfere with comprehension. Adding a few word-identification skills increases the likelihood of accurate prediction. These skills are discussed further on in the chapter.

Using material that is too difficult decreases the likelihood of accuracy and success in prediction. Unfamiliar context is not effective in narrowing down the choices of what the unfamiliar word may be. Using it encourages random guessing (Hood, 1978), definitely to be avoided. Such behavior can become a habit difficult to change. Instructional-level materials should be provided, additional helpful context included, and an environment encouraging prediction structured. Smith (1975, 1978) points out that using context and prediction is something to be encouraged, not necessarily taught, because the process has been used in learning new words from the beginning stages of spoken language acquisition. Reading print is a process of language comprehension, and teaching reading should capitalize on skills available in normal systems of language acquisition.

Skills teaching

The assumption that the ability to read is a composite of identifiable subskills requires that constituent subskills be laid out in a hierarchy or scope and sequence for the purpose of teaching. Some of these skills are necessary because they comprise the basis of the teacher's instructional talk. If a teacher uses the word *letter,* the the child must know what letters are, or there will be no comprehension of the directions. Terms like *letter, word,* or *sound* represent only a few of the constituent items that may appear in the early part of some reading programs. Literally hundreds occur in various reading programs. Many of these subskills must be learned because they are a part of the reading program, and progress in the program is measured against mastery of its constituent skills. The skills that must be learned are those defined as important to the reading program in use. This is often the only reason for teaching them. As Morrone (1958) effectively pointed out, there is no incontrovertible evidence that most of the "skills" presented are essential in learning to read.

There is much evidence that the ability to apply the skills and mental ability are correlated (Bond & Dykstra, 1967; Dolch & Bloomster, 1937; Spache, 1976). The overemphasis of these skills in reading programs for the retarded is to their disadvantage. There is also little value in encouraging many of these "skills" in reading programs for use with hearing impaired children, who have no familiar spoken counterpart of the printed word to decode.

The importance of the various skills is largely determined by the definition of reading held by the authors of the particular reading program, or test. If reading is defined as being largely a set of subskills, which subskills to include will be important. But if reading is first and foremost a receptive language process, the subskills included should be useful. How helpful is a given skill in developing independence in reading? The utility should further be judged relative to the handicap of the group or individual for whom it is to be included. Rather than a lexicon of the hundreds of reading subskills included in reading programs in this chapter, those with the most practical applicability in fostering independence (in learning to read and in reading itself) should be emphasized.

A variety of terms is associated with the various skills. Some clarification may be helpful before proceeding with further discussion. The term *metalinguistics* has come into frequent use in the discussion of some of the reading skills. In regard to reading, metalinguistic terms are those used to describe or analyze printed language. Even the terms *letter, word, sentence,* and *paragraph* are metalinguistic. Any terms seen as part of the reading program that a child needs to understand when hearing about various aspects of print and reading can be considered metalinguistic.

Concepts about print may or may not be associated with metalinguistic terms. These concepts have to do with conventions of the printed form of language relative to the spoken form. They may seem simple, but often they are very important. Children's metalinguistic awareness does not always keep pace with the demands of classroom instruction (Blachowicz, 1978). The temporal order of spoken language becomes the top-to-bottom and left-to-right sequence of printed English. Books must be held a certain way, pages turned in a certain direction and read in sequence. Letters follow from left to right. Words have spaces of a certain size between them to denote their boundaries. Children must learn to segment the essentially continuous flow of spoken language into the visually discontinuous flow of separate words in printed form.

A variety of terms is associated with learning to read words. Some of the more common are *phonics, decoding, word attack, word analysis, word perception, word recognition,* and *word identification.* These seem at times to be used interchangeably. Here the terms *word recognition* and *word identification* are differentiated. *Word recognition,* in this book, indicates the instant recognition of printed words. Children sufficiently familiar with words in print recognize them instantly, as they do familiar spoken words. Word identification, here, is the process of identifying words not yet sufficiently familiar to be instantly recognized.

The term *phonics* is probably best defined as the relationship between spelling and sound, even though it is often used in a generic sense to denote a supposed method of teaching reading. Other terms used in a similar way are *grapheme-phoneme correspondence, sound-symbol relationship*, and *spelling-sound correspondence*. The term *structural analysis* refers to the use of specific spelling conventions having to do with syllabication, accent or stress, inflectional endings, and affixes in the identification of words.

LETTER-SOUND ASSOCIATIONS

Word-identification skills cover a broad range of items. Smith (1978) mentions the 300-plus spelling-to-sound correspondences that have been identified in twenty thousand common English words. In the six thousand one- and two-syllable words from this group, no fewer than 211 correspondences occur. Studies of individual sounds in English usually only consider about 45, however. This is obviously a greater number of sounds than there are letters in the alphabet, so combinations of letters are used to represent some sounds. In an analysis of over twenty thousand words, 52 "major spelling units" were found: 20 for the vowels and 32 for the consonants (Venezky, 1967). The 21 consonant letters are used to represent about 26 consonant sounds. Sometimes 2 consonant letters must be used to represent a single sound. These combinations are called consonant digraphs. The most common ones are *sh, th,* and *wh. Th* actually represents different sounds, the one heard at the beginning of *think* and the other at the beginning of *these*. The latter *th* is voiced and the former not voiced. A significant number of people, experienced teachers, have difficulty distinguishing between the two sounds. This may be because placement of the articulators is identical for both. The only difference between the two sounds is the use of voice with one and only breath with the other. Obviously there is implicit knowledge of the distinction because these are consistently used correctly in speech. Conscious awareness of the distinction, however, is difficult for many to grasp. This notion of implicit and conscious knowledge is an important perspective in both understanding and teaching reading. Some phoneticians are unlikely to credit the *wh* as having a sound distinct from the *w* when it is a part of a word in connected discourse. The *ch* spelling sequence is usually listed with the digraphs. It frequently represents the sounds heard at the beginning and end of *church*. It is, however, the blend of the sounds *t* and *sh*.

Two consonant letters are particularly troublesome in that each may frequently represent two sounds. One, the letter *c*, has no sound distinctly its own; it can have the sound of *s* or *k*, depending upon what vowel or consonant letter follows it. Followed by the letter *h*, it most often has the sound indicated by the digraph *ch*. The rules and generalizations that have evolved around predicting the sounds that the letter *c* has are varied and complex. The letter *g* can have its own "hard" *g* sound or the same sound that the letter *j* often has. Which sound it has usually depends on what consonant or vowel follows it. If *g* is followed by the letter *h*, it usually produces the *f* sound. The rules or generalizations associated with the letter *g*, as with *c*, are varied, complex, and very difficult for the beginning reader to learn, let alone apply. They are even difficult for the adult in training as a reading teacher or a special educator. The difficulty is with conscious mastery, not implicit knowledge already demonstrated.

The letter *x* has no sound of its own. In more common words, it represents the sound of *k* and *s*, as in the word *box*. Here, the sound is a final consonant blend of *-ks*. It does not always represent a consonant blend, however. In words like *exercise*, the *k* sound ends the first syllable, and the *s* sound begins the next. This pronunciation follows if the *x* ends an accented syllable and is followed by a vowel. In words like *exclude*, if the *x* is followed by a consonant the *-ks* blend ends the syllable. In words like *exact*, the *x* ends an unaccented syllable and is followed by a vowel. In such instances, *x* represents the sounds of *g* and *z*. Less frequently, and depending on etymology of the word containing it, the *x* can represent the sound of *z* as in *xylophone*.

The spelling sequence *qu* represents the sounds of *kwh* or *kw* as in *quick* or *quiet*.

One consonant sound in English has no consistent spelled representation at all. This is the sound you hear represented by the spelling sequence *si* in vi*si*on and the letter *z* in azure.

These are some of the major problems with the consonant letters and their correspondent sounds. By and large, however, they are relatively consistent when compared to the letter-sound problems associated with the vowels. As Smith (1978) points out, in the six thousand most-common one- and two-syllable words, there are 83 different letter-sound associations for the consonants and 128 for vowel sounds. These fewer vowel letters—*a, e, i, o, u* and occasionally *y* and *w*—represent an even more varied group of sound associations than do the consonants. The letter *r* following any of the vowel letters indicates special additional pronunciation conditions. Vowel sounds and their letter associations are much less stable than consonants in two major respects. The first of these is dialect. The most significant distinction among regional dialects is in vowel pronunciation. Consonants represent the same sounds across dialects, but some vowels can represent as many distinctly different sounds as there are distinguishable dialects in spoken English. The second is in regard to place of accent of syllables within words. Regardless of the letter representation of vowels within syllables, place of accent determines whether a vowel with full value can be produced. Unaccented syllables have reduced vowel sounds. All vowel sounds may be reduced to either of two forms. These are represented by the phonetic symbols *I* or *ə* (schwa), depending upon what vowel is being reduced. This problem is especially noticeable in derived forms of words in which the pattern of accent changes but the vowel letter representing each of the syllables cannot. Consider the pairs *telegraphic-telegraphy* and *orthographic-orthography*. Notice that the vowel sounds change with the pattern of accent. The vowel letters, however, cannot change. No matter what the vowel letters are in a syllable, the sounds they actually may represent in speech are dominated by placement of accent. Take the two words *homophone* and *homophene*. In *homophone*, the vowel in the last syllable is the long *o*. In *homophene*, the vowel in the last syllable is the long *e*. If the suffix *-ous* is added to both of the words, the pattern of accent changes. The vowel in the last syllable in the root word is reduced to *schwa* in both instances. Two vowel sounds are changed to the same sound by the change in accent. The reduction in both cases *(homophonous, homophenous)* causes them to be pronounced identically! Complex systems of accent or stress operate in words and sentences in English. These systems are regulated by complex rules (Chomsky &

Halle, 1968) and are only now being systematically analyzed. In multisyllable words, there is a system of alternation between accented and unaccented syllables. It is basically inevitable, therefore, that some vowel sounds in most multisyllable words do not represent the vowel letters in the printed form. Accent (stress) and dialect dominate the actual vowel sound represented by any vowel letters. Attention to vowel sounds in word-indentification programs must be carefully moderated by this knowledge. Even though we demonstrate implicit knowledge of the rules through spoken language, the nature of these rules in their relationship to print poses a great challenge to conscious mastery. Adults who are competent readers inevitably forget how difficult it is to match the appropriate vowel sound with the vowel letters in unfamiliar words. They may be reminded, however, if they are required to pronounce words with which they have little familiarity. Take for example, words such as *tragedian, automaton,* or *microscopy.* Usually, when using a dictionary to determine the pronunciation of a word, one must check the vowel sounds in the word, not the consonants.

Determining the vowel sounds in printed words that are unfamiliar in speech is usually most accurately done by consulting a dictionary or asking someone who knows the word. It is possible to use a complex set of rules to determine placement of stress and sounds in a word, but these are far too complex to include in beginning reading programs. Besides, at this level of instruction, we are not trying to teach children to pronounce strange words but to identify an otherwise familiar word from the unfamiliar printed form. As will be demonstrated later, the most important reading skill for dealing with vowels in beginning reading is not their letter-to-sound association or complex syllabication and stress rules but the effective use of context and prediction!

STRUCTURAL ANALYSIS

Structural analysis considers more extensive units of words than individual letter-sound associations. It includes syllables, compound words, contractions, inflectional endings, accent, prefixes, and suffixes. Common inflectional endings are often introduced in the first grade. Syllabication, accent, prefixes, and suffixes are usually introduced later, and their study frequently extends over several years. This latter group forms a highly complex body of rules and generalizations that have varying degrees of consistency, not to speak of their relative utility. Most adults have no conscious knowledge of the system. Adults in teacher training have considerable difficulty in learning many of the structural-analysis generalizations. A good many of these are used primarily in regard to vowel sounds, as mentioned earlier. Their utility in beginning reading programs for most children should be carefully considered before time is devoted to them at the expense of that engaged in actual reading.

HOW MUCH EMPHASIS ON SKILLS TEACHING

From Huey (1908) to Smith (1971), we find an ebb and flow of emphasis on meaning as the main concern of word identification. As Huey stated:

> Careful observation, however, reveals the fact that words are seldom or never heard as mere sounds. What seems to be their sound is really mainly the meaning which we read into them . . . when we are occasionally able to attend mainly to the raw sounds of a word divorced from meaning, the word sounds as strange and unlike itself . . . as any letter or figure when unduly stared at. (p. 164)

In the process of fractionating reading into sets of subskills, the meaning is divorced from skills teaching. The focus and approach to word identification presented in this chapter emphasizes meaning. Word-identification skills are used to identify a word through its meaning, not through a set of abstract sounds that have no psychological reality for a child. Meaning and meaningfulness should be central factors in beginning reading programs.

Another consideration in emphasis of skills teaching is the utility of the skill and its relative order of teaching, considering its difficulty or "learnability." Considerable attention has already been paid the multitude of problems in the hierarchical placement of various reading skills. However, placing the skill in sequence, in terms of its relative difficulty, is given extra consideration in this chapter. It is important not to dilute reading time with teaching subskills more difficult than ones more readily learned and, possibly, applied. This is certainly true of teaching skills that are more difficult to attain than some actual reading ability would be. One must remember that reading achievement can occur without learning the supposed subskills. This is most obviously apparent in languages represented ideographically. These do not have a phonic component to break into subskills. Profoundly deaf children must learn to read any language as if it were ideographic.

Often the word-identification skills are isolated in such a way that meaning cannot be a part of their use. They are unnecessarily difficult and have even less psychological reality for children. Word-identification skills should be used to identify words (meaning), not the sounds of words.

Remember that fragmentation of speech into isolated words seldom occurs in the physically real world of the child, and the fragmentation of words into phonemes never occurs. Children do not hear words, let alone parts of words, fragmented and segmented as they are often presented in reading programs. It is only when appropriate word-identification skills are used to identify word meaning that the skills themselves can actually be applied in identifying words.

The number of skills that can or should be taught is variable. One cannot assume that an invariant number must constitute any part of the reading program. Reading programs that most strongly emphasize phonics have the highest correlation between achievement and IQ (Bond & Dykstra, 1967). With retarded children, the teaching approach, as well as the method of reading emphasized, should capitalize on their strength in rote-associative learning. The generalization of skills to the identification of new words cannot be assumed with retarded students. The skills emphasized with them must be the most straightforward and utilitarian; and they must be presented as a meaningful reading activity, not in isolation divorced from application. If the benefits gained from the teaching of word-identification skills are at the expense of time and improvement in reading ability, skills teaching should receive reduced attention relative to time spent in reading at appropriate instructional levels.

As IQ declines to the moderate range, this intellectual approach to reading (teaching of skills), should be decreasing rapidly. As retardation becomes more severe, emphasis should become increasingly attuned to survival and functional reading. Independent identification of words through a decoding process must be replaced by associative signal responses to important selected words and phrases.

WORD-IDENTIFICATION SKILLS FOR THE HEARING IMPAIRED

Conventional use of word-identification skills with hearing impaired children is simply not appropriate, though unfortunately this is often the practice. Letter-sound association or phonics by definition is inappropriate for children who have no perceived speech sound to which they may make an association. This is especially significant for the most profoundly hearing impaired. The "deaf" population is not constituted of people with no hearing, however. Over 80 percent of deaf children have residual hearing in at least three speech-reception frequencies. Almost half of the population has residual hearing in all speech frequencies. The current generation of effective high-fidelity hearing aids and auditory-training equipment makes this residual hearing an increasingly significant asset for hearing impaired children in language and speech development. Even the best hearing aids, however, are unlikely to make spelling-to-sound correspondences possible for the forty-odd sounds. How much emphasis on how many of these word-identification skills, for which they have no auditory model, must be determined case by case. Here, the printed form is used as a guide or visual aid in teaching each of the speech sounds. The Northampton Charts were developed at the Clark School for the Deaf in Northampton, Massachusetts, for this purpose (Yale, 1946). These charts contain the most common spellings that represent the various speech sounds. The purpose of the charts was to help deaf children recognize the various spellings of speech sounds so that they could gain some independence in using print as a guide to pronunciation. In fairly wide use in American schools for the deaf, they were also employed as the basis for the Phonovisual Method (Schoolfield & Timberlake, 1974) for the teaching of word-identification skills to hearing children.

In speech-reading activities the appearance of the various speech sounds are related through instruction to different spelled forms of the sounds. The Northampton Charts are commonly used for this purpose also. These activities are often a natural outgrowth of speech teaching. Auditory training is related to spelling in much the same way. Whatever words or sounds are the focus of discrimination are further related to their printed form. As these additional language arts for the deaf are integrated, the symbol associations can be incorporated in the reading program.

SYNTHETIC AND ANALYTIC METHODS

Harris and Sipay (1975) provide a detailed but concise description of the origin and evolution of both synthetic and analytic reading methods. Reading methods that begin by teaching letter-sound associations before they present words, phrases, or sentences are said to be synthetic methods. After the children learn letter-sound associations they are expected to use them to "sound out" unfamiliar printed words. The scope and sequence for spelling-to-sound associations can vary greatly. Analytic methods start with words and use the known ones as the basis for forming letter-sound associations. The number of words learned first and the letter-sound associations contained in them vary considerably.

Major criticisms of synthetic methods include that overemphasis of word analysis tends to produce slow, labored reading, at the expense of meaning and comprehension. "Word calling" has been associated with the behavior of children who characteristically labor haltingly over the production of each word, one at a time, in oral reading. It is also almost impossible to depend entirely on sound-by-sound analysis to produce the correct pronunciation of a word.

Major criticisms of some analytic methods concern a selection of words initially introduced to help form the letter-sound associations. This criticism has been especially hard on "linguistic" or "programmed" materials greatly concerned with regularity in controlling letter-sound associations. Printed discourse comes to bear little relationship to comprehensible language usage, at times approaching nonsense.

With handicapped children, a direct approach to beginning reading—one that makes reading a meaningful language experience—is probably best. Word-identification skills are most effectively added as the teacher witnesses the progress and needs of children in learning to read.

WHICH SKILLS SHOULD BE EMPHASIZED

Earlier, the use of context was emphasized as the most important word-identification skill. In reading material at an instructional level, context alone is sufficient to predict exactly more than one-third of the missing words deleted through the Cloze procedure. Syntactic and semantic clues provided by the surrounding discourse provide the basic information for word identification. Context reduces the number of alternatives for any given new word. Any placement in discourse provides contextual information that reduces the number of alternative possibilities for the new word. Context aids in prediction. It is often not sufficient for the identification of a new word, but it is always necessary except for the most common structure words. Take for example the word *contract*. Only in context can one determine whether the word is a verb or a noun. The location of stress changes and the pronunciation depend on whether it is in a verb or a noun position. Consider these sentences:

> They signed the *contract*.
> They will *contract* the disease.

When checking entries in a dictionary, one usually finds multiple definitions. Words in isolation are often ambiguous in meaning and pronunciation. Consider, besides the example above, the words *address, record, contest, object, permit, graduate, duplicate, estimate,* and *alternate,* for example. Only context can determine whether these are verbs or nouns. Note also that the consonant sounds are stable but that the accent and the vowel sound shift.

Use of context coupled with the knowledge of a relatively few letter-sound associations, primarily for consonants, increases accuracy. Without the use of context, as is necessarily the case when words appear in isolation, a great many more phonic skills are required. It is, in fact, much less likely that an unfamiliar printed word can be correctly identified if it appears completely apart from context. It is fortunate that actual reading situations do not demand reading isolated words. Words in isolation frequently appear as labels or signs whose direct referent or situational placement provides important nonlinguistic context. The words isolated on flash cards, in word lists, on "word wheels," or in "games" unfortunately do not have this context to assist in their identification.

Using context is a skill already available as part of the normal language-acquisition process—that is, if the child's handicap is in no way definable in terms of language deficiency. This available skill should be treated as valuable capital and its use encouraged at every opportunity. It certainly does not make sense to discourage its use by the overemphasis of identifying words in isolation. There should be continuous opportunity for practice with the use of context.

Concepts about print   The first skills to present should be those that have to do with concepts and insights about print. These concepts are best presented while reading to the children. In group work, the reading can be done from experience charts, bulletin boards, or "big books." The children can learn the spatial concepts related to the order of print on a page and the order of pages. The meaning of *letter, word,* and *sentence* can be gained implicitly as the teacher reads and points to the words, and during the writing and reading of experience charts. Preparing and reading labels, signs, and bulletin boards provide similar experience with these concepts. No metalinguistic terms need be introduced to present or to learn these concepts.

Children need to become aware of the sequence of words in a sentence, sentences on a page, and pages in a book or on an experience chart. They must recognize the boundaries of words and the direction of the sequence of letters that words contain. The notions of juncture and punctuation should begin here as well.

Using spoken context   Before children are able to recognize any words independently, or before they can recognize a sufficient number of words to use as familiar context, the teacher should provide exercises using spoken context. As a sentence is being read, the teacher should pause and ask what word comes next. As words are being written on an experience chart teachers can stop and ask the students if they know or remember what word comes next. Sentences with words omitted from various positions can be read and the child asked to supply the missing word. Any reasonable response that fits the context should be encouraged. A secure atmosphere that fosters prediction should be established.

Recognizing letter forms   It is very helpful to recognize the forms of both capital and lowercase letters and to know their names. This is true not because it is a part of reading per se, but because it is convenient and helpful in talking about words, what sounds the letters have, and for comparing printed words. It is also necessary if the language arts are to be most effectively integrated with reading. The teaching of handwriting and spelling can be used as a part of reading at the outset and can readily lead to making letter-sound associations.

With hearing impaired children, depending on the mode of communication used in the school, the letter names may not be in spoken form. The printed association may be the letter formed by the one-hand manual alphabet. The finger-spelled letters may be related to their printed counterparts. With some hearing impaired children the letters and letter combinations may be related to their form in the production of speech sounds on a speaker's lips.

Letter-sound associations   The consonant sounds provide the most helpful information, when coupled with the use of context, in identifying unfamiliar printed words. These letter-sound associations should not be taught as abstract isolated relationships. They should be learned as parts of words. After children recognize a letter they can learn that the letter has the sound heard in a word that contains it. The sound need not be isolated from the word. Sounds isolated from words are not heard the same way as when coarticulated with the word's other sounds.

The beginning letter-sound associations should be made with the consonant letters that begin words. These first words should be common concrete nouns. They should have a clear picturable referent that can be a conceptual tie to facilitate the learning of these letter-sound associations. There are many sources of word cards with their pictured referents. They accompany many reading materials, basal reader programs, and many speech therapy materials.

After children learn the letter-sound associations for the beginning consonant sounds in words, they will be better prepared to associate them with the letters that occur at the end or the middle of words. This is more difficult, however, and should be dealt with later.

As the children learn to recognize the letters, the sound associations for some of the consonants they are learning can be presented. These include the voiced consonants $b, d, g, j, l, m, n, r, v, w, y$; the unvoiced consonants c (hard), f, h, k, p, s, t; and the digraphs ch, sh, th, wh. As mentioned previously, the sound associations for these letters should be presented, whenever possible, as the beginning sound of common nouns. As these associations are being made, the children should have the opportunity to use context and the letter-sound association for beginning consonants to identify new words. With the addition of beginning consonants, prediction becomes more accurate. The opportunity for using context with initial consonants should now regularly be provided. Of all the word-identification skills involving letter-sound associations, context in connection with initial consonants is the most helpful. The following consonant associations can be presented next: soft c, soft g, z, and qu. The associations for the voiced s (with the sound of z) as in *his* and the voiced th as in *these* can be presented now, but they are less important. The voiced s does not appear in the initial-consonant position, so its teaching may be deferred until final consonants are presented. It will appear in extremely common words such as *is*, *was*, *as*, and *his*, however, and the association may well have been learned already. The need to make a distinction between the voiced and unvoiced forms of th is usually eliminated if the words containing them are learned in meaningful context and the use of context encouraged.

The sound sometimes produced by the letter sequence ng as in *hang* is emphasized by some. The author believes that there are too many exceptions to warrant teaching it. Exceptions to this association include words like *danger*, *stranger*, and *angel*. In some cases the *ng* sound is produced along with the *g* sound as in *angry, hungry,* and *hunger.* Sometimes the letter *n* has the *ng* sound when it is followed by some consonants as in the words *think, thank, sink, blink, uncle, anchor,* and many more. Words or common spelling patterns are learned more readily than more specific letter-sound associations, with many exceptions.

When final-consonant sounds have received some attention, a second type of letter-sound association can be presented. These are the common endings of words. The sound associations can be related to the whole spelling unit. They are *-ing, -ed,* as in *wanted* (a syllable is added), *-ed* as in *borrowed* (no syllable is added), *-ed* as in *walked* (*t* sound, no syllable is added), *-er, -ly, -est, -es,* as in the verb *watches* and the noun *peaches,* *-y, -less,* and *-ness.* One common ending, *-le* as in *little* and *tickle,* forms an unaccented syllable. The sound association for this syllable has considerable utility.

The spelling-to-sound associations covered so far are the most utilitarian. They should be presented as parts of words, and their use in word identification should be emphasized in context. The order of their presentation should be first in the initial, then in the final, position in words. Presentation of consonants in the final position should be in one-syllable words at first. This is not to say that children cannot be learning multisyllable words. It simply means that the presentation of final-consonant letter-sound associations can be more clearly focused in one-syllable words. Then the transition to associations for consonants that end and begin syllables within multisyllable words is relatively easier.

The next spelling-to-sound associations are for the vowels. The complexity of the vowels has already been stressed. Certainly the spelling patterns for vowel sounds should become familiar to the students if for no other reason than to make sure they are contrasted with the consonants and to help the students develop the notion of the syllable. Some words begin with vowel sounds, so the students should become familiar with sounds of vowels that begin common words. McKee (1966) recommends using the qualifying statement: "This is the sound that ___ sometimes has."

As the letter-sound associations for the consonants are presented, the students can be told that the letters *a, e, i, o, u* are letters that have many different sounds. They can also be told that if they use context and consonants, they usually will not need to know what sound the *a, e, i, o, u* have. Consider this example in which the vowels are deleted:

> Th_ b_ _ w_nt t_ th_ c_rc_s t_ s_ _ th_ f_nn_
> cl_ _ns _nd th_ _ _ _m_ls H_ _t_ L_ts _f p_ _c_ _n
> _nd h_ l_ _gh_d _nd l_ _gh_d _t th_ cl_ _ns.

As you can see, the context provided by the sentence structure, story content, and the consonants is sufficient to make the words known.

Teaching the vowels initially should be limited to introducing their various spelled forms. In this way they can act like the blanks in the selection above, and the students can identify new words using context. When the students become more familiar with a variety of words containing the various vowel spellings, they often will learn the common letter-sound associations on their own. Before teaching the associations for vowels, therefore, test the students' knowledge of them. There is no point in presenting something already known.

The spelling patterns that a child needs to recognize in words are these: the single vowel letters *a, e, i, o, u*; the double letters, both together and final-*e* type; *oo* for both *moon* and *book*; *o-e* and *oa* as in *home* and *boat*; the *ow* for both *tow* and *now*; *aw* and *au*, as in *raw* and *author*; *ee*, as in *need*; *ea* for both *meat* and *bread*; *a-e, ai, ay*, as in *name, pain*, and *pay*; *i-e*, as in *time*; *ie*, as in both *field* and *cried*; *ou* (the most varied of the vowel sounds represents six different vowel sounds besides schwa), as in each of the words *soup, pour, could, cough, rough, house*; *oi* and *oy*, as in *oil* and *boy*; *u-e* as in both *tune* and *cute*. For each of the final, or silent-*e*, spelling sequences, it should be pointed out to the students that the *e* in these cases does not represent a second vowel sound.

The vowel-letter sequences formed with consonants may cause difficulty unless they are shown to represent vowel sounds. These are *ow, aw, ew, oy, ay*. The letter *r*, when it follows a single vowel letter, produces some additional special conditions. *Er, ir, ur* as in *her, girl*, and *hurt* should be dealt with as vowels that represent the same sound. The letter *r* following the single vowel letters *o* and *a*, as in *corn* and *barn*, produces two vowel sounds.

Attention may be directed to the letter-sound associations for the vowels by underlining them in newly introduced words and by comparing them to those in known words.

The number of vowel sounds can be directly related to the number of syllables in words. The auditory training of hearing impaired children can focus on vowels and syllables because the vowel sounds have the greatest low-frequency components and the greatest volume or intensity. As the language arts are integrated for hearing impaired children, vowel sounds can be a basic component.

Some reading programs place considerable emphasis on teaching consonant blends, but where is the great need to dwell on teaching the associations for them? Once the students recognize the letter-sound associations for the individual consonants and *qu*, which is in fact a blend, they have a sufficient basis for dealing with the blends. McKee (1966) recommended that when a new word beginning with a consonant blend appears, attention should be directed to the blend and the students reminded that they know the individual letter sounds. Students can be told that when the letters come together in a word, they have the sound heard at the beginning of some other familiar words that contain the blend. Final blends can be treated similarly. The most common initial blends are *bl, br, dr, dw, fl, re, gl, gr, cl, cr, qu, pl, pr, tr, tw, sl, st, str, sp, spl, spr, sc, scr, sw, squ, sm, sn,* and *shr*. The procedure mentioned above can be used to introduce them. If the individual consonant sounds that make up the blend are known, this introduction should be sufficient.

Some reading programs emphasize syllabication rules. McKee (1966) found that syllabication rules were not needed for students who used context, letter-sound associations for consonants, and a few other items. These rules may help hearing impaired children learn to pronounce words that they are still unable to say, but as for reading skills they are much less important.

A child spending increased time in reading may learn many of the letter-sound associations without direct teaching. The teacher should screen for mastery of each of the various skills to be presented. The procedures for the assessment of letter-sound associations illustrated in Chapter 3 are recommended for this purpose.

New words appearing in a reading selection should receive some introduction. They should be presented in context that may be spoken at the earlier levels. Point to the new word and call attention to the beginning sound and other familiar sounds. Ask the students to identify the word. If they cannot, direct their attention to other words that contain relevant letter sounds. If they still have trouble, simply tell them the word and direct their attention to the important associations. As the students read more widely, they will encounter many new words that need receive no introduction. If they learn to use context and relatively few letter-sound associations, they can develop considerable independence in identifying unfamiliar printed words.

It demoralizes a teacher to have students show inconsistent or unreliable responses in the various reading skills being taught. The child may seem to know it one day and not the next, a common complaint about children who attain very little reading skill even after lengthy periods of instruction. As these children fail to achieve, the skills being taught become increasingly removed from meaningful reading. The reading program becomes more and more isolated—skills centered. When this happens, there is no firm ground for rooting the skills teaching and no meaningful way to apply the skills. The teaching of skills should be directly related to comprehensible reading. The emphasis on context and the skill help keep meaning and skills integrated. As reading skill emerges and the child attains a level of functional literacy, none of the word-identification skills presented earlier will be needed except for context.

Oral reading

Children facing beginning reading instruction have an often-unappreciated range of personality traits. Some are reticent and shy, some assertive and outgoing. These traits, and all shades in between, are present in most first-grade classrooms. Regardless of where the children stand on this continuum, they must all face the demands of oral reading. Teachers must learn to respect a child's natural inclinations. The apprehension and fear a child may have for reading before a group can be enormous. This condition will be worsened if the child is not doing well or lacks confidence in his ability. A substantial number of serious reading problems stem from oral reading.

In the worst cases, with the least sympathetic teachers, apprehension and fear can produce a block to the attention or the perception of words in this reading activity. A form of negative learned behavior similar to the blocking incriminated in stuttering can emerge. A blocking fear that prevents reading has caused the label *dyslexia* to be applied in some cases. Continued inappropriate attention to oral reading will compound the problem.

Oral reading differs from silent reading dramatically. Silent reading, like listening, requires only comprehension. Seldom appreciated is oral reading's requirement for language comprehension *and* production skills used simultaneously. This is a burden of complexity unprecedented in the child's prior experience. In life's discourse to this point, these aspects of language were separate. You listened (comprehension) to someone's communication and spoke (production) your thoughts, but not at the same time.

Oral reading constitutes a significant portion of some reading programs. If "round robin" reading or a "reading circle" is used, it may not only pose problems for the child whose turn it is to read but for the children waiting their turn. The reading pace of all the children is limited by that of the child doing the reading. This is a very unnatural process, particularly for the better readers when children less fluent than they are reading.

Oral reading is a useful and important part of reading instruction when used appropriately. Do not make a child deal with comprehension and pronunciation at the same time as other features of spoken language. Let the child read silently at first, even in assessment situations, allowing attention to focus first on the comprehension aspect through silent reading and then on production alone in oral reading. In instructional situations, help the child with any words that cannot be identified independently, when the selection is read silently. Then let the child read the selection orally. Always be sensitive to a child's apprehension about oral reading.

At sight, oral reading can disrupt a child's comprehension in the struggle to pronounce words. Comprehension is lost because when the child is focusing on pronunciation he or she cannot correct errors.

There are a number of appropriate purposeful reasons for including oral-reading activities. A student may want to share an anecdote, joke, or poem. If they have been read by and are familiar to the student, they can be read to the class with more confidence. Reading parts in plays or skits may be motivating oral-reading activities that provide as well an opportunity for integrating other language arts. Oral reading is important for use in informal assessment, but it can be made less stressful by permitting silent reading first and by making sure that some parts of the test are relatively easy for the student.

Sight words

The terms *sight words* or *sight vocabulary* generally refer to very common words that should be introduced early and made a part of a child's instant word recognition reading vocabulary. The most prominent list of sight words has been the Dolch Basic Sight Word List (Dolch, 1948). Johnson (1971) recommended an updated form of the list to accommodate the changes over the years in frequently used words. He developed an updated 220 Basic Sight Word Vocabulary. Other sight-vocabulary lists are available. The Harris-Jacobson Core Words (Harris & Sipay, 1975) is a list of first-grade-level words. Hillerich (1974) developed a list of 240 words through the analysis of fourteen vocabulary studies. These word lists and others are based on studies of word frequency and contain terms that children are likely to encounter in their reading material. As such, they are valuable teaching aids.

There is another way to view and to develop a sight-word list. This is the "survival" or functional word-list approach for moderately and severely retarded students. Important labels or signs in the environment are selected for teaching as sight words. These include terms that warn of danger, alert to traffic, direct to restrooms, and others. Vocabulary appropriate to a specific environment or vocation may be selected to help individual retarded persons perform more independently. Polloway and Smith (1981) provide a good treatment of functional words that includes lists.

Concerning the former group of sight words that occur with high frequency, Kirk, Kliebhan, and Lerner (1978) have this to say on the subject:

> The teacher of atypical learners should be acquainted with the various word lists so the necessary words will be included in the children's prebook work. Other words may also be used, but unless the child masters by sight the words that appear most frequently in books, reading will become too laborious a process. Mastery of the words used most commonly in primers and first readers helps the child read fluently and with meaning. (p. 98)

It is in the teaching of such sight words that considerable difficulty may arise for the handicapped student. The difficulty of teaching isolated sight words has been emphasized already. Various classifications and characteristics of words, whether they are form or structure words and whether they have high-imagery or low-imagery values, make a great difference in the teaching and learning characteristics of words (Hargis & Gickling, 1978, 1980). These are characteristics that are more important than phonic composition or configuration. The terms that appear most frequently are largely structure words at the first-grade level. It is paradoxical that what seem to be simple, common words can be extremely difficult to learn—that is, they are extremely difficult to learn as they are frequently presented, in isolation. The words most readily learned as isolated sight words are high-imagery nouns. They are the least frequent constituents of lists to be taught as sight words, however. Innumerable flash cards, games, and gimmicks have been developed to teach sight words. Most of these activities emphasize teaching these words in isolation, the hardest possible way for many children to learn. A child "behind" in reading and receiving remedial help or any special reading instruction is likely to get increasingly larger doses of this isolated sight-word instruction. As it is with word-identification skills, increased fragmentation from meaningful reading seems to be a problem with teaching the so-called sight words to handicapped students. Again, what the student needs is not *isolation from* meaning with these words but *increased contact* with them in meaningful reading situations. Experience and research points to the benefits of teaching such words in meaningful contexts. Even high-imagery nouns are learned more readily if they are associated with their even-more-concrete picture referents (Arlin, Scott, & Webster, 1978–1979).

The characteristics and type of word to be taught must receive consideration if they are to be taught in isolation. Concrete nouns are learned most readily, even more so if associated with their picture referent. This is a form of context. Structure words, low-imagery nouns, and other, less-tangible words should be placed in meaningful contexts. Phrases or sentences may suffice. For example, in teaching the word *this*, place it in a noun phrase with a known concrete noun such as *this dog*. For even more clarification, pictures can be used.

Survival or functional words to be taught in isolation do not necessarily have the intrinsic difficulties that words used with high frequency have. If they are taught from lists or on flash cards with no regard to whether or not their meaning is understood, however, or without associating them concretely to the environment or situation they label, they may be unnecessarily difficult to learn.

In his pioneering studies on the development of reading vocabulary, Gates (1930) found the average number of repetitions required for word-recognition mastery. The figures he reports are for children of various IQ ranges who were between the chronological ages 6.1 and 7.5 at the beginning of the school term. Children in the IQ range of 90 to 109 required thirty-five repetitions, 80 to 89 IQ forty repetitions, 70 to 79 IQ forty-five repetitions, and 60 to 69 IQ fifty-five repetitions. It was emphasized that these numbers of repetitions were averages, not necessarily required for every word. These numbers of repetitions were for "running" words (words in connected discourse), not for those that occurred in isolated repetitions.

Gates further pointed out that in reading materials the vocabulary burden should be light enough to enable the pupils adequately to master recognition of new words (about one new word in sixty). In the primary grades there should be thirty to fifty-five (depending on IQ) running word repetitions for each new word introduced. This repetition should be in meaningful reading material instead of in phonetic drills or other types of isolated-word study. Gates's tests showed "from every point of view" the superiority of learning words through repetition in context over mere isolated repetition in phonetic analysis and word study.

Approaches to beginning reading

Reading methods can be described as developmental or remedial. Developmental methods are usually comprehensive and provide for levels of reading readiness through various levels of actual functional reading skills. Remedial methods usually are not comprehensive. They are geared to the remediation of some assumed specific deficit or learning weakness.

Basal reader programs dominate developmental beginning-reading instructional methods. They provide a sequenced set of materials for reading that control the introduction rate of new vocabulary. Truly reasonable word-introduction rates began to appear only within the last fifty years. Up to the time of Gates's (1930) research, beginning readers commonly introduced more than one new word in twenty. The moderation in rates of word introduction was a truly significant change for the basal reader programs.

Basal reader programs present sets of skills through workbooks, supplementary materials, and activities spelled out in considerable detail in the teacher's manuals. These skills are supposed to be coordinated with the actual reading material. Basal programs are the most comprehensive. Using a teacher's manual, a teacher can provide minute-by-minute instruction in the instructional talk to use for each lesson. Basal reader programs, by and large, have made a creditable contribution to the teaching of reading in the United States.

The language-experience approach can be considered developmental, though it does not have the same scope and structure as a basal reading series. It did prove essentially as effective as basal approaches in the extensive study of beginning reading programs sponsored by the United States Office of Education (USOE) in the 1960s (Bond & Dykstra, 1967). The major criticisms of the approach have been its failure to follow a predetermined skills sequence and possible lack of control over vocabulary introduction and repetition. There has been considerable detail in the explanation of its use (Allan, 1966; Braun & Froese, 1977; Spache, 1976).

For a variety of reasons, discussed in previous chapters,

some children have difficulty within comprehensive basal reader curricula, so a myriad of specialized supplementary- or remedial-reading techniques and materials have been developed over the years. Some are specific exercises and drills, and some define a method of presentation. Some have become comprehensive in scope themselves. The materials, of course, are as varied as their developer's theoretical perspectives on the cause of reading difficulty. I will not attempt to summarize all of these methods. Good descriptions of the programs can be found in Cook and Earlly (1979); Gillespie-Silver (1979); Harris and Sipay (1975); Kaluger and Kolson (1978); Kirk, Kliebhan, and Lerner (1978); and Spache (1976).

The general slant on beginning reading discussed so far has been toward developmental rather than remedial approaches. There are, however, students who are not beginners with reading instruction but are still beginners in terms of reading skill. These students constitute two instructional groups with some distinct needs. Special methods applying to the older group of students are considered specifically further on in the chapter. Some simple methods are effective with older students who have experienced chronic failure and who have not acquired any appreciable reading skill.

The language of children's reading material should be meaningful and firmly rooted in experience. Only then can they make ready transition to language represented by print. Reading aloud to the children regularly helps them gain some necessary concepts about print. In fact, there are some peculiarly literary grammatical styles of beginning reading material (in particular the variations on the direct-discourse form) with which a child can only become familiar by being read to. Writing and reading experience charts can bring the concepts about print into clearer view. Concepts of the printed word, spatial sequencing, and others can proceed gradually to reading the printed form—using context and adding some utilitarian word-identification skills. Only then is it advisable to increase the amount of meaningful independent reading.

When the teacher is faced with an older child who has not made this progression into reading print, a considerably different approach or temporary alternative intervention may be called for. Some of the same guidelines should be followed as for the more developmental approach. The reading activities should be meaningful.

Many of these children are almost overwhelmed by isolated drills on sight words and word-identification skills. Still, their progress in reading may be at an apparent standstill. A recommended approach to helping these children is really a variation of a simple method that has seen widespread use. The essential component of the procedure is to tape record a reading selection and have the student follow the printed text word by word as he listens to it. The student follows this procedure repeatedly until he or she has memorized the selection, not just the spoken part but the printed part as well. The memorization process should continue until the child can read the selection from beginning to end, or start reading at any point in the selection, or identify upon request individual words in the selection without the tape. The child may have to "read" with the tape for a considerable number of times in order to attain complete mastery. Chomsky (1978) reports that approximately twenty repetitions of a selection were required for mastery over the first selections attempted using this procedure. A short book takes about fifteen minutes of recording time. A selection of this length, repeated twenty times, would take about five hours in total.

The number of repetitions a child needs, of course, depends on at least two factors. The first is the difficulty level of the chosen reading selection relative to the child's ability level. The other is the amount of repetition that words receive within the selection. Sufficient repetition of the words within the selection reduces by that amount the number of listening-reading times for the total taped selection. If the teacher prepares or identifies material that controls these variables, the trials to mastery for individuals can be fairly well managed. If the child makes the selection based on interest alone, the trials to mastery may be fairly extensive. The number of trials necessary to complete mastery of the selection depends on the words that receive the fewest repetitions within the selection. Clearly, the process can be made more efficient by preparing or selecting material that provides increased word repetition within the selection. There are, though, real advantages in using this approach even if it requires that the student spend a month or more learning a very hard selection of his own choice. It is a "no fail" activity. There need be no frustration involved. The spoken context and counterpart of the printed word are always there. The student is aware of progress made as words become familiar. A complex selection can be learned, if the language is meaningful and mastery over it demonstrated, much more quickly than with a slower developmental approach. One can learn a great many new words that can be recognized independently and can use more varied material requiring much less care in selection and preparation. The student can use the procedure independently at school or at home. Also very important, the time is engaged in meaningful reading activity.

Some disadvantages include the potential for boredom because the necessary repetition to mastery may seem excessive. The less the within-text repetition of vocabulary required, the greater the number of trials to mastery. However, a growing feeling of competency and successful engagement in a reading activity is usually sufficient reinforcement to keep these students on task.

Learning to use the system can take some time. Some children may need to work on very short selections until they learn to coordinate eye movements with the tape without losing their place. It is necessary to provide some auditory signal on the tape to help them locate their place or signal when to turn pages. These signals are learned rather quickly.

Older students, even with little actual reading ability, usually know the basic concepts about print, a necessity before a child can learn to use this system.

Some variations on the system can be used. The student may listen to the tape before reading or the tape can be used at a second reading. Some students may find these tapes helpful to use occasionally, some as a regular means of checking their own progress.

This listening-reading method is only an interim remedial measure that should lead to more independent reading. To this end, there are a number of procedures which can be used effectively. If you wish the child to work in a book or a basal reading series, make sure that the taped selections contain the vocabulary appropriate for independent transition into that material. To reduce the total number of times the student must listen to and read a tape, increase the number of within-text repetitions (the number of times a word appears in the selection) of the vocabulary. Gates's estimates for number of repetitions in context can be used as tentative targets. Simply add the number of within-text repetitions of the least frequently appearing words to the number of listening-reading trials. The total should approximate the Gates figure.

This procedure can be an effective morale-boosting activity, but it should not be considered a total program. A student's independent use of context in identifying and learning new words receives little exercise. As soon as possible, reading material within the child's instructional reading level should be provided. This can be expedited if the vocabulary used in the listening-reading activities parallels that of the instructional-level materials to be read independent of the tape.

A procedure that requires the child to attempt oral reading simultaneously with listening resembles another called the neurological impress method (Heckelman, 1969; Langford, Slade, & Barnett, 1974). Here the student and instructor read together, using a finger as a locator for each word read.

The *Distar Reading Program* (Engelmann & Bruner, 1974, 1975) emphasizes highly structured oral-reading activities that are used for groups of children. The teacher reads the selection first, providing the model of expression. Children, in turn, read the selection with appropriate expression. This routine is repeated until each child reads the selection with expression (Carnine & Silbert, 1979). As with other group oral-reading activities, however, inattentiveness and losing the place are problems. In the Distar program unison oral reading is used for beginning reading of connected discourse. Each student points to each word as the group reads in unison. Periodically, each student takes a turn so that progress can be checked and attention maintained. Providing adequate practice for slower students, while avoiding boredom and insuring adequate progress for the faster students, is a major difficulty with group work of this kind.

Students able to read much less well than their actual grade placement or chronological age will frequently lead the teacher to expect sometimes have difficulty with content or interest level of books that match their actual reading level. A number of books are available in the high-interest, low-vocabulary category. These can appeal to an appropriate type and level of interest using a relatively easier vocabulary load. Some publishers of such books are listed in Appendix E. A note of caution about using these books is in order. The primary control in them is the vocabulary load. For those children whose handicapping problem is definable in terms of a language deficiency, this control alone may not be sufficient. These books have very limited use with hearing impaired children because the controls must extend to the introduction of syntactic and figurative structures as well.

Adaptions for children with sensory impairments

VISION

The primary adaptions in reading instruction for children with visual impairments have to do with physical environment of the place of instruction and the format of the material used.

In terms of the classroom, illumination and seating are primary considerations for the partially sighted child. Some of the same considerations are appropriate for the child with marginal vision problems also. Glare from windows, frequently a problem, can be controlled by use of blinds, shades, or even certain paints. Artificial lighting should be used if brightness levels are too low in parts of the room where the visually impaired student will work.

Illumination should be checked by a light meter during various parts of the day and through seasonal changes.

Seating should be arranged to permit light to fall over the shoulder so that students will not work in a shadow. The source of light should be outside their field of vision. Children should be permitted to change their seating according to need or changing light conditions. Desks or work surfaces should be directly in front of them, at a slant of approximately twenty degrees, to assist in using binocular vision and to reduce muscular effort. Desk height may need adjusting.

In terms of formats, all chalkboard writing should be large and clear. Chalkboards should be cleaned frequently. White chalk makes the best contrast on green and black chalkboards. Accommodate individual needs. Optical aids may be used to increase the size of print without using special materials. See Harley and Lawrence (1977) for information on magnification. All books or materials selected should have nongloss surfaces with appropriate clear contrast. These materials must be kept clean or replaced as necessary. Duplicating materials should have clear reproduction and appropriate type size and ink color. A large-print typewriter with a good ribbon is important. Students should have nongloss paper, soft lead pencils, and black felt-tipped pens. Experience charts require extra-heavy felt-tipped pens with black ink.

The scheduling of instructional time may have to be varied. The varying visual efficiency may require different amounts of time to read material. Some children may require equal amounts of time for close and distance work. Daily schedules should be planned to account for fatigue, and less visually demanding activities should be prepared and integrated.

HEARING

Some hearing impaired children may require adaptions to the acoustic environment in regular classrooms. Arrangements should be made for preferential or flexible seating. Carpeting to reduce distracting background noise for the hearing aid wearer may be very helpful. Ambient-noise levels can be checked to determine the amount of sound reduction required. Radio transmitters or induction-loop amplification systems can be helpful in amplifying and isolating the teacher's instructional talk from distracting classroom sounds. Tape recorders with head sets also help ease speech-discrimination problems.

A significant language deficit associated with the hearing loss warrants major adjustments in the preparation of reading materials. These adjustments, mentioned earlier, will be further described in the next chapter.

VISUAL PERCEPTION

There is little evidence, other than testimonials, that the effect of the many varied visual-perceptual training programs have any significant beneficial effect specifically related to reading achievement. Possibly this lack of effect has to do with the process orientation of the training programs. The "visual perceptual" activities suggested here will be more directly related to reading. These suggested activities could be readily described as visual discrimination training or more simply as reading readiness activities. Some activities necessarily integrate motor and auditory components, but these activities relate only to learning some basic *visual* concepts about the *visual* form of the language.

Educators often overlook the fact that children do not always start reading instruction with the necessary concepts about print. Some do not acquire the concepts as readily as others. Certain children simply have not been exposed to reading at home. No matter what the cause of the difficulty, the transition from the auditory temporal order of language to the visual spatial order may take more time. The term *visual activities* here refers only to the visual conventions of print that represent language, not to actual reading. It is important to note that reading can only proceed when the child has some experience in how to look at the printed form of language and what to start looking for. The activities should provide this experience and help the child attain the essential visual concepts about printed language.

It is necessary to learn some metalinguistic terms in association with these visual concepts. The words *letter* and *word* as they relate specifically to what they mean in print, as well as in speech, are such terms. The word *sound* is another important part of the specialized beginning-reading vocabulary.

These terms are used to direct a student's attention to the visual forms. The associative link between *word* and its referents in print, and between *letter* and its printed forms, should be established early. When children learn what the letters are, conceptual view of a letter is established. Students may then proceed to learn to recognize each letter. Certain procedures facilitate a child's learning to recognize the printed forms of a letter. Organizing letters into smaller groups of more discriminable forms eases the difficulty of this learning task. See Carnine and Silbert (1979) or McKee (1966), among others, for suggested groupings of the letters. The print size and type style is a consideration. Ease of visual discrimination influences the rate of learning. Sufficient visual-discrimination skill to match letter form to letter form, given a mixed group of letter pairs, presupposes sufficient visual discrimination skill to learn the letter names.

Forming letters or words is not the only proof that they have been learned. If a child can point to a letter or a word upon request, the child can make the discrimination and so has learned the metalinguistic terms. There is no point in using the various kinesthetic-tactile activities that have been widely suggested. Their use is often equivocal, and they seem to be of little benefit in teaching letter recognition (Miccinati, 1979). Their extended or expanded use is only appropriate for those children who have trouble acquiring the basic visual concepts about printed language. Two-dimensional activities include such things as tracing, following dot patterns, and using templates. Tracing may follow a visual pattern and/or a tactile pattern. In three-dimensional activities, letters are manipulated or traced. While forming or tracing words or sentences, students' attention is drawn to the pertinent features of letters and words and to other characteristics of print.

It is important that activities be comprised of meaningful words and sentences. If the word being traced or copied has no meaning for the children, its boundaries and letter sequence can have no particular significance to them except as marks on their paper.

For some children the extra-motor component may in fact be more difficult than the visual discrimination involved. If these children make more progress using vision alone, the activities should emphasize vision. Physically handicapped children are obvious examples. Children normally have considerable variation in maturation of motor coordination and somewhat older children are likely to benefit more than younger ones.

For beginning readers, use large, clear print on labels of concrete items in the room, name tags, and picture dictionaries. These help form the visual concept of words with meaningful referents. Some simple activities help establish visual concepts about larger discourse units. These include following the teacher in the preparation of experience charts, for example, and reading and rereading experience charts and other large chart material as the teacher points to each word. The reading and pacing can be done by the teacher, tutor, and/or student. Handwriting activities can be correlated with experience charts, but there may be a developmental lag in fine-motor skills of younger or less-mature students.

REFERENCES

Allen, Roach Van. *Language experiences in reading*. Chicago: Encyclopaedia Britannica, 1966.

Arlin, Marshall, Scott, Mary, & Webster, Janet. The effects of pictures on rate of learning sight words: A critique of the focal attention hypothesis. *Reading Research Quarterly*, 1978–1979, *14*, 645–660.

Blachowicz, Camille L. Metalinguistic awareness and the beginning reader. *The Reading Teacher*, 1978, *31*, 875–876.

Bond, Guy L., & Dykstra, Robert. The cooperative research program in first-grade reading instruction. *Reading Research Quarterly*, 1967, *2*, 5–142.

Braun, Carl, & Froese, Victor. *An experience-based approach to language and reading*. Baltimore: University Park Press, 1977.

Carnine, Douglas, & Silbert, Jerry. *Direct instruction reading*. Columbus: Charles E. Merrill, 1979.

Chomsky, Carol. When you still can't read in the third grade: After decoding what? In S. Jay Samuels (Ed.), *What research has to say about reading instruction*. Newark: International Reading Association, 1978.

Chomsky, Noam, & Halle, Morris. *The sound pattern of English*. New York: Harper & Row, 1968.

Cook, Jimmie E., & Earlly, Elsie C. *Remediating reading disabilities: Simple things that work*. Germantown: Aspen Systems, 1979.

Dolch, E. *Problems in reading*. Champaign: Garrard, 1948.

Dolch, E. W., & Bloomster, M. Phonic readiness. *Elementary School Journal*, 1937, *38*, 201–205.

Engleman, S., & Bruner, E. *Distar reading level 1*. Chicago: Science Research Associates, 1974.

Engleman, S., & Bruner, E. *Distar reading level 2*. Chicago: Science Research Associates, 1975.

Gates, Arthur I. *Interest and ability in reading*. New York: Macmillan, 1930.

Gillespie-Silver, Patricia. *Teaching reading to children with special needs*. Columbus: Charles E. Merrill, 1979.

Hargis, Charles H., & Gickling, Edward E. The function of imagery in work recognition development. *The Reading Teacher*, 1978, *31*, 870–874.

Hargis, Charles H., & Gickling, Edward E. *Word recognition development as a function of imagery level and syntactic classification.* Paper presented at the regional conference of the International Reading Association, Norfolk, Va., November 1980.

Harley, Randall K., & Lawrence, G. Allen. *Visual impairment in the schools.* Springfield: Charles C Thomas, 1977.

Harris, Albert J., & Sipay, Edward R. *How to increase reading ability* (6th ed.). New York: David McKay, 1975.

Heckelman, R. G. A neurological impress method of reading instruction. *Academic Therapy*, 1969, *4*, 277–282.

Hillerich, Robert L. *Word lists—getting it all together. The Reading Teacher*, 1974, *27*, 353–360.

Hocevar, Susan Page, & Hocevar, Dennis. The effect of meaningful versus non-meaningful reading material on oral reading errors in first through third grade children. *Journal of Reading Behavior*, 1978, *10*, 297–299.

Hood, Joyce. Is miscue analysis practical for teachers? *The Reading Teacher*, 1978, *32*, 260–266.

Huey, Edmund Burke. *The psychology and pedagogy of reading.* New York: Macmillan, 1908.

Johnson, Dale D. The Dolch list reexamined. *The Reading Teacher*, 1971, *24*, 449–457.

Kaluger, George, & Kolson, Clifford J. *Reading and learning disabilities* (2nd ed.). Columbus: Charles E. Merrill, 1978.

Kirk, Samuel A., Kliebhan, Sister Joanne Marie, & Lerner, Janet W. *Teaching reading to slow and disabled learners.* Boston: Houghton Mifflin, 1978.

Langford, Kenneth, Slade, K., & Barnett, A. An explanation of impress techniques in remedial reading. *Academic Therapy*, 1974, *9*, 282–291.

McKee, Paul. *Reading: A program of instruction of the elementary school.* Boston: Houghton Mifflin, 1966.

Miccinati, Jeannette. The Fernald technique: Modifications increase the probability of success. *Journal of Learning Disabilities*, 1979, *12*, 139–142.

Morrone, Victor Eugene. *A critical analysis of scientific research on phonics.* Unpublished doctoral dissertation. University of Pittsburgh, 1958.

Polloway, Edward, & Smith, James. *Teaching language skills to exceptional learners.* Denver: Love, 1981.

Schoolfield, L. D., & Timberlake, J. B. *The phonovisual method* (rev. ed.). Washington, D.C.: Phonovisual Products, 1974.

Smith, Frank. *Understanding reading*. New York: Holt, Rinehart & Winston, 1971.

Smith, Frank. The role of prediction in reading. *Elementary English*, 1975, *52*, 305–311.

Smith, Frank. *Reading without nonsense*. New York: Teachers College Press, 1978.

Spache, George D. *Diagnosing and correcting reading disabilities*. Boston: Allyn & Bacon, 1976.

Venezky, R. L. English orthography: Its graphic structure and its relation to sound. *Reading Research Quarterly*, 1967, *2*, 75–106.

Yale, Caroline. *Formation and development of elementary English sounds*. Northampton, Mass: Clark School for the Deaf, 1946.

6

SELECTION AND PREPARATION OF READING MATERIALS

Control of vocabulary

Control of idiomatic
and figurative structure

Control of syntax

Problems with direct discourse

Controlling known context

Introducing and using reading selections

Appropriate reading materials

6

Frequently overlooked as the source of reading problems is the material used in reading instruction. Usually the reading problems are thought to be a deficiency of some sort in the student, not the material. The structure and difficulty of the reading material, however, is a primary cause of reading problems and a major part of their ultimate solution. In order to deal with reading material as a part of the problem, it is necessary to shift the focus of assessment to include it. The vocabulary, syntax, and nonliteral structure of the material must be compared directly to the student's ability to deal with them. The major emphasis of this assessment must be on what the student knows. Reading material can then be provided to satisfy the requirement for the ratios of knowns to unknowns needed at the instructional and independent reading levels.

Once the basic concepts about print have been learned, the most consuming part of teaching reading to most handicapped children is the selection and preparation of materials that match the student's needs. Although basal reading materials are quite adequate for most nonhandicapped students, these materials are too difficult for handicapped children. For most children with reading problems, the interaction of word-repetition rates and word-introduction rates is the primary problem in regular material. This interaction produces reading material that is more difficult than is instructionally appropriate. If there were more material that provided appropriate controls over repetition, many problems would be alleviated. Failure often occurs precisely because the child is too far out of synchronization with the vocabulary's introduction and repetition rates. Preparation of reading material requires attention to repetition within the selection and/or repetition of the selection as well as repetition from one selection to the next.

The material must be sufficiently close to an instructional level for benefit from word-identification skills—even fairly utilitarian ones. There must be sufficient known context and comprehension to use the other word-identification skills effectively. If materials are too hard, comprehension drops and context will not be available to help identify unfamiliar printed words. For a child to use emerging word-identification skills adequately, reading material that makes it possible to apply them is needed. Further, the introduction of these skills and the provision for their application should be an intrinsic part of the use of reading selections. In this way word-identification skills can be applied more meaningfully, and transfer of training is much less of an issue.

Most readability measures offer relatively little help in the preparation and selection of reading materials at the primary levels. The general limits of readability measures were discussed in a previous chapter. Beyond those limitations, readability measures provide no specific information as to introduction or repetition rates of vocabulary. In order to prepare reading material to match the instructional needs of specific children, individual assessment is necessary. These procedures were outlined in Chapter 3. The focus of this assessment must shift to what a child knows. Known context must comprise the largest part of any instructionally appropriate reading selection. Precision in identifying what is known is necessary to structure material that works with handicapped students.

Failure continues to occur until focus shifts to what is known and this information is used to prepare reading material. Children fail because material is too hard, not because of skill deficiency. Moreover, assessment is often directed to correcting skill deficiencies, further fractionating reading activities for children who are failing. Little attention is given to assessment aimed at preparing materials and activities that a child can actually use.

Teachers may select materials for the handicapped learner from myriad sources and reasons, but this is seldom done with precise regard to the instructional level of individuals, which requires appropriate assessment techniques and direct application of their results. Those whose instructional-level needs fall outside the scope of available instructional materials are unfortunate indeed. Teachers have become conditioned to seeking a published remedy for all classroom ailments. These materials seldom match the specific needs of individuals. This chapter is devoted to the specifics of preparing material that is instructionally appropriate for children whose needs fall outside that available in published form.

Control of vocabulary

Older children who have severe reading problems may be able to recognize so few words in print that virtually nothing is available for them to read successfully. Success in a reading activity, however, is precisely what these students need most. In order to insure success in a real reading activity, the material should be structured according to individual needs. The words that they know should be the basis for developing success-inducing reading material.

Students having severely limited reading vocabularies (fewer than thirty words) can benefit from approaches that are helpful in the preparation of reading material. The approach depends on the severity or level of deficiency within an already extremely limited word-recognition vocabulary. If a child seems to recognize essentially no words with any consistency, a highly repetitive use of words and sentence frames may be needed to start off. The only unifying theme to the discourse may be the repetition of an activity. This may simply have to suffice until a larger stock of words has been acquired. Repetition provides the known context and the necessary trials to mastery of newly introduced words.

BUILDING ON RECOGNIZED WORDS

Material prepared for children at this most basic level has included the following selection:

I see a chair.	I see a book.
I see a table.	I see a car.
I see a desk.	I see a dog.

Most older students will recognize *I* and *a*, if for no other reason than that names of these letters are also the same as (or a form of) the pronunciation of the words. The noun objects of the sentence can be selected from the students' limited stock of known nouns or from labeled objects in the room. Common concrete objects in the room should be labeled, until as Huey (1908) described, the room looks as though it had an attack of the measles. The labels, then, are high-imagery nouns well within the students' experience. The room itself is the necessary reference if some of the words in the selection are still unfamiliar. The unfamiliar verb *see* may pose limited difficulty because of its repetition. As the stock of recognized nouns grows, or as the student learns to recognize the names of other students or persons, the sentence frame can begin to vary:

I see Joe.	Joe sees a chair.
Joe sees a dog.	Joe sees a car.
Joe sees a desk.	Joe sees Pete.

Next new verbs can be added to the simple sentence frame:

I have a dog.	Joe has a bike.
I have a bike.	Pete has a bike.
Fred has a bike.	Pete has a dog.

It may be helpful in the initial stages to line up repeated sentences vertically so that the visual impression of the vertical repetition of newly introduced words provides additional context for helping insure success. Comprehension activities at this time should be limited to matching pictures or drawing pictures for the selection or sentences in the selection.

As subjects vary in the sentence frame, the inflectional forms of the verb changes. If the same verb is predictably used in the selection, the change in the subject makes the identification of the new inflectional form of the verb easier:

I ride a bus.   Joe rides a bus.
Pete rides a bus.   Fred rides a bike.

This is true even in the highly irregular forms of the verb *be*:

Joe is a boy.   Pete is a boy.
Helen is a girl. I *am* a boy.
Mary is a girl.

Ease in identification can be verified by introducing the sentence with a blank instead of the verb form *am*. The context of the selection and the sentence should be enough to permit prediction of the verb. Cloze-type activities with and without multiple choices can be used as a comprehension check, as well as an opportunity for further repetition.

In order to make discourse more connected and less a list of sentences, it is important to introduce the definite article *the*. To make the strongest contextual placement possible, an indefinite article should introduce the first occurrence of each noun. Subsequent use of a noun that applies to the same referent will require the use of *the*:

A boy rides a bike. The boy has a hat.
The boy has a book. The boy has an apple.

The prepositions *in*, *on*, and *at* are very helpful in varying simple sentence structure. These can be introduced in strong contexts to enhance predictability. A picture or demonstration of the placement of the objects can be used with each sentence in which the preposition is used:

A cat is in a house.
A dog is on the house.
A bird is on the dog.

A few common intransitive and transitive verbs should be introduced early. The action verbs *run, jump,* and *walk* are very helpful. These, as isolated words, can constitute sentences if they are used imperatively. They can be used in games in which the printed command is to be acted upon while the word is held up by the instructor. Three or four concrete transitive verbs should be introduced at about the same time. The transitive verb *ride* has been illustrated already. A few adjectives can be introduced also. *Big* and *little* are helpful, and the color words are easily pictured in conjunction with sentences. Past-tense forms of previously used verbs can be introduced by changing the selections used before.

One personal pronoun, *I*, has been recommended for use as the subject of the beginning sentence frames. The stock of nouns in these frames can be increased via the labeling procedure and the use of the names of fellow students and friends. If names of people or objects are not yet recognized in print, a rhebus procedure recommended by Huey (1908) can be used. In this technique a simple line drawing of a high-imagery noun can be substituted for the unknown noun. This is the most unambiguous rhebus approach:

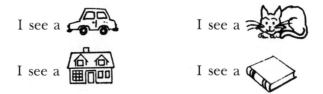

I do not recommend the use of homonyms in the rhebus approach where the name of the pictured item reflects only the sound of the word that should go in the space but is not consonant with the meaning. Of course, this will restrict the use of rhebus to point where high-imagery nouns fit. This will suffice, however, for the initial periods when successful experience in reading is needed but the fund of recognizable printed words is extremely limited.

The type of words just introduced is limited to use in simple sentences. This is just fine for the moment, however, when the fund of words surpasses about twenty of the type just illustrated, the repetition of and within the sentence frame need not be so restricted. The reading selections can then become more varied, and attention to discourse or story features can much more readily be incorporated:

A boy had a dog.
The boy was in bed.
The dog jumped on the bed.
The dog licked the boy.
The dog ran.
The boy saw the dog.
The boy ran.

MAKING READING INTERESTING

It can be very difficult to prepare such material when the controls are very restrictive. Usually, however, skill at preparation emerges with practice. Materials that produce success are more important than those that are interesting at these beginning levels. Fortunately, as the stock of words grows, a student's interests can be considered more easily in the preparation of materials. Here is a selection that was read with considerable enjoyment by a student for the very first time:

Joe sees a *motorcycle*. The motorcycle is in a store. Joe buys the motorcycle. Joe rides the motorcycle. Joe is happy. Joe rides home. Joe has a jacket. The jacket is new. The jacket is black. Joe puts a *skull* on the jacket. Joe rides the motorcycle. Joe has a friend. The friend is Sam. Sam likes the motorcycle. Sam rides on the motorcycle. Sam sees a jacket. The jacket is in a store. Sam buys the jacket. The jacket is black. Sam puts a skull on the jacket. Sam puts on the jacket. Joe rides the motorcycle. Sam rides on the motorcycle. Joe rides the motorcycle fast. The motorcycle *hits* a tree. Joe is hurt. Sam is hurt. Joe is sad. Sam is sad. Joe walks home. Sam walks home.

The unfamiliar words are italicized at their point of introduction in the selection. A labeled picture of a motorcycle and a skull were used to introduce the story. Otherwise the student could read it independently. The story may seem repetitious and, with the repeated use of short simple sentences, choppy. But the important consideration is that the student is having success in reading for the first time, and clear objectives for making continued progress can be formulated.

When a student is able to read at this simple level, a decision should be made about the vocabulary to be selected for introduction in subsequent selections. This decision depends on several factors. If the student can potentially be integrated in a basal or developmental reading program, the word lists from these books should be used as a primary source. The words necessary to read instructionally at any given level should be introduced through this approach of special preparation. When sufficient words from a given book have been learned, the child can be given the book for instruction.

With older students, word lists associated with some high-interest, low-vocabulary books may be best. Words systematically selected from these lists can expeditiously ease the student into reading books more appropriate in content and format than those of primary-grade level.

Other students who have a cognitive limitation on ultimate reading achievement may need to be introduced to reading from functional or survival reading lists. This, of course, depends on how severe the cognitive deficit is.

Even if the vocabulary selected for subsequent teaching is appropriate, it is essential to remember to start with what the student knows or can do. If this is not a foremost consideration in assessment and the preparation of material, the activities and materials may be composed largely of unknowns. This will induce failure again.

Gates's (1930) general guidelines for introduction and repetition of words are fundamentally sound. The number of word repetitions is twenty to fifty-five corresponding to the IQ range of 129 to 60 (p. 35). The number of repetitions increase by about five for each ten-point reduction in IQ. This number of word repetitions should be considered a minimum average per word in a meaningful contextual setting. Repetitions should be considered aside from any other incidental or isolated presentation of the word. Some words as a matter of course receive much repetition; but others must receive minimum consideration, as well.

Teachers often complain about inconsistent responses from students who have severe reading problems. "They seem to know the words one day but not the next." This observation reflects a problem of children not introduced to words in meaningful context with sufficient repetition and who have not as yet been able to do any meaningful reading—often after years in school. Fragmented exposure to skills and words in the primary reading program causes such inconsistent response behaviors in these students. They fall into this predicament because there are no published materials with sufficient controls to permit meaningful reading activities. The teachers often select isolated-word teaching activities that only burden short-term memory functions. These are not learned consistently through this method.

Severely disabled readers are likely to get more isolated skill training to help them identify words in passages that they are assigned to read. On the premise that there are too many unknown words for them, they receive more attention to word-identification skills. It is impossible for them to cope with a selection loaded with unknown words and unreasonable to expect them to identify the words using only the skills we are teaching them. Then, if such students fail, we often assume that they need more skills teaching, not less! The attention to remediation for these children must shift to the preparation of reading material that these children can handle. This means taking care in the introduction and repetition of words. Only when the student is reading can skills be applied to identify words in a *reading* situation. In material appropriately structured (containing a sufficient number of known words), the context helps identify unfamiliar words. Even if context and other word-identification skills when used together do not identify the word (maybe because it is an unknown spoken word also), the comprehension of the selection may be retained and some semantic features of the word processed and stored.

Control of idiomatic and figurative structure

Idiomatic and figurative structure are ubiquitous parts of the language. They exist in all cultures and dialects but vary from one to another. To cope with them requires certain language sophistication. Such structures beyond the developmental reach of the students or from another culture or dialect give students trouble. Comprehension problems occur in this area as often as with the strange words.

One problem with nonliteral structures is that they may be composed of apparently familiar words. As such they will be entirely overlooked by readability formulas, as well as by a teacher during conscious examination. The latter case is especially true if the structure is of the most common idiomatic form.

I have found that the most direct way to deal with nonliteral structure is to analyze the material intended for use. A page-by-page, word-by-word analysis is necessary to identify specific nonliteral structures. Because they appear frequently and are randomly introduced without any consistency in basal programs at any given reading level, they can constitute major comprehension problems. The particular challenges of the material selected for a particular student must be examined. This can be done in much the same way as vocabulary after completing analysis of the material. The specific nonliteral structures introduced should be sequentially listed according to the level and page on which they occur. In this way the teacher will be aware of the problems to be encountered. Even if the structure is an uncommon idiom having relatively little utility in terms of general frequency of use, the teacher can plan to help the child cope with it when it does occur. It is only through thorough analysis of regular reading materials, however, that one can prepare a scope-and-sequence chart of nonliteral structures to use as a guide for instruction. An analysis of figurative and idiomatic structure of a reading program (Ruddell, Shogren, & Strickland, 1978) was prepared for use at the Tennessee School for the Deaf.* This analysis illustrates the scope and sequence of the structures as they appear in this series. It can also serve as a guide for the review and evaluation of any regular reading material. The nonliteral structures and the definitions used for identifying them are included at the end of the book, in Appendix D.

Many feel that the publishers of developmental and remedial reading materials should provide detailed information about idiomatic and figurative structure just as they do for vocabulary. Such information is relevant for handicapped children who, because of sociolinguistic or cultural differences, have varying levels of skill in coping with nonliteral language. Such differences pose many more problems than other dialect variations.

As the words that comprise nonliteral structure may be known in their usual literal sense, exercises that help children understand what they mean in these unfamiliar uses are valuable. Certainly children should not encounter a word for the first time in a nonliteral context. The nonliteral structures that a child needs for reading should be presented orally and explained. This presentation may be necessary for each idiomatic structure in the reading program. Language arts activities can focus on the more common figurative devices to help students gain independence in coping with their meaning.

Control of syntax

A scope-and-sequence chart that illustrates the normal acquisition of syntax is essential in the preparation of reading materials for use with children with language impairments. One such chart is included in Appendix B. A basic readiness requirement for beginning reading instruction, or reading at any other level for that matter, is mastery of syntax. It was emphasized earlier in the book that all syntactic structures are used without attempt at control from the beginning levels of reading instruction. A child who has not completed comprehension mastery of the scope of English syntax will not have successful access to currently available instructional material in reading.

If a child's level of syntactic development falls short of complete mastery, reading materials must be accommodated to

*This analysis was prepared as a part of the reading curriculum for figurative and idiomatic structures by a committee comprised of Elaine Alexander, chair; Betty Lawson; Janet Matthews; Sharon Wade; Charles H. Hargis, consultant; and Lana Doncaster, coordinator; July 1980.

that area of deficiency. The level of development must be identified on the scope-and-sequence chart. Appropriate instructional material must comprise most syntactic structures within the threshold of known structures. As with vocabulary, in syntax what is known must be the primary focus of assessment and materials preparation. Preparing materials with controlled syntax requires identifying the known structures constituting the threshold of communication. The proportion of known structures must predominate in instructional material so that active communication in reading is possible. New syntactic structures should be introduced from the next level of development on the scope-and-sequence chart. This process is followed to mastery of the scope of English syntax.

When and if the reading language arts program is effective in helping a child master the normal sequence of syntactic development, the rigorous controls required in the preparation of these materials can be eased, and standard available materials can be introduced. At the point where students can begin using regular materials, vocabulary and nonliteral structure specific to that selected become the dominating consideration in making the transition from controlled syntax to the published material.

Some vocabulary, structure words, being an intrinsic part of the various syntactic forms, are introduced as a necessary constituent of the structure. Form words such as nouns, verbs, adverbs, and adjectives are not so tied to specific syntactic structures and therefore may be subject to more arbitrary selection. Utility and concreteness of form words should be major considerations when they are chosen for the beginning levels that require controlled syntax. New form words should be introduced within familiar syntactic structures. Conversely, familiar form words should be used within and with new syntactic structures when they are introduced.

Using syntactic controls when preparing reading materials at beginning levels may cause the material to look strange. If in fact a child is functioning at that level, however, you must stay within this threshold of communication.

CONTROL PROCEDURES

The material begins to appear more natural as development progresses and the array of vocabulary and syntactic structures permit more varied sentence and discourse grammar. The student's comprehension of syntactic forms dictates progress along the sequence of development of these structures. Syntactic structures outside the threshold of development are totally unfamiliar, not just unfamiliar in print, so the meaning associated with them must be basic to their introduction. Each new structure must be associated with a concept or activity for understanding to occur. A still-unfamiliar syntactic form being introduced in print must have this introduction.

The following selections illustrate procedures for controlling the use of syntactic forms in the preparation of reading material. References to syntactic structures used are found in Appendix B. Structures being introduced are italicized. The remaining structures in the selection were already known by the students for whom the selections were prepared. The known structures provide the known context necessary for adequate comprehension. The relatively few new structures being introduced in each selection must receive preliminary teaching or illustration.

The procedure of repeating in print syntactic structures required for mastery is essentially the same as that suggested by Gates (1930) for the repetition of vocabulary. As previously pointed out, however, syntactic structures affect comprehension approximately twice as heavily as vocabulary per occurrence. In other words, one may introduce only half the number of new syntactic structures as new vocabulary.

CONTROL SELECTIONS

The first selection was written for a student who had completed the first three rows of the scope-and-sequence chart. The structures being introduced for him are in row 4. The specific structure being introduced in this selection is a noun clause (item 8, column h, of the scope-and-sequence chart), first introduced as the object of a familiar transitive verb:

Bill's birthday is October 31. Ed wants to buy a present for Bill. Ed goes to some stores. He looks at many toys. He sees some skates. He likes to skate. He thinks *that Bill may like skates.* He sees many board games. He likes to play board games. *He thinks that Bill may like a board game.* He sees some basketballs. He likes to play basketball. *He thinks that Bill may like a basketball.* He sees some footballs. He likes to play football. He knows *that Bill likes football.* He bought the football for Bill.

The next selection was written for a student who had completed only row 1 on the scope-and-sequence chart. The structure being introduced in this selection is a transitive verb complement. It is listed as Vt$_{to}$ on row 2 of the scope-and-sequence chart in Appendix B.

A boy liked dogs. His friend had a dog. The boy liked *to pet the dog.* He liked *to throw a ball to the dog.* He wanted a dog. He wanted *to buy a dog.* He went to a pet store. He looked at the puppies. He bought a puppy. He took the puppy home. The puppy liked *to play.* The puppy liked *to catch the ball.* The boy liked *to pet the puppy.* The boy was happy. The puppy was happy.

The next selection was written for a student who had completed the first two rows of the scope-and-sequence chart. The structures being introduced are the "prearticles" *one of, two of,* and *all of.*

One day five dogs came to school. *One of* the dogs was brown. *One of* the dogs was black. *One of* the dogs was white. *Two of* the dogs had spots. *All of* the dogs were big. *All of* the dogs wagged their tails. *All of* the dogs ran into the school. *Two of* the dogs ran into our room. *All of* the children petted the dogs. *All of* the children liked the dogs. *All of* the dogs were nice. The teacher petted *one of* the dogs. *One of* the dogs licked the teacher. The teacher was angry. We laughed.

The next selection was prepared for a student who had completed the first six rows on the scope-and-sequence chart. The structure being introduced is an adverbial clause form, listed as T-adverbial clause *so . . . that* on row 7 of the scope-and-sequence chart.

Our class went to the zoo last Friday. It is a very good zoo. The zoo has *so* many animals *that we did not see all of them.* The monkeys were funny. The monkeys were *so* funny *that all of the kids laughed.* The lions were scary. They were growling. One lion growled *so* loud *that some of the kids ran.* The giraffes were very tall. They were *so* tall *that they could eat the leaves from the tree tops.* All of the bears were *so* tired *that they were sleeping.* Most of us had a good time at the zoo. But one boy ate *so* much candy *that he threw up.* We had *so* much fun *that we want to go back to the zoo again soon.*

It should be noticeable that the more structures mastered and made available for use, the more interesting and varied the structure of the selections becomes. The child's level of comprehension mastery of syntax, however, must determine the threshold within which these selections are prepared. Comprehension and success must be structured from what a student knows. These considerations must take precedence over concerns for style. It is difficult to exercise or incorporate creativity and interest in the preparation of materials that need severe controls over both vocabulary and syntax. A child's success, however, must predominate over the teacher's or critic's literary impulses. The further along in scope and sequence that the student progresses, the more easily these considerations can be incorporated. Even with such restrictions, some teachers use remarkable creativity and inventiveness in preparing materials for students who work within a very limited range of language skills.

Problems with direct discourse

Some language forms are peculiar to, and seem to be very largely a function of, print. By far the most common syntactic peculiarity specific to the printed form has to do with the structure of direct discourse (Hargis, 1973, 1974, 1977). Direct discourse is a syntactic procedure used to represent conversation in print. The following sentences contain examples of direct discourse:

1. Billy said, "Do you like being a policeman?"
2. "I am not a policeman," said Mr. Smith.
3. "Then what are you?" Billy asked.
4. "I thought you knew, Billy," Mr. Smith said.
5. "I am a fireman."

These examples seem common enough. Similar structures appear on virtually every page of primary-level basal reading material. In the attempt to represent conversation in print, direct discourse must be used. It is indeed ironic that this vehicle for representing normal conversation in print is not itself a common part of everyday conversation. These structures are not familiar enough components of conversation that children hear before they start school.

Forms of direct discourse such as those represented in sentences 1 to 5 have certain things in common. The subject is a speaker, the predicate has to do with speech (*said, asked*), and what was said exactly is enclosed in quotation marks. The quoted portion of the sentences is comprised, in fact, of complex direct objects of the same type of transitive verb. The most usual sequence of sentence components is subject (S), predicate verb (V), and object (O). This is the sequence that is represented in sentence 1.

STRUCTURE VARIATIONS

Direct discourse, however, is subject to more syntactic manipulation than any other syntactic form. Some of this variation is illustrated in the remaining examples. In example 2, the word order is O-V-S. In example 3, the order is O-S-V. The sentences in examples 4 and 5 are syntactically bound by the form of direct discourse. Although sentence 5 is punctuated as a separate sentence, it is the direct object of the predicate verb *said* in sentence 4. Examples 4 and 5, therefore, produce the sequence O-S-V-O. Many separate directly quoted sentences can follow or precede the verb form of *say*. This increasing distance from the main subject and predicate verb can cause confusion or difficulty in identifying the speaker subject, especially in selections in which there are a number of characters involved.

These problems would probably be considerably lessened if direct discourse, as represented in print, were the norm or a frequent format of the language children hear and use. It is occasionally used in speech but is by its very structure a device peculiarly literary. It is used when conversation is represented in writing. The variation in the subject-predicate-object word order is another problem. Authors, to make their writing more interesting or to avoid stereotyped patterns and redundancy, manipulate this word order at every opportunity. This makes it much more difficult for children who are unfamiliar with the process and who are at the same time trying to learn to read.

The subject noun and the predicate verb of the "say" class are seldom used in real conversation. These words serve the same function as the balloon in a comic strip. The balloon itself functions as the quotation marks. As a matter of fact, the cartoon balloon format is superior to the formal structure of the foregoing sentences in presenting conversation in print for children who may have difficulty reading direct discourse.

Direct discourse has an abstract capacity for showing in type the expression and the emotion or manner of conversation. This is accomplished through the use of a variety of "say"-class verbs. Verbs other than *say* itself can be used to indicate these notions. They include verbs like *ask* or *request* for questions and *screamed, shouted, cried, snorted,* and *purred*—among an enormous number of others that may be used to express emotion. Children are accustomed to seeing emotion or manner in the physical appearance of speakers and/or hearing it in their voices. The cartoon and balloon, therefore, can be used especially effectively at beginning levels of reading. In this way the student can see emotion or manner conveyed through characters' words *and* their expressions as pictured.

The cartoon balloon connects reality and print. The pictured speaker represents the concrete subject noun. The line enclosure of the balloon that leads to the speaker represents both quotation marks and the "say" predicate verb. The only words that need be used in the balloon, then, are those really being said. Again, the added advantage of the cartoon-and-balloon format is that emotion and manner need not be immediately transferred to the "say" class of verbs. The adverb of manner, which may be associated with the direct-discourse framework, can also be transferred to the image of the speaker in the cartoon. The cast of characters is much easier to manage when what is being said is associated with their images.

MANAGING THE PROBLEMS

Several things can help manage the use or introduction of direct discourse to students for whom it causes difficulty. First, children should be familiarized with this form, as well as with other structures that may be outside their experience, by being read to. This is the only way they can become familiar with direct discourse before they start reading. Reading to children is an essential readiness activity, particularly in this regard. The second procedure that can be used to manage this form is to delay its introduction, using narrative style or the cartoon-and-balloon format to represent conversation. The second procedure cannot be used indefinitely, of course, and the students must begin dealing with this extremely common form. The last procedure, then, is to make a gradual, controlled transition to representing conversation in print. The cartoon balloon can be directly translated into direct discourse for the students. Experience charts representing familiar conversation can be prepared. In the initial stages of use of direct discourse, the S-V-O sequence should be maintained until the student recognizes the "say" verbs and the punctuation associated with them. Then systematic variations in word order can be used for those students who may need extra help. Continued reading to the students should make the forms increasingly familiar and accessible.

Controlling known context

The use of context is an exceedingly important word-identification skill. As such it must receive careful attention in the beginning reading program and in the selection and preparation of beginning materials. As Gates (1930) stated forcefully more than fifty years ago:

To introduce new words in printed context successfully and without secondary ill effects, the primary requirement is that each new word first appear in a meaningful setting, sufficiently rich in clues to insure the pupil's success in a very high proportion of his efforts to "make it out." If the contextual clues are too few, the pupil will often "make it out" wrongly and thus practice an erroneous perceptive reaction and probably distort the meaning of the whole passage. Even if he does work out the correct pronunciation and meaning of the word after a time, he may do so only at the cost of undue interruption in, and distraction from, the process of reading. Introducing new words too rapidly has these effects . . .

   To insure that the pupils "make out" the new words with few errors and disturbances, the material must be very carefully organized, especially during the first and second years of experience. The setting for each new word can and should be carefully planned. Words should not be thrown in hit or miss, but presented at intervals in a setting of clues so suggestive that the pupil can "guess" from the meaning what the word must be. As he gains in experience, the pupil becomes more and more capable of "guessing" words from context. New words may then be introduced more rapidly and with less ample context clues. The introductory settings should, throughout the basal materials, be organized to give full play to the pupil's growing power to work out the perception and meaning of new words. (pp. 197–198)

Structuring a "meaningful" setting sufficiently rich in clues that permit accurate "guessing" requires giving fundamental consideration to the instructional level. The ratio of known words to those being introduced or still unfamiliar is basic to structuring this context. When over 95 percent of the material is comprised of familiar words, the general discourse of the selection can be comprehended, and the unfamiliar words that appear within it are relatively near the point of identification. Because of the buoyancy provided by this environment, the identity of the new words is forced to the surface.

The need to encourage prediction requires facilitating it through structuring context. Of course, the use of context implies that a student has at least some reading skill. To encourage prediction and use of context at the beginning levels of reading instruction, therefore, alternate sources of context or means of structuring context may be necessary. Spoken context can be used in a variety of ways to aid in the prediction of a word selected for teaching. A sentence or selection can be read aloud, the student then guessing at the targeted printed word or words. At the outset, the new word should be the last one in a sentence. Students may be used to this kind of activity if they have been exposed to exercises that require using spoken context to supply the missing word, such as the following:

The dog likes to chew on a ———.
Joe got a new jacket for his ———.
The bike had a flat ———.
Fred was climbing over the fence and he ripped his ———.

After this, instead of supplying words from their imagination, the students will have to use the context of the sentence to identify an unfamiliar printed word given in place of the blank. Gradually letter-sound associations may be added and the words placed at a variety of locations in sentences. Words beginning with letter sounds that are the focus of instruction can be introduced. Students can be permitted to choose from a list of learned words beginning with different sounds to replace the missing word. This kind of multiple-choice response, using context and letter-sound associations, can be incorporated in each reading selection for students who need extra help or added practice. Besides introducing and encouraging practice with letter-sound associations, such an exercise can also facilitate the learning of word families, in which specific common spelling patterns often appear. For example, these patterns are contained in groups of words such as *cold, told, fold,* and *mold,* or *light, bright, tight,* and *fight.*

As experience charts or stories become relatively familiar, students can be encouraged to read and guess at the words by recalling previous spoken contacts with the selections. A new selection can be read to the student before he reads it himself. Methods of simultaneously providing the spoken form while reading have already been discussed. In these cases there is relatively little opportunity to predict or to foster prediction.

Pictures to illustrate aspects of a selection or story serve as a nonlinguistic context to help in prediction. Labels in the classroom illustrate a form of nonlinguistic context. The object or picture labeled usually provides very strong context. The rhebus form, discussed earlier, can provide context at beginning levels, using pictures within a sentence for students without sufficient reading vocabulary to use context effectively.

Introducing and using reading selections

As noted, the context of a selection sufficiently strong may require relatively little introduction to be read by a student. It is not always easy or convenient to manipulate context in such ways, however. In such instances, new words or experiences that the child may need to read the passage independently may be introduced, possibly with spoken context, before the selection is read. If the new words contain known letter-sound associations, attention may be directed to these. In some instances the letter-sound association necessary to identify a specific word may be presented.

It is often helpful to stimulate students' interest in reading a selection. Direct their attention to the title and to some interesting pictures to arouse curiosity about the story. In the case of longer selections being read in parts, it may be helpful to review what has happened to that point each time the story is resumed.

If possible, follow the silent reading with discussion. This activity serves to check comprehension and to encourage students to keep in mind what the story is about. The questions the teacher asks about the story can act as the basic summary outline for the selection. Other questions can attend to conclusions drawn about the story that may not be explicitly stated in it.

Activities that combine comprehension exercise with the opportunity to gain additional practice with word-identification skills can end many reading selections. This is the basic form that Gates (1930) called the "intrinsic method," in which comprehension and word-identification activities are meaningfully integrated. The following exercises were developed to accompany a teacher-made reading selection:

1. What did the boy buy?
   A cap, a ball, a cat, a hat

2. Where did the cat have the kittens?
   under the bed
   under the shed
3. Which kitten did the boy keep?
   Blackie, Fatty, Brownie, Puff
4. Where did the kitten sleep?
   on the bed
   on the box

The comprehension of the story can be checked, with these exercises and practice with word-identification skills provided in the selection of the correct answer.

The advantage of incorporating the word-identification work here is that transfer of training is not an issue because the exercise is related to the reading process. The word-identification skills taught or presented must be drawn from the list of words being introduced, not from some isolated listing that may not relate to what is actually being read.

The word-identification skills presented this way foster the use of context and can be structured to focus attention on common syllables, spelling units, and inflectional endings, as well as letter-sound associations.

Children whose education has overemphasized isolated word identification may progress only to the point of "word calling." These children may need extra direction in the use of context that requires comprehension of the selection in order to break the habit of word calling. To redirect the student toward using context and attending to understanding, simple Cloze-type activities can be used. This requires the periodic deletion of words from passages being read by the student. The exercises should be quite simple at first, much like the sentences that were used to illustrate the use of spoken context. Even easy passages can have periodic word deletions to make the selection comprehensible, allowing the student to supply sensible, grammatically appropriate words for the blank spots. Easy multiple choices may be required at first for the most confirmed word callers. The continued use of Cloze-type activities may be necessary to redirect these children toward using and attending to context and comprehension. They also need a great deal of encouragement to engage in purposeful "guessing."

If comprehension seems to pose continual problems with some students, questions that ascertain comprehension may introduce the story. This may help reduce the extra rereading that some students seem always to need. The comprehension checks that follow a reading selection should also be used to appraise the difficulty of the reading selection for each student. The responses to the comprehension items should tell whether or not the selection is at an appropriate level of difficulty for instructional use.

Appropriate reading materials

Preparation and selection of reading materials require a shift in the focus of educational assessment to what the student knows. The vocabulary, the syntactic structures, and the nonliteral structures familiar to a child are essential information for structuring material for students whose needs are often not met by available published material.

Word-identification skills can only be learned and applied when a child is actually doing some reading. This can only be accomplished by preparing or selecting materials that are at an appropriate instructional level. Meaningfulness can only be associated with material at this readable level. Appropriateness is also the fundamental requirement for context to be used with effectiveness, and context is the foundation of word-identification skill development.

Important results of formulating appropriate instructional-level materials are success and engaged time. Appropriately prepared instructional-level material induces success, the fundamental reinforcement needed in reading instruction. Materials with these characteristics permit students to remain engaged in actual reading, the activity that is basic to a maximum rate of progress and achievement.

The final chapter considers measurement of readability. It is possible to find various published materials that suit the skill level of children with substantial measurable independence in reading ability. Measuring or assessing readability can become increasingly helpful in the selection of reading material that is within the student's threshold of reading ability.

REFERENCES

Gates, Arthur I. *Interest and ability in reading.* New York: Macmillan, 1930.

Hargis, Charles H. *An analysis of the syntactic and figurative structure of popular first grade level basal readers.* Paper presented at the 12th meeting of the Southeastern Conference on Linguistics, Washington, D.C., 1974.

Hargis, Charles H. *English syntax: An outline for clinicians and teachers of language handicapped children.* Springfield: Charles C Thomas, 1977.

Hargis, Charles H., & Evans, Carol. A criticism of the direct discourse form in primary level basal readers. *The Volta Review,* 1973, *75,* 557–563.

Huey, Edmund Burke. *The psychology and pedagogy of reading.* New York: Macmillan, 1908.

Ruddell, R. B., Shogren, M., & Strickland, R. *Pathfinder reading program, levels 1–14.* Boston: Allyn & Bacon, 1978.

7

READABILITY

Laurence J. Coleman

The major variables in readability

General issues

Reliability and validity

A review of specific methods

The procedure in practice

Suggestions for use

Readability techniques

7

Everyone has had the experience of trying to read something too difficult to understand. Sometimes this happens throughout a selection. At other times one may encounter a paragraph or a page that is difficult to read. Most people in such a situation either skip quickly over the part they do not understand or abandon reading that material entirely. Writers, librarians, editors, and teachers have long been cognizant of this problem.

Readability concerns attempts to understand and do something about this phenomenon. This chapter explores the topic of readability. The assumptions, advantages, and disadvantages of various readability procedures, as well as the technical concepts of reliability and validity, are discussed.

In a book of this type, it would be possible to analyze over thirty techniques (Klare, 1974–75). As this text is devoted to improving instruction for children, this chapter will primarily discuss readability techniques in terms of instruction. Therefore, only seven techniques most used by educators and librarians will be considered. These techniques will be introduced later in the chapter.

Readability techniques were developed to try to estimate how well persons at different levels of reading skill could comprehend written materials. These techniques were necessary because of the complex nature of the phenomenon and the scope of the problem.

Reading experts realized that the public inaccurately thinks that an adult reader can read almost anything. The fact is that written information comes in a variety of formats and deals with diverse topics. This variety can cause individual readers problems in comprehending materials. The problems are not confined to technical information. There is actually a great range of difficulty within common adult reading materials.

Powers and Ross (1959) examined this range after studying 100 selections from a large number of publications using four different readability methods. They categorized these publications into five designations with each representing a range of difficulty levels. The grade range of each category varied from readability measure to readability measure. Powers's and Ross's categories were scientific and academic, quality, standard, slick fiction, and pulp fiction. Each category was described, and the average grade levels from four different readability measures were summarized.

Scientific and academic materials were calculated to be at grade levels of from 7.4 to 11 +. Examples were *Science,* and *Annals of the American Academy of Political and Social Sciences.* Quality as a category referred to *Harper's* and *Atlantic Monthly,* with an average grade-level range of from 6.3 to 7.5. *Reader's Digest* is an example of the standard category, with an average grade range of from 5.4 to 6.3. The slick-fiction category was represented by stories in *Good Housekeeping* and *Ladies' Home Journal.* Pulp fiction included magazines such as *True Confessions.* The grade level of these categories was from 4.6 to 5.4 and 4.0 to 4.6 respectively. The range of adult materials is probably wider than this study shows. Nevertheless, one can readily see that an adult reader can be expected to encounter a wide variety of reading levels.

A similar situation exists for children's materials. Children too come in contact with material, in and out of school, that is written on many different reading grade levels. Guidry and Knight (1976) have demonstrated this in recreational reading materials. Lavely, Lowe, and Follman (1975) have shown this to be the case with classroom materials.

Those who seek to come to terms with this situation require a set of procedures for understanding what makes a passage difficult to read. Readability research is based on the assumption that reading takes place best in situations where the reader's abilities and purposes are congruent with the writer's style and intent. This assumption recognizes that any given passage is not always appropriate for readers of the same ability level.

Readability research offers a clearer picture of the complexity of written materials by studying the specific elements within the material. A considerable number of variables have been found to influence the readability of a passage. Literature shows substantial agreement about these variables. None of the techniques developed to measure readability, however, consider all the possible variables. In practice, two variables are studied by the many readability techniques to ascertain the readability of a passage. It is possible to estimate the reading difficulty of an article, book, or other written material by studying these elements in them.

The major variables in readability

Readability procedures make assumptions about the factors responsible for affecting the readability of a passage. Most literature shows substantial agreement about these factors (Klare, 1974–75).

Although numerous variables have been proposed, the entire group may be treated as constituting three types: word frequency, sentence length, and word length. The last of the variables is actually a variation on the other two. Almost everyone agrees that word frequency influences comprehension. This variable has to do with how often a reader encounters certain words. Thorndike and others established that much written material uses a limited number of words. It was reasoned that frequency of use increased comprehension of any word. Although this reasoning has not been proven, we do know that the inclusion of the variable increases the accuracy of readability estimates.

Most authorities agree that sentence length influences comprehension (Standal, 1978). The hypothesis most frequently advanced about this variable is that larger sentences contain more dependent clauses, more subordinate ideas, and more concepts that place a burden on the reader. This contention has not been empirically validated, but it is practicable. Sentence length is an important variable.

The third variable listed is word length, most often referred to in terms of syllables. (Sometimes this variable is measured in terms of number of letters in a word.) A common tactic is to determine word length by counting the number of syllables in a passage. The reasoning is that long words, having more syllables, are frequently more complex in meaning and less frequently encountered by readers than short ones. Strong support is available for the notion of frequency but not for the idea that larger words have more complex meaning.

These three variables have been used because of their relationship to each other in what are called regression equations. These variables are combined and weighted to predict the difficulty of a passage. Vocabulary (word frequency) and sentence length have continued to produce the highest loadings in the equations. For this practical reason they continue to be used (Hittleman, 1978). An adequate theory to explain the phenomenon has not been advanced. Thus, it appears we can calculate readability, but we are not certain why.

General issues

Readability procedures do bring definite advantages that should lead to improved instruction. Armed with these techniques the teacher can be more in control of instructional material. They allow teachers to make rational decisions about the purchase, modification, and creation of instructional materials.

Teachers in most schools are provided with a very limited budget for the purchase of materials. How does one choose from the vast array of materials in existence? Which ones should the teacher select? A publisher's advertising is not trustworthy. It is not uncommon for publishers' estimates of readability to be unreliable (Lavely, Lowe, & Follman, 1975).

ADVANTAGES

Readability techniques allow the teacher to calculate the readability of commercial materials before purchase. Materials that appear to be too difficult, too easy, or too variable may be eliminated.

Readability techniques have the advantage of helping teachers modify existing materials. The formulas give information on how to alter instructional levels. The teacher may adjust a too-difficult story downward a grade level and still preserve the integrity of the materials. Coleman (1979) has described how this may be accomplished.

Another advantage of readability procedures is their usefulness for creating or constructing written class materials. It is not unusual for students to have difficulty with traditional materials, but it *is* unusual for published material to present concepts exactly as the teacher wishes to convey them to students. Teachers can write their own materials and control for the students' reading levels with readability procedures.

LIABILITIES

For all their advantages, readability techniques do have some drawbacks. These may be seen as limitations of readability techniques. The problems are similar to those in standardized tests because readability techniques are themselves tests. Readability procedures are a type of test that is applied to materials—that is, to written passages rather than to persons. The results permit one to judge the suitability of written material for persons with different reading skill levels. Readability methods typically express skill levels as a reading grade score—for example, in the third grade. The issues to be discussed apply to most readability procedures but not to all. Exceptions are noted when specific procedures are described.

GRADE SCORES

Most readability techniques yield grade scores specifying that a typical child at a given grade level could probably read the selection. The concept of grade score is an elusive idea for many teachers.

A grade score represents a range of scores with the final score being the average of all. Different readability techniques produce different ranges and scores for the same material. Furthermore, for readability techniques, the norm group is comprised of passages, not people. Taken together, these points illustrate that grade scores derived from readability measures are relative, not absolute, scores. The meaning of any single grade score varies from technique to technique.

One final point about grade scores is that their meaning decreases inversely with grade level. Secondary grade scores are much less meaningful than those obtained at the elementary level. Reading is not taught as a separate subject having specified content at the secondary level as it is at the elementary. Instead, reading is tied to subject areas with specialized vocabularies. This discussion of grade scores helps explain the general problem about why readability techniques, which purport to measure the same thing, do not agree on the specific grade to which a particular reading selection should be assigned. This point, and others, have raised questions about the accuracy, reliability, and validity of the techniques.

Reliability and validity

The issue of reliability is really a question of how consistent the results of a technique are. Stated simply, the reliability question is do different users of the same technique get similar results on the same passages? The general answer is yes. Persons trained in a specific method tend to rank material similarly.

This does not mean that the methods are without error. Like all tests, readability techniques do not yield true scores; they produce scores that contain error. The rate of error, called the standard error of measurement (SEM), may be calculated. The smaller the SEM, the greater the accuracy of a procedure.

Another reliability question is does a specific technique consistently rank a group of reading selections from least difficult to most difficult? Many studies have been conducted on this point. The general answer is yes; when readability procedures are compared, they tend to place the individual selections in a similar order. This does not mean, however, that different techniques assign the same grade score to these individual selections. Research on the accuracy of scores is described in the next section.

The issue of validity has to do with whether the procedures measure what they claim to. In other words, do they predict how well one might read a book? The earlier evidence of reliability contributes to a discussion of validity.

Any discussion of validity needs a restatement of what readability procedures try to do. Readability techniques attempt to make predictions about how well a person can be expected to understand or comprehend a reading selection. This assumption about reading comprehension is the real meaning of readability. Unfortunately, as Spache points out, "This assumption has seldom if ever been tested in the development of . . . readability formulas" (1978, p. 189). Comprehension is a complex phenomenon. Many ideas have been advanced about how it operates. Unfortunately, there is no real agreement about what comprehension is.

In practice, comprehension is defined according to the means by which it is measured. Several approaches are possible for judging the probability that a person will understand a selection (Klare, 1974–75).

DETERMINING VALIDITY

One approach is to ask experts, or people trained to make judgments about reading materials, or readers themselves to suggest who could read these materials. Several studies have tried this approach (Klare, 1963), which Carver (1974) has shown to be valid. The difficulty with this technique is the problem of standardizing procedures for making judgments.

A second approach is to construct special comprehension tests that may be keyed to different reading selections, unlike the usual tests of reading. Such an approach requires a great deal of effort and careful development. Little work has been devoted to this approach because it would require special skills in test construction and development to put it into practice.

The third approach to ascertaining the validity of readability procedures is to compare the complexity of new written material against some known standard or criteria of comprehension. The McCall-Crabbs *Standard test lessons in reading* (1925, 1950, 1961) has been used extensively as a standard. Another version of this approach is to use textbooks of known reading level or existing readability procedures (Fry, 1968; Spache, 1978).

The essence of this technique is that whatever criterion or standard of comprehension is selected becomes operationally defined by that standard. In other words, comprehension is whatever the standard is. If there are problems with the standard, there are problems with the meaning of comprehension. Since the McCall-Crabbs *Standard test lessons in reading* (McCall & Crabbs, 1925, 1950, 1961) have been used as the measure of comprehension by many readability formulas, these lessons are really what comprehension is. Many of the most popular techniques use these lessons—the Flesch (1943) and its revisions (Powers, Sumner, & Kearl, 1959), the Dale-Chall (1948) and its revision (Powers et al., 1959), and the SMOG (McLaughlin, 1969), as examples.

If there are any problems with the construction of these lessons, one may raise questions about the meaning of comprehension. Stevens (1980) has pointed out such issues. She remarked that these lessons were never really standardized or developed intentionally for use as a standard of comprehension. Rather, they were intended to provide practice in reading. Apparently the creators of readability techniques did not question McCall or Crabbs about their feelings as to the appropriateness of using their lessons as a criterion of comprehension. If they had, they might have discovered problems with the standardization. The norm group for the *Standard test lessons in reading* was a number of New York City schoolchildren in grades three to six. Some tests may have been given to grades three, five, and seven. Perhaps two hundred children were used in each grade, but there may have been "thousands" of subjects. Another problem of standardization was the means by which comprehension levels were assigned to the lessons. In the *Standard test lessons in reading,* children were asked to answer questions about each lesson. The number of correctly answered questions was related to the Thorndike-McCall Reading Test. The final comprehension levels were obtained by averaging the reading grades of the subjects. Later editions used the Gates Reading Test to establish levels of comprehension. Thus, reading grade scores of the *Standard test lessons in reading* are clearly an approximation of reading levels (McLaughlin, 1969; Stevens, 1980). Realizing this, one should be careful in assuming that comprehension has been clearly defined by these procedures.

These particular comments about comprehension do not apply to the Cloze procedure, the Harris-Jacobson formula, and the Fry method, which did not use McCall-Crabbs. Little can be said about comprehension, regarding the Fry and the Harris-Jacobson, because their developers did not really pay attention to the issue and this aspect of validity. Unlike these methods, the Cloze procedure is concerned directly with the issue of comprehension.

The Cloze procedure is a readability technique to which this issue of comprehension has been very important. Taylor (1953) announced this new technique and discussed this issue. Subsequent studies have compared scores on Cloze-type tests to those derived from an independent measure of comprehension. Standardized tests of reading have generally been the independent measure. Many of the most widely used tests, such as the Metropolitan Achievement Test (Gallant, 1965) and the Stanford Achievement Test (Ruddell, 1964) have been used. The evidence is substantial and supports the notion that Cloze tests are valid measures of comprehension (Bormuth, 1968; Rankin, 1971). In sum, the Cloze procedure may be the better procedure in terms of comprehension.

ASCERTAINING ACCURACY

Accuracy, the final major issue in need of attention, can be defined as the ability of a procedure to produce grade scores consistently and to produce scores similar to those of other procedures. Accuracy is related to the previous discussions of reliability and validity. It is important as an issue because teachers tend to have favorite procedures that they use. If one's favorite procedure yields results that differ from another's, these teachers have problems talking to each other about different textbooks.

Several studies have looked at accuracy. The present discussion is confined to the accuracy of procedures contained in this chapter.

Guidry and Knight (1976) conducted a study in which they calculated the grade levels on fifty-three Newbery Award winners using the Flesch, Dale-Chall, and Fry techniques, and one other procedure. A mean readability score or grade score was computed by averaging the results for each book from all the formulas. An interesting variability was found among the procedures, which ranged from two grade levels in one book to a spread of seven grades in several others. The authors concluded that the Dale-Chall method tended to assign consistently higher grade levels and the Fry consistently lower readability scores than the other procedures. The Flesch revealed no consistent trend. On the basis of these findings, Guidry and Knight suggested that teachers use an "adjustment factor" to correct the imprecise estimates of the formulas. They proposed that an adjustment of −.891 be made to the Dale-Chall scores and +.805 to the Fry scores. Although these findings give some indication of the variability of grade scores, note that the authors were assuming that "true" readability was an average of all the formulas.

Harris and Jacobson (1980) compared one of their primary-grade formulas to the Fry and Spache methods, using two recently revised basal readers. One series had a phonic emphasis and the other a meaning emphasis. The complete series, which included all books (i.e., preprimer to high third grade) and all the text in each book of the series, were studied. Two hundred-word samples were consecutively drawn from each test. A total of the findings showed that 247,494 words were analyzed. The assigned grade levels were dissimilar across the methods. All procedures showed a sequential increase in reading difficulty, an indication of good reliability. The authors noted that Fry "seriously overestimates" second- and third-grade reading abilities. The Fry grade-level ratings were much higher, not only than the Harris-Jacobson and the Spache, but also than publisher estimates. Findings also indicated that Spache underestimated the reading levels established by publishers at the late second- and third-grade levels.

Pauk (1969) reported a study in which readability scores

were computed on twenty articles. The study was conducted to determine if fast procedures (i.e., Fry and SMOG) were accurate. The Dale-Chall formula was used as the criterion of the best readability score. Such a practice was deemed acceptable because the Dale-Chall is generally recognized as the most valid method. Results indicated that the SMOG produced a wider variety of scores. The Fry and the Dale-Chall grades agreed in 45 percent of the cases and in 10 percent was two grades off. Pauk concluded with a critique of the SMOG. McLaughlin (1969) responded by computing correlations among the three procedures using Pauk's data. McLaughlin noted similar correlations, which meant that all the formulas were predicting similar phenomena, another sign of good reliability.

Vaughn (1976) replicated and extended Pauk (1969), increasing the number of selections to eighty-seven. These articles represented a diverse set of reading materials. The results were that (1) the Dale-Chall and the Fry "agreed consistently"; (2) the SMOG "consistently disagreed" with the Fry and Dale-Chall; (3) the SMOG produced grade scores two grades higher than the Fry and Dale-Chall scores; and (4) all the methods correlated significantly ($p < .001$) with each other— that is, Dale-Chall to Fry ($r = .89$), Dale-Chall to SMOG ($r = .87$), and Fry to SMOG ($r = -.80$).

When these three studies are considered together, several conclusions may be drawn. If the correlations indicate that the methods are measuring something similar, why do they not give the same scores? Several explanations are reasonable. The fact that these methods use different variables to compute readability scores may explain some of the variation in scores. The Fry, the Flesch, and the SMOG use syllables, but the Dale-Chall uses word frequency as the basis for testing. Another explanation is that all procedures contain some error that causes the difference. A third explanation is that the procedures use different size samples for computing scores. A final explanation is that the differences in accuracy depend on how the standard of comprehension is defined.

Although all of these explanations are good, the last one is probably the best one because the difference in grade scores tends to be consistent in comparisons of the Fry, SMOG, and Dale-Chall. Consistency is shown by the formulas' agreeing to order the same group of articles from highest to lowest readability in a similar sequence, and the formulas' disagreeing on a grade score. In these studies, a two-grade difference between SMOG and the others consistently appears. The agreement and disagreement are probably because the formulas do not really yield grade scores that mean the same thing. The grade difference is probably a reflection of the different levels of comprehension used by the formulas. The Dale-Chall and the Fry use 50–75 percent comprehension; whereas the SMOG uses a 90–100 percent level. Obviously, a score dependent upon a higher level of comprehension requires that readers be more competent. In other words, comprehension requires higher grade levels of reading in one method than another. Thus, one would get grade scores two grades higher with the SMOG than with the others. This point is important to remember when choosing a procedure to evaluate materials.

In summary, readability procedures in general have strengths and limitations. Their strengths outweigh their limitations, but the limitations remind one not to become overconfident about decisions made using readability procedures. Readability techniques are reliable and valid measures of the difficulty of written materials. In the following section specific procedures will be reviewed.

A review of specific methods

Dozens of readability procedures are available for teachers to assess the comprehensibility of reading materials. Within this group some procedures are more popular with educators than others. Their popularity seems to be a consequence of many factors, including the variables measured, the criterion of comprehension, the standard error of estimate, the time needed to use the procedure, and the grade level of materials for which the procedure is intended. In this chapter, these factors and others will be discussed in terms of seven methods used to determine readability: Flesch, Dale-Chall, Spache, SMOG, Fry, Harris-Jacobson, and Cloze.

FLESCH

The Flesch formula (1948) was originally published in 1943 and was quickly changed because of problems within it. The formula, published to measure typical adult reading materials, used as its two variables number of syllables and sentence length. The formula in its present form (Powers, et al., 1958) is as follows:

Reading Ease (R.E.) $= -2.2029 + .0778sl + .0455wl$

where: sl = average number of words per sentences
wl = number of syllables per 100 words.

The Flesch formula was validated with the McCall-Crabbs *Standard test lessons in reading* (1925). A correlation of .70 was obtained using a 57–75 percent standard of comprehension. In the update of the formula, a newer version of McCall-Crabbs (1950) was used. A correlation of .64 was calculated (Powers, et al., 1958).

The accuracy of the Flesch formula has been calculated. The standard error for this formula is .85 school grades. Thus, if one wants to be sure 97 of 100 times about the true reading level of a passage, the error is ± 1.71 grades (Powers, et al., 1958).

The time needed to use the Flesch formula has been a concern. Powers and Ross (1959) developed an easy graph for teachers to use. This is a rapid procedure.

DALE-CHALL

The Dale-Chall system was published in 1948 to be used with adult materials—that is, fourth grade and above (Dale & Chall, 1948). The procedure employed two variables: average sentence length and word difficulty. The actual formula as recalculated by Powers, Sumner, and Kearl (1958) is this:

$X_{c}50 = .1155_{x1} + .0596_{x2} + 3.2672$
where: $X_{c}50$ = reading grade with 50-percent comprehension
X_1 = percentage of words not on Dale list of three thousand (Dale score)
X_2 = average sentence length in words

The percentage of words is determined by comparing each word against a list of three thousand words. A series of nineteen rules must be used to judge whether a word is on the list.

Dale and Chall were careful to be specific about the criterion of comprehension used to substantiate the value of their work. Using the first edition of McCall-Crabbs (1925), they reported a correlation of .70 using 50-percent comprehension (Dale & Chall, 1948). Powers, Sumner, and Kearl (1958), using the 1950 version of the *Standard test lessons in reading* (McCall-Crabbs, 1950), calculated a correlation of .71. Compared to standardized tests this is an acceptable level.

The standard error of estimate for the revised formula is .77 grades, which makes it more precise than other formulas.

The Dale-Chall technique is rather time-consuming because one must compare each word using the nineteen rules and three thousand words. Pauk (1969) reported various times for using several formulas. Although this was not clearly stated, it appears to have taken forty minutes to estimate the readability of any one article. This estimate seems a little high. Pauk did not report using any of the shortcuts available with the Dale-Chall. Powers and Ross (1959) have constructed a graph to aid calculation, Williams (1972) has built a table, and Koenke (1971) has a graph for decreasing the time needed to calculate the formula.

SPACHE

The Spache formula was constructed in 1953 to assess primary-level children's material (Spache, 1978). Unlike the previously described methods, reading materials from first to third grade were the target. In this sense the Spache formula is a downward revision of the others.

Spache made use of two variables to ascertain grade level, average sentence length and word difficulty. The latter variable is ascertained by comparing each word to a list of known words. This list has changed twice since 1953. Stone (1956) showed how a modified list could increase the accuracy of the method. More recently, Spache (1978) in the tenth edition of his book, revised the word list to accommodate stylistic changes in primary textbooks. He modified the word list by reviewing (1) a study done by his publisher on primary words, (2) a 1970 word list prepared by Dale, and (3) the Harris-Jacobson (1972) *Basic elementary reading vocabularies.* The revised word list was expanded to 1,041 words. A series of eleven rules for evaluating specific words was also slightly modified. The new regression equation is

Grade level = $.121_{x1}$ + $.082_{x2}$ + $.659$

where: x_1 = average sentence length in words
x_2 = words not on revised word list

The criterion of comprehension is difficult to discuss because, as Spache (1978) has noted, it has not been extensively studied. As the formula has been shown to correlate well with other indicators of grade levels, one may infer something about the formula's ability to assess comprehension (Spache, 1978). Spache (1978) cites a study by Staiger that used the earlier formulas in which a correlation of .70 was found between ratings of student performance in oral reading and comprehension and ratings.

The standard error of estimate for the Spache is probably ± 2 months 68 percent of the time, which makes it an accurate formula. The amount of time needed to use this formula has not been reported in literature. Given the smaller number of words one needs to locate on the revised word list, the time consumed by a teacher is less than with the Dale-Chall and Harris-Jacobson methods. Spache (1978, p. 195) provides a chart for reducing the time it takes to calculate the formulas.

SMOG

The SMOG was introduced by McLaughlin (1969) as a more reliable and faster procedure than other methods used for adults. The acronym SMOG has been attributed to a recognition of another technique called the FOG Index and McLaughlin's birthplace, London, and to an acronym derived from "Simple Measure of Gobbledy-gook" (McLaughlin, 1969). The formula follows:

Smog = 3 + estimated square root of polysyllable count
where: polysyllable = the number of words of three or more syllables

The SMOG takes samples in a manner different from other methods. The user is advised to select ten consecutive sentences from the beginning, middle, and end of a text. These thirty sentences are used for ascertaining the syllable count. McLaughlin (1969) claims that this produces a sample of about six hundred words—double the standard number.

The criterion of comprehension is based upon the 390 selections in McCall-Crabbs *Standard text lessons in reading* (1961). The SMOG differs from other readability formulas in that comprehension is defined as answering all of the comprehension questions correctly. Other formulas use 50–75 percent correct (McLaughlin, 1969). This practice seems to result in the SMOG's yielding grade scores two years higher than the Dale-Chall (Klare, 1974–1975; Vaughn, 1976).

The standard error of estimate for the SMOG is ± 1.5 grades (McLaughlin, 1969). If one wants to estimate the difficulty of a passage as accurately as 97 out of 100 times, the SMOG accuracy is ± 3.0 grades. McLaughlin claims that SMOG may be more indicative of actual reading difficulty than other methods because of the 100-percent comprehension level. The time needed to use the SMOG is nine minutes (McLaughlin, 1969) per text. In a comparative study of methods, Pauk (1969) confirmed this figure.

FRY

The Fry graph was announced in 1965 as a rapid method for calculating the readability of materials (Fry, 1968). The technique may be used from preprimer to adult level (Maginnis, 1969).

The Fry differs from other procedures in that it is not a formula. Rather, one counts variables and plots them on a graph. The variables used with this method are syllables and sentence length. Samples of 100 words are taken from the beginning, middle, and end of a book. Bradley and Ames (1977) have presented data suggesting that perhaps two dozen samples are needed for optimum sampling.

The criterion of comprehension for the Fry is impossible to determine. Fry (1968) used an uncommon procedure. Apparently, he took publisher estimates of grade levels from an unknown number of books and plotted their difficulty.

In the same article Fry presented further evidence about comprehension with variables on a graph that reported high correlations between scales on a graduate-student-constructed comprehension test and readability scores on ten books.

The standard error of estimate according to Fry was within one grade level. As no statistics were cited, it is not possible to make a statement (Harris & Jacobson, 1980). However, Pauk (1969) found that the Fry agreed with Dale-Chall grade levels less than half of the time.

Because Fry developed the procedure to speed up estimating readability, one would expect it to be a fast procedure. Pauk (1969) has found fifteen minutes to be the time needed to do an article, comparable to that needed to do the SMOG procedure.

HARRIS-JACOBSON

The Harris-Jacobson readability formulas are the newest techniques discussed in this book. Harris and Jacobson proposed two formulas (Harris & Sipay, 1975), which were based on their research into the words used in reading materials (Harris & Jacobson, 1972). Several versions of the basic formula based upon the level of the material and the variables measured are available. Harris and Jacobson proposed two formulas using these variables: word difficulty, as determined by percentage of words not on their word list, and average sentence length (Harris & Sipay, 1975). One formula was for primary materials and the other for above third grade. Harris and Jacobson (1980) described another version of the formula that used a third variable, the average number of letters in a word. Even though there are some changes in the values of the formulas, the index of word difficulty remains relatively constant because the word list remains constant. The Harris-Jacobson formulas require no special rules for considering each word. In this manner they are easier to use than the Spache formula and the Dale-Chall procedure.

The criterion of comprehension is difficult to judge. Evidence is available to show that two versions of the formula rank textbooks from lowest to highest grade (Harris & Sipay, 1975). In a third version similar evidence is available (Harris & Jacobson, 1980). Unfortunately, this evidence addresses itself somewhat indirectly to the issue of validity. The evidence does not directly show how Harris-Jacobson readability scores predict other indicators of comprehension, such as the McCall-Crabbs materials or comprehension tests, as other formulas have attempted.

The standard error of estimate is dependent upon the version of the formula being used. Harris and Sipay (1975) calculated an error of ± .38 grades and ± .71 grades for a primary formula (grades one through three) and a formula for grades one through eight-plus, respectively. For the three variable formulas an error of ± .3 grades was found (Harris & Jacobson, 1980).

The amount of time needed to use this formula has not been stated in the literature. Harris and Sipay (1975) point out that Harris-Jacobson formulas are probably faster than Dale-Chall (1948) because the Harris-Jacobson has no cumbersome rules to apply when counting unfamiliar words. In the Harris-Jacobson system, any word not on the list is unknown. In an informal study by the author, the amount of time for the procedure was about twenty minutes per article.

CLOZE

The Cloze procedure differs markedly from the others. The predominant difference is that this method does not make predictions about how some students at a future time might do on reading a particular passage. Instead the Cloze procedure measures how a student can read a specific passage in the present because the person is asked to read that particular selection. Klare (1974–75) has discussed this distinction at length.

Other differences between the Cloze procedure and other methods should be noted. The Cloze is not a mathematical formula. It is not a regression equation. It does not count factors such as sentence length, word difficulty, and syllables. These differences should not lead one to conclude that these variables are not important; they are simply treated in another manner. The essence of the Cloze procedure is that it seems to explore most of the many factors in a passage that might affect a person's ability to read the selection. Other variability procedures do not take this factor into account.

The manner in which the Cloze procedure works is to recognize that written language is composed of patterns of words. The structure and variability of these patterns is what a reader must decode. The notion of language patterns recognizes the importance of the commonly used variables like vocabulary and sentence length, syntactic complexity, and lexical density as readability factors. In brief, "one can think of cloze procedure as throwing all potential readability influences in a pot, letting them interact, then sampling the result" (Taylor, 1953, p. 917).

The Cloze procedure accomplishes this simply by removing words from a selection. A frequent method is to remove every fifth word. Figure 1 illustrates the technique. Readers are

---

Figure 1   Example of Cloze test

"Don't make such a ___ deal out of such ___ little dent!" "Little dent! ___ you little turkey, I'll ___ you a little dent," ___ shouted, shaking his fist ___.

"I've just had this ___ for an hour and ___ run it into the ___." "How was I to ___ that you shouldn't use ___ front brake by itself?" ___ Freddy said sheepishly.

"Oh brother, ___ just told you not ___ do it and you ___ ahead and did it ___ the same. You always ___ the opposite of what ___ tell you. I'll never ___ you again. Get away ___ my bike."

Jason pushed ___ hands from the new ___. Freddy wistfully withdrew, and ___ a final longing look ___ the shiny bike turned ___ slowly along the curbing ___ toward his house. Freddy ___ unhappily, "I tried to ___ which handle was for ___ rear brake, but the ___ was too close. If ___ could only have turned ___ faster. Jason will never ___ me ride the bike ___. I guess I don't ___ blame him either."

As ___ looked down at the ___ triangular dent in the ___ perfect fuel tank, he ___ both anger and remorse. "___ Jason," he thought. "Why ___ I yell at him ___ why did I let ___ ride my new bike."

___ realized that the bike ___ get plenty of dents ___ scratches soon enough. After ___ hadn't he dreamed of riding ___ all the old cow ___ on Jake's farm. Jason ___ that he was only ___ that he didn't do ___ first damage himself.

required to read the passage and supply the missing word, usually in writing. By counting the number of times that a reader supplies the missing word it is possible to state at what level a person understands that selection. Rankin (1971) has described these levels.

Research on the Cloze procedure has addressed the issue of an independent measure of comprehension quite extensively. Numerous studies have correlated Cloze-procedure scores with scores on comprehension tests (Bormuth, 1968). The results indicate that the Cloze procedure can be interpreted to measure different percentage levels of comprehension. These levels are a direct measure of a person's ability to read that book.

The Cloze procedure is appropriate for material above third-grade level. It is unreliable below this point.

It is difficult to compare the time needed to employ the Cloze procedure with other methods because the procedure is so different from others. With the Cloze the most time is devoted to constructing the tests for the students to take. Considerable time is spent typing the samples and deleting the words. The actual calculation of a person's performance takes only a few minutes because it is necessary only to count all the correct responses.

The seven procedures have been reviewed. They appear to differ in which variables they measure. Table 1 summarizes the discussion by permitting a quick comparison of the seven procedures. Obvious differences appear between methods in terms of accuracy, speech, validity, age/grade levels, and format. Each of these factors is important in choosing a method. The next sections are directed at helping a teacher decide on a method of use.

In sum, readability procedures appear to be reliable and valid predictors of the difficulty that readers will encounter when reading instructional materials. These methods can be useful tools for teachers and librarians.

Readability techniques, on the other hand, have several serious deficiencies. The criterion of comprehension has not been standardized. These techniques do not really explain why one selection is more difficult to read than another. Questions may also be raised about the factors that they do not measure and their accuracy in specifying grade level. Nevertheless, these are useful techniques.

Table 1 Summary of Characteristics of Techniques

Age/grade range	Name	Variables	Sample size	No. of samples[3]	Special features	Standard error[4]	Criterion of comprehension
Primary	Spache	Words re: 1041[1] ASL[2]	100 words	3	Formula	± .4 grades Spache, 1978	Unclear Spache, 1978
Mixed	Fry (K-adult)	Syllables ASL	100 words	3+	Uses graph	unknown—probably more than 2 grades Fry, 1968	Unclear
	Harris-Jacobson (1-3; 1-8)	Words re: 2792 ASL	200 words	3–5	Several formulas; computer based	± .76 grades; ± 1.4 grades Harris & Sipay, 1975	Unknown & Harris & Sipay, 1975
Adult	Flesch	Syllables	100 syllables	systematic		± 1.71 grades Powers et al., 1958	50%[5]
	Dale-Chall (3-12)	Word re: 3000 ASL	100 words	throughout or 3		± 1.80 grades Powers et al., 1958	50%[5]
	SMOG	Words with 3 or more syllables	10 sentences	3	Very fast	± 3 grades McLaughlin, 1969	100%[5]
	Cloze	Unspecified	250 words	6-12, possibly less	Every 5th word deleted		Relative to percent correct—varies from 75% to 90%

[1]compared to word list of that size [2]average sentence length [3]the general practice is to take sample at beginning, middle, and end [4]recalculated to ±2 SEM [5]based on McCall-Crabbs

The procedure in practice

The review of the procedures was to provide some background to offer a more thorough understanding of the techniques. The discussion suggests that readability scores differ with the techniques used. Such a conclusion is correct. To illustrate this point, readability scores were calculated on the same material using the seven methods. A reading series was selected at random from a curriculum-materials center. Two books were selected. One was *Whispering ghosts*, level 9 (Eller & Hester, 1976), estimated by the publisher to be at the beginning third-grade level. The other was *Patterns*, level 12 (Eller & Hester, 1978), estimated to be at the fifth-grade level.

A random sample was taken at the beginning, middle, and ending of each book and readability techniques applied to each book in order to make comparisons. Some liberties were taken in using the techniques.

The results are reported in Table 2. It reports the readability of each sample according to method in one column. The spaces for nonapplicability mean that no calculation was possible with that method. By reading across Table 2 one can see the readability score for each passage as calculated by each method. Other differences are also apparent. The variability may seem unsettling, but it is no problem when several samples are taken. The readability levels of the books for the various techniques generally fall within one year of each other.

Several points can be made about specific techniques from Table 2. Note that none of the methods give the same value as the publishers' estimates. This is a common occurrence. The Spache, Fry, and Harris-Jacobson are appropriate for primary materials. Of these three, the Spache seems to yield slightly more consistent scores. In terms of standard error, however, they yield the same scores. The Fry and Harris-Jacobson were also used with the level-12 textbook, as were the Dale-Chall, Flesch, and SMOG.

The SMOG produced a grade level two years beyond all the procedures. This fact is consistent with the literature.

Not surprisingly, the Cloze procedure did not yield a readability score. Unlike the other methods, the Cloze proce-

Table 2 Readability of two reading textbooks with different techniques by grade level

FORMULAS

	Publisher Estimate	Spache	Fry	Harris-Jacobson[1]	Dale-Chall[2]	Flesch[3]	SMOG	Cloze
LEVEL 9								
Page 13		2.4	2nd	high 2nd	NA	NA	NA	NA[4]
Page 121		3.1	6th	4th	NA	NA	NA	NA
Page 276		3.5	5th	5th	NA	NA	NA	NA
average readability	3.1	3.0	3.3	3.7	NA	NA	NA	NA
LEVEL 12								
Page 48			mid 6th	5th	6.4	4.8	9 wds.	NA
Page 142			high 5th	high 3rd	5.5	4.6	3 wds.	NA
Page 256			3rd	low 3rd	5.1	4.0	7 wds.	NA
average readability	5	NA	4.6	4.0	5.7	4.5	15 wds. (7th g.)	NA

[1] used formula 2 with 100 words [2] using table of Koenke (1971) [3] Powers & Ross (1959) [4] NA = not applicable

dure is typically administered to students. The other methods may be calculated without the presence of students.

The data in Table 2 taken as a whole provides support for earlier statements about the functioning of readability materials. In the concluding section recommendations are made about when to use these procedures.

Suggestions for use

The selection of readability procedures to suit a teacher's purpose requires that the teacher examine his or her goals. The present discussion assumes that the teacher has done that. The final section discusses the advantages and disadvantages of each method and makes specific recommendations.

THE SPACHE METHOD

The Spache (1978) has been used extensively for many years to evaluate materials from levels one to three. One advantage of the Spache is that it appears to be more accurate for the primary grades than the other methods reviewed here.

Teachers who work with children reading the 3.9 grade level will find this procedure most useful. The emphasis here is on reading levels, not age. Special educators should particularly note this point because most special children read below fourth-grade level.

As the Spache uses a list of 1,041 words for determining unfamiliar words, the formula has the disadvantage of consuming much teacher time. The rules needed to evaluate each word also add to the time; speed is greatly decreased by frequent reference to the list.

The presence of the revised word list of 1,041 words, however, has a converse and beneficial effect for the teacher. Because the list represents a recent analysis of commonly used words in primary materials, a child who is to become a competent reader needs to learn these words. A word-study program based on unfamiliar terms from the revised word list should improve the child's reading skill and increase the reliability of the teacher's readability estimates. Other uses of the word list may be the construction or adaption of reading materials or the development of a diagnostic test (Coleman, 1979).

Some persons have found the mathematical calculations of the Spache formula to be awkward and confusing. Safier (1959) devised a graph that eliminates calculations. Spache (1978) has published a similar graph to overcome this minor disadvantage. A last disadvantage of the Spache is that one cannot assume a child's comprehension of the material at more than an average level.

The Spache (1978) is a very good method for assessing primary materials. It seems to combine features of accuracy and speed in predicting how well primary-level readers may read a textbook.

THE FRY GRAPH

The Fry graph is a relatively new procedure for assessing materials. A modification by Maginnis (1969) enables one to evaluate material from preprimer to college level. The Fry method has been the focus of much attention in recent years on a wide variety of materials—children's picture books (Hunt & Reuter, 1978), basal readers (Bradley & Ames, 1977), and Newbery Award winners (Guidry & Knight, 1976). Other studies, discussed elsewhere in this paper, have compared the Fry formula to others.

The Fry has two important advantages: the range of materials it can assess and speed of calculation. The speed is brought about by making a syllable count instead of referring to a word list with its accompanying rules. The speed enables one to assess a large amount of material in a short period of time. If a person's job requires consultation about a wide range of materials, this is an important advantage.

The advantage of speed has another side. The Fry seems to sacrifice some accuracy for the sake of speed. In fact, less is known about its accuracy than that of most other formulas. Loss of accuracy may be caused by the fact that words of fewer syllables are not necessarily more familiar than long ones to a reader. Some evidence suggests that the Fry underestimates reading difficulty (Guidry & Knight, 1976). Other evidence contradicts the findings by reporting that the Fry overestimates second- and third-grade material, compared to the Spache (1978) and Harris-Jacobson (1980). Another study has showed the Fry scores to be comparable to these in Dale-Chall (1948) and more accurate than those in SMOG (Vaughn, 1976). These latter findings refer to adult (above third grade) formulas.

The Fry does not seem to offer any clear indication of comprehensibility, a shortcoming worth remembering, but it is a useful and speedy method.

The findings suggest that the Fry method might best be used with adult materials as a fast means for estimating the readability of a wide number of books, articles, and other written materials.

THE HARRIS-JACOBSON FORMULA

The Harris-Jacobson readability procedures are a series of formulas that measure different variables to account for the readability of a variety of written materials from first to eighth grade (Harris & Jacobson, 1980; Harris & Sipay, 1975). These are the newest formulas, reviewed here, to make use of a word list. Their word list, developed from extensive studies of the terms used in primary reading series (Harris & Jacobson, 1972), is representative of the latest trends and comparable to other word lists (Harris & Jacobson, 1973–1974). Spache (1978) used their words to revise his own word list.

A significant advantage of the Harris-Jacobson formula is that no special rules are necessary for using the word list. If a word is not on the list, it is considered an unfamiliar or hard word. In practice this approach reduces the time and error involved in using other methods that employ word lists. Other advantages of the word-list approach are the same for the Harris-Jacobson as for other methods. The lists are useful for word study and for writing and adapting materials. A final advantage is that the Harris-Jacobson formulas seem to be accurate. One version of their formula appears to agree with publisher criteria more readily than does the Spache (Harris & Jacobson, 1980).

The Harris-Jacobson also has several shortcomings. One disadvantage is that the time needed to use the word list may be excessive. The procedure apparently has not been used by teachers, probably because of its relative newness or because it has been presented in a format that may be threatening to potential users (Harris & Sipay, 1975). Furthermore, the fact that different versions of the formula have been reported may have led to hesitation about using these formulas. A final reservation about the Harris-Jacobson formula might be that it has not been validated against an acceptable measure of comprehension.

The Harris-Jacobson formulas are appropriate for primary- and secondary-level materials. The nature of the procedure suggests it might be best used by school systems doing an extensive review of curricular materials.

THE DALE-CHALL FORMULA

The Dale-Chall formula (Dale & Chall, 1948) has been used for assessing material at above a fourth-grade level. The procedure is generally accepted as the most reliable of the adult formulas (Klare, 1963). It has become the standard criterion for establishing the value of newer formulas. The Dale-Chall has been recommended for use in research projects (Klare, 1974–75).

Besides this distinct advantage, the Dale-Chall employs a three-thousand-word list to evaluate words in any passage. This word list can be applied for rewriting materials and for devising a word-study program. The word list is particularly helpful in these two endeavors because it represents words that primary readers have probably mastered.

The word list, however, contributes to a shortcoming of the Dale-Chall. Formulated in the 1940s, it may be becoming outdated. Furthermore, the three thousand words and nineteen rules require that considerable time be spent using the technique.

Not only has the length of time needed for arriving at a readability estimate reduced the use of the procedure; the presence of mathematical calculations has also influenced some persons to avoid the technique. Proposals have been offered to deal with these shortcomings. Powers, Sumner, and Kearl (1958) recalculated the values in the formula in terms of vocabulary changes. Others have devised procedures for eliminating calculations through the use of graphs and tables (Koenke, 1971; Powers & Ross, 1959; Williams, 1972). Each modification has contributed to making the Dale-Chall more attractive to teachers.

One final note on the Dale-Chall refers to the level of comprehension that it assumes. The Dale-Chall uses a 50-percent level, which means that teachers should not assume a student's ability to master the information independently. Furthermore, the teacher should recall that the standard error is almost two full grades. This means that a given book may be that much above or below the estimate given by the formula.

The Dale-Chall formula is a most useful procedure. It takes longer to use than other adult-level formulas, however. The potential user of this procedure is encouraged to organize a group of teachers to use it as a means for establishing the readability of books that the group may want to purchase. In this manner, the amount of time any one person spends can be reduced, and the number of books assessed can be increased considerably.

THE FLESCH FORMULA

The Flesch formula assesses adult materials too. One difference between the technique and the Dale-Chall is that the Flesch uses a syllable count, not a word list. This makes it a faster procedure. The Flesch is less accurate but is comparable to Dale-Chall (Powers, et al., 1958). The Flesch is similar to the Dale-Chall in that it also has a 50-percent standard of comprehension. It requires mathematical calculation.

When considered together, the Flesch offers the advantage over the Dale-Chall of speed and accuracy. The Flesch procedure has been used for many years, and many people are familiar with it.

THE SMOG PROCEDURE

Another procedure which employs a syllable count to assess adult materials is the SMOG (McLaughlin, 1969), a relatively new procedure. The SMOG differs from other procedures in that it counts only one variable, words with three or more syllables. Consideration of sentence length is presumed to be operating in the selection of samples of ten sentences each.

The format of the SMOG makes it a very fast procedure. Like other speedy procedures, however, it appears to give up accuracy for speed. The SMOG has a standard error of ± 1.5 grades (McLaughlin, 1969). Furthermore, the SMOG tends to estimate grade levels of the same materials at two years higher than Fry or Dale-Chall (Vaughn, 1976).

Unlike other fast methods, which have a criterion of comprehension of about 50–70 percent, the SMOG uses a criterion of 90–100 percent. This significant difference may make the SMOG a very desirable formula to use in looking for or constructing materials for independent study or homework.

A 90-percent criterion is significant because this comprehension level is similar to that usually accorded the term *independent reading level.*

The SMOG procedure is fast and probably provides a more realistic estimate of how well students above fourth grade can handle written materials (assuming current classroom grouping procedures) than other measures of readability.

THE CLOZE PROCEDURE

The Cloze procedure is for intermediate and adult-level materials. The major advantage the procedure has over other types of readability is that it is a direct measure of whether one individual or a group can read and understand a passage at the instructional (a Cloze score of 44 percent) or independent (a Cloze score of 57 percent) level (Bormuth, 1969). The Cloze also has significant advantages relating to its direct form of measurement. It requires only that one be able to count to use it. Use of formulas is not necessary.

The Cloze procedure examines the probable effects of content, language complexity, syntax, and more factors, which other readability materials cannot. Accompanying this advantage is the fact that the Cloze procedure may be applied to any subject or topic. It is possible to assign pupils to specific texts. The Cloze is a reliable and accurate but time-consuming process. Unlike other methods, it requires spending time in preparing the materials rather than calculating the readability. The user must type separate 250-word selections from the reading material to be measured. These selections should conform to the rules discussed earlier.

To use the Cloze procedure persons must be available to take the tests, whereas other methods do not require the presence of children. Some may consider this a major disadvantage, as it is not always convenient to find individuals to test. A final limitation of the Cloze procedure is that it does not readily yield data useful for diagnosing problems or modifying materials.

Before concluding this review of readability techniques, several points need stating to keep the selection in perspective.

1. No standard word list can accommodate itself to all procedures. Thus, a person who wishes to use different methods in different circumstances must be familiar with different word lists.
2. There is no convention or standard procedure for counting total number of words or for counting different word forms, such as different verb tenses or prefixes, as familiar or unfamiliar. Each technique has its own rules. If one plans to use different methods, the rules must be rechecked.

3. The terms *instructional level* and *readability level* are not the same. Instructional level is typically considered a person's ability to read a selection with 95 percent accuracy and at least 75 percent comprehension. Readability level is the grade score assigned to a particular selection. The grade score does not make a direct statement about an individual's capacity for instruction. Furthermore, most readability methods also assume 50–75 percent comprehension.

4. The readability score or grade level is an estimate. It represents a statement about an average person in an average grade. As no "average" person or grade exists in any absolute sense, the readability score is only an estimate.

5. One needs to be careful about high school grade levels. They are not measured the same way as primary grades because reading is not typically taught beyond sixth grade. Instead, a student reads books in special subject areas. Thus, estimates of readability are probably more suspect and subject to error at the secondary-school levels than those for earlier grades.

6. Remember that adult reading level refers to reading beyond third-grade level. "Adult" has nothing to do with high school graduation or age.

7. The articulation between primary-level and adult methods is not well done. One who is confronted with a passage written at high third- or low fourth-grade level must be careful that the formula is not overestimating or underestimating its readability.

Readability techniques

This examination of seven readability techniques has considered theoretical and practical issues before making specific recommendations about each.

The chapter did not attempt to explore all the issues in readability research, but discussed techniques popular with, and useful for, teachers, in the author's opinion. None of the techniques serves as an absolute measure of readability. What each provides is a reliable estimate of a passage's difficulty. Such information can help a special-education teacher create a learning environment in which the learner's capabilities, the material's complexity, and the lesson's objectives can meet in a way that results in student learning and teacher satisfaction.

REFERENCES

Bormuth, John R. The Cloze readability procedure. *Elementary Education,* 1968, *45,* 429–436.

Bradley, John, & Ames, Wilbur. Readability parameters of basal readers. *Journal of Reading Behavior,* Summer 1977, *9,* 175–183.

Carver, Ronald P. *Improving reading comprehension: Measuring readability* (Final Report, Contract No. N00014-72-C0240). Silver Spring: Office of Naval Research, American Institutes for Research, May 14, 1974.

Coleman, Laurence J. Using readability data for adopting curriculum materials. *Education and Training of the Mentally Retarded,* October 1979, *14,* 163–169.

Dale, Edgar, & Chall, Jeanne S. A formula for predicting readability. *Educational Research Bulletin,* January 21, *27,* 11–20; and February 17, 1948, 37–53.

Eller, William, & Hester, Kathleen B. *Whispering ghosts.* River Forest: Laidlaw Brothers, 1976.

Eller, William, & Hester, Kathleen B. *Patterns.* River Forest: Laidlaw Brothers, 1978.

Flesch, Rudolf F. *Marks of readable style: A study in adult education.* New York: Bureau of Publication, Teachers College, Columbia University, 1943.

Flesch, Rudolf F. A new readability yardstick. *Journal of Applied Psychology,* June 1948, *32,* 221–233.

Fry, Edward. A readability formula that saves time. *Journal of Reading,* April 1968, *11,* 513–578.

Gallant, R. Use of Cloze tests as a measure of readability of materials for the primary grades. In J. A. Figurel (Ed.), *Reading and Inquiry,* 286–287. Newark, Del.: International Reading Conference, 1965.

Guidry, Hoyt, & Knight, Frances. Comparative readability: Four formulas and Newbery books. *Journal of Reading,* April 1976, *19,* 552–556.

Harris, Albert J., & Jacobson, Milton D. Harris-Jacobson core words for first grade. *Basic Elementary Reading Vocabularies,* New York: Macmillan Publishing Co., 1972.

Harris, Albert J., & Jacobson, Milton D. Some comparisons between basic elementary reading vocabularies and other word lists. *Reading Research Quarterly,* 1973–74, *9,* 87–109.

Harris, Albert J., & Jacobson, Milton D. A comparison of the Fry, Spache and Harris-Jacobson readability formulas for primary grades. *The Reading Teacher,* May 1980, *33,* 920–926.

Harris, Albert S., and Sipay, Edward R. *How to increase reading ability* (6th ed.). New York: David McKay, 1975.

Hittleman, Daniel. Readability, readability formulas and Cloze: Selecting instructional materials. *Journal of Reading,* November 1978, *22,* 117–122.

Hunt, Adrianne, & Reuter, Janet. Readability and children's picture books. *Reading Teacher,* October 1978, *32,* 23–27.

Klare, George. *The measurement of readability.* Ames: Iowa State University Press, 1963.

Klare, George. Assessing readability. *Reading Research Quarterly,* 1974–75, *10,* 62–102.

Koenke, Karl. Another practical note on readability formulas. *Journal of Reading,* December 1971, *15,* 203–208.

Lavely, Carolyn, Lowe, A. J., & Follman, John. Actual reading levels of E.M.R. materials. *Education and Training of the Mentally Retarded,* December 1975, *10,* 271–274.

Maginnis, George. The readability graph and informal reading inventories. *Reading Teacher,* March 1969, *22,* 516–559.

McCall William A., & Crabbs, Lelah M. *Standard test lessons in reading* (1st, 2nd, & 3rd eds.). New York: Bureau of Publications, Teachers College, Columbia University, 1925, 1950, 1961.

McLaughlin, G. Harry. SMOG grading—A new readability formula. *Journal of Reading,* May 1969, *12,* 639–646.

Pauk, Walter. A practical note on readability formulas. *Journal of Reading,* December 1969, *13,* 207–211.

Powers, Richard, & Ross, J. E. New diagrams for calculating readability scores rapidly. *Journalism Quarterly,* Spring 1959, *36,* 177–182.

Powers, Richard, Sumner, W. A., & Kearl, B. A recalculation of four adult readability formulas. *Journal of Educational Psychology,* 1958, *49,* 99–105.

Rankin, E. F., Grade level interpretation on cloze readability scores. In Frank P. Greene (Ed.), *Reviews: The right to participate.* Twentieth Yearbook of the National Reading Conference, 1971. 30–37.

Ruddell, R. B. A study of the Cloze comprehension technique in relation to structurally controlled reading material. *Improvement of Reading Through Classroom Practice,* 1964, *9,* 298–303.

Safier, Daniel. Notes on readability. *Elementary School Journal,* May 1959, *59,* 429–431.

Spache, George. *Good reading for poor readers* (10th ed.). Champaign: Garrard, 1978.

Standal, Timothy. Readability formulas: What's in what's out? *Reading Teacher,* March 1978, *31,* 642–646.

Stevens, Kathleen. Readability formula and McCall-Crabbs *Standard test lessons in reading. Reading Teacher,* January 1980, *33,* 413–415.

Stone, Clarence R. Measure difficulty of primary reading material: A constructive criticism of Spache's measure. *Elementary School Journal,* October 1956, *57,* 36–41.

Taylor, Wilson. Cloze procedure: A new tool for measuring readability. *Journalism Quarterly,* Fall 1953, *30,* 414–433.

Vaughn, Joseph. Interpreting readability assessment. *Journal of Reading,* May 1976, *19,* 635–638.

Williams, Robert. A table for rapid determination of revised Dale-Chall readability scores. *Reading Teacher,* November 1972, 158–165.

APPENDIXES

Tests

Reading readiness

Clymer-Barrett Prereading Battery. Personnel Press, 191 Spring Street, Lexington, MA 02173.

Gates McGinitie Readiness Skills Test. Teachers College Press, Columbia University, 1234 Amsterdam Ave., New York, NY 10027.

Harrison Stroud Reading Readiness Profiles. Houghton Mifflin, One Beacon St., Boston, MA 02107.

Macmillan Reading Readiness Test, Revised Edition. Macmillan, 866 Third Ave., New York, NY 10022.

Metropolitan Readiness Tests. Harcourt Brace Jovanovich, 757 Third Ave., New York, NY 10017.

Monroe Reading Aptitude Tests. Houghton Mifflin, One Beacon St., Boston, MA 02107.

Murphy-Durrell Reading Readiness Analysis. Harcourt Brace Jovanovich, 757 Third Ave., New York, NY 10017.

Walker Readiness Test for Disadvantaged Preschool Children (ERIC ED 037 253). United States Office of Education, Bureau of Research, P.O. Box 190, Arlington, VA 22210.

Group intelligence

California Test of Mental Maturity, Pre Primary Battery. California Test Bureau/McGraw-Hill. Del Monte Research Park, Monterey, CA 93940.

Kuhlman-Anderson Measure of Academic Potential. Psychological Corp., 757 Third Ave., New York, NY 10017.

Otis-Lennon Mental Ability Test, Primary I. Harcourt Brace Jovanovich, 757 Third Ave., New York, NY 10017.

Pintner-Cunningham Primary Test. Harcourt Brace Jovanovich, 757 Third Ave., New York, NY 10017.

SRA Primary Mental Abilities Test. Science Research Associates, 155 North Wacker Dr., Chicago, IL 60606.

Slosson Intelligence Test. Slosson Educational Publications, 140 Pine Street, East Aurora, NY 14052.

Individual intelligence

Nonverbal

Columbia Mental Maturity Scale. Harcourt Brace Jovanovich, 757 Third Ave., New York, NY 10017.

Goodenough-Harris Drawing Test. Harcourt Brace Jovanovich, 757 Third Ave., New York, NY 10017.

Leiter International Performance Scale. Stoelting Co., 424 North Homan Ave., Chicago, IL 60624.

The Nebraska Test of Learning Aptitude. Marshall S. Hiskey, 5040 Baldwin, Lincoln, NE 68508.

Raven Progressive Matrices. Psychological Corp., 757 Third Ave., New York, NY 10017.

The performance halves of the following only

Wechsler Adult Intelligence Scale (WAIS). Psychological Corp., 757 Third Ave., New York, NY 10017.

Wechsler Intelligence Scale for Children—Revised (WISC-R). Psychological Corp., 757 Third Ave., New York, NY 10017.

Wechsler Preschool and Primary Scale of Intelligence (WPPSI). Psychological Corp., 757 Third Ave., New York, NY 10017.

Verbal

The Stanford-Binet Intelligence Scale. Houghton Mifflin, One Beacon St., Boston, MA 02107.

The verbal halves of the following only

Wechsler Adult Intelligence Scale (WAIS). Psychological Corp., 757 Third Ave., New York, NY 10017.

Wechsler Intelligence Scale for Children—Revised (WISC-R). Psychological Corp., 757 Third Ave., New York, NY 10017.

Wechsler Preschool and Primary Scale of Intelligence (WPPSI). Psychological Corp., 757 Third Ave., New York, NY 10017.

Language

Northwestern Syntax Screening Test. Northwestern University Press, 1735 Benson, Evanston, IL 60201.

Peabody Picture Vocabulary Test. American Guidance Service, Publishers Bldg., Circle Pines, MI 55014.

Tennessee School for the Deaf Language Curriculum Tests. Tennessee School for the Deaf, 2725 Island Home Blvd., Knoxville, TN 37920.

Test for Auditory Comprehension of Language. Learning Concepts, 2501 North Lamar Blvd., Austin, TX 78705.

Test of Language Development, PRO-ED 333 Perry Brooks Building, Austin, TX 78701.

Test of Syntactic Abilities. Dormac, IWC., P.O. Box 752, Beaverton, OR 97075.

The following may be used as a reading capacity or listening comprehension test.

Spache Diagnostic Reading Scales. California Test Bureau/McGraw-Hill, Del Monte Research Park, Monterey, CA 93940.

Achievement adapted for the deaf

Special Edition of the Standford Achievement Test. Office of Demographic Studies, Gallaudet College, Washington, DC 20002.

Oral reading

Gilmore Oral Reading Test. Harcourt Brace Jovanovich, 757 Third Ave., New York, NY 10017.

Gray Oral Reading Tests. Charles C. Merrill, 4300 West 62 Street, Indianapolis, IN 46268.

Reading Miscue Inventory. Macmillan Publishing, 866 Third Ave., New York, NY 10017.

Spache Diagnostic Reading Scales. California Test Bureau/McGraw-Hill, Del Monte Research Park, Monterey, CA 93940.

Vision

Standard

Keystone Visual Survey Tests. Keystone View Division, Most Development Co., 2212 East 12 Street, Davenport, IA 52803.

Ortho-Rater. Bausch and Lomb Optical Co., Rochester, NY 14602.

Professional Vision Tester. Titmus Optical Co., Petersburg, VA.

Titmus Biopter. Titmus Optical Co., Petersburg, VA.

Supplementary

Keystone Tests of Binocular Skills. Keystone View Division, Mast Development Co., 2212 East 12 Street, Davenport, IA 52803.

Spache Binocular Reading Test. Keystone View Division, Mast Development Co., 2212 East 12 Street, Davenport, IA 52803.

Scope-and-sequence chart for the acquisition of English sentence structure

The scope-and-sequence chart represents the developmental sequence in which the syntactic components and transformations of sentences are normally acquired. The notational system is that used by Hargis in *English syntax: An outline for clinicians and teachers of language handicapped children* (Springfield: Charles C Thomas, 1977).

The chart is composed of eight columns (a-h) and eight rows (I-VIII). It is to be read from top to bottom. Normal acquisition occurs simultaneously across the columns, with constituents from several squares in each row comprising the sentence forms that emerge in the comprehension capability of the normal child. Each row represents roughly six months in the average child's life. Row I begins at about age two for average children and ends at about age six. Here too constituent items from boxes across the chart are acquired simultaneously. This chart represents language comprehension of sentence structure. Expressive use is on a different timetable, incrementally later in development.

The chart does not include syntactic relationships produced in discourse units larger than the sentence. The syntactic relationships between sentences that occur in dialog, paragraph units, plots, and jokes, for example, are also of interest and should be considered both in terms of comprehension and production. Acquisition of the comprehension of sentence syntax, however, is a fundamental readiness base for all subsequent language growth.

Scope-and-sequence chart

	a	b	c	d
	Determiner Components	**Nouns**	**Auxiliary Components**	**Verbs**
I	1. Articles *(a, an, the, some ∅)* 2. Cardinal number *(one, two)*	1. Singular/plural 2. Count/noncount 3. Human/nonhuman 4. Personal pronouns *(I, me, you, we)* 5. Possessive pronoun *(my)*	1. Present tense 2. Past tense 3. Be + *ing*	1. Be 2. Have 3. Simple transitive + intransitive verbs *(see, like, walk, run)*
II	1. Proximities *(this, that, these, those)*	1. Possessive nouns 2. Possessive pronoun *(your)* 3. Personal pronouns *(he, she, they, it)*	1. Modal *(can)*	1. Transitive phrasal verbs 2. VT to 3. Intransitive phrasal verbs 4. Sense verbs + copular verbs in addition to *be* 5. Be + *for* 6. Copular verb + *like*
III	1. Pre-articles *(one of, some of, all of, two of, none of)*	1. Possessive pronouns *[(their(s), her(s), his, its, our(s), mine]* 2. Personal pronouns *(him, her, them, us)*	1. Modals *(may) (should) (ought to) (will)*	1. VTing
IV	1. Ordinals *(first, next, last)* 2. Pre-articles *(both of, each of, every one of, any of, several of, a few of, a lot of, a bag of, a piece of)* 3. *Other, another*	1. Indefinite pronouns *(someone, anyone, everyone, somebody, anybody, everybody)*	1. Quasi-modals *get to* *be about to* *have to* *be going to* *be supposed to* 2. Modal *(must)*	1. VT *(to)*
V	1. Pre-articles *(either of, neither of)*			1. VT*(be)*
VI	1. *Superlative (-est of)* 2. Pre-articles of comparison *(-er of)*	1. T-*for . . . to* (form nouns)		
VII		1. Reflexive pronouns *(yourself, myself, herself, himself, themselves, ourselves)*		
VIII		1. T-possessive -*ing*	1. *(have + en)* 2. *(had + en)*	

e	f	g	h
Adverbs 1. Adverb of place (single words and phrases)	**Sentence transformations**		1. T-*who?* (question)* 2. T-*yes/no* (question) 3. T-*what?* (question)
1. Adverb of time (single words and phrases) 2. Intensifier *(very, too)* + adjective		1. T-conjunction—*and* word and phrase conjuncts	1. T-negative 2. T-*how many?* 3. T-*what (be)* . . . *do(ing)?* 4. T-*where?* 5. T-*whose?* 6. T-*when?* 7. *first . . . then* 8. T-VT*(to)*
Prepositions 1. *With* 2. *For* (helping *for*) 3. *For, to* (with indirect objects) 4. Adverb of manner 5. Adverb of frequency *(after, everyday)*	1. T-*more . . . than* T-*er . . . than*	1. T-conjunction *(and)* sentence conjuncts 2. T-conjunction *(and) too*	1. T-*what—do(es)* . . . *do?* 2. T-direct discourse 3. T-*what . . . for?* (purpose) T-*who . . . for?* 4. T-relative direct object *(who, that)* 5. T-relative *that who* (subject-subject) 6. T-noun modifier 7. T-adverbial clause *(because)* 8. T-*for . . . to* 9. T-VTing
1. Intensifier—*very* + adverb	1. T-*as . . . as* 2. T-*as . . . much as* 3. T-*as . . . many as*	1. T-conjunction—*or* 2. T-conjunction—*either . . . or* 3. T-conjunction—*but*	1. T-*how (?)* 2. T-*how many?* much? 3. T-*why?* 4. T-*what . . . for?* 5. T-*how come?* 6. T-adverbial clause *(if . . . then)* 7. T-*which?* 8. T-noun clause 9. T-relative indirect object *(who, that)* 10. T-relative *which*—subject 11. T-VT *(to)*
1. *Ever, never* 2. Adverb of time *(then, now)* 3. Adverb of place *(here, there)*	1. T-*fewer . . . than* 2. T-*less . . . than* 3. T-*enough . . . to*	1. T-conjunction *and . . . also*	1. T-relative *who(se)* 2. T-adverbial clause *before* 3. T-adverbial clause *after* 4. T-adverbial clause *so* (consequence) 5. T-*so that* (consequence) 6. T-noun clause *wh* question 7. T-VT *(be)*
1. *Almost, about* 2. *Just, even, only*		1. T-conjunction—*neither . . . nor*	1. T-*too . . . for . . . to* 2. T-*enough . . . or . . . to* 3. T-*there* 4. T-adverbial clause *(when)* 5. T-relative object of preposition 6. T-relative *(where)* 7. Nonrestrictive relative clause
1. Sentence adverbs (modal) *probably* *maybe* *perhaps* 2. *Instead of*		1. T-conjunction *and neither do(es)*	1. T-*so . . . that* 2. T-adverbial clause *(while)* 3. T-adverbial clause *(until)* 4. T-passive direct/indirect object 5. T-*such . . . that* 6. T-participial phrase 7. tag question
1. Sentence adverbs (evaluative) *fortunately* *luckily* *strangely (enough)* *oddly*		1. T-conjunction—*all of . . .but/all . . . except* 2. T-conjunction *none of . . . but/except* 3. T-*rather . . . than* 4. T-*other than*	1. T-indirect discourse—*ask* (yes/no questions) 2. T-indirect discourse—*ask* (wh questions) 3. T-indirect discourse—*ask* (wh———to) 4. T-word order 5. T-extra position 6. T-cleft position 7. T-nominative absolute 8. T-indirect discourse *(said* and *tell)* 9. T-adverbial clause *although* 10. conjunctive adverbs *(however, therefore)*

*The capital letter *T* stands for transformation.

Sentence illustrations
of syntactic structures

Locate these examples on the foregoing scope-and-sequence chart through the grid (roman numerals vertical, letters of the alphabet horizontal).

Ia *A* boy bought *an* apple. *(a, an)*
The boy ate *the* apple. *(the)*
_____ apples grow on _____ trees. *(∅)*
Some apples are yellow. *(some)*
The boy bought *two* apples. *(two)*
One apple is red. *(one)*

Ib A *boy* saw a *cat.* (singular nouns)
Cats have four *legs.* (plural nouns)
Cats drink *milk.* (noncount)
Cats drink milk. (count)
Cats drink milk. (nonhuman)
I see a cat. (personal pronoun)
The cat likes *me.* (personal pronoun)
My cat is big. (possessive pronoun)

Ic I *see* a cat. (present tense)
I *saw* a cat. (past tense)
The cat *is running.* *(be + ing)*
The cat *is climbing* a tree. *(be + ing)*

Id The cat *is* big. *(be)*
The cat *is* a tiger. *(be)*
The cat *was* in a tree. *(be)*
The cat *has* whiskers. *(have)*
The cat *climbed* a tree. (transitive)
I *see* a cat. (transitive)
The boy *ran.* (intransitive)
The cat *walked.* (intransitive)

Ie   The boy is *upstairs*. (adverb of place)
The cat is *in the tree*. (adverb of place)

Ih   *Who* saw a cat? (T-*who?*)
What did the boy see? (T-*what?*)
Did the cat *climb* a tree? (T-*yes/no?*)
Is the cat in a tree? (T-*yes/no?*)

IIa   *This* cat is big. (proximity)
The cat climbed *that* tree. (proximity)
These apples are red. (proximity)
Those apples are yellow. (proximity)

IIb   The *boy's* cat saw a dog. (possessive noun)
Your cat climbed a tree. (possessive pronoun *your*)
He has a cat. (personal pronoun)
They have two cats. (personal pronoun)

IIc   Birds *can* fly. (modal, *can*)

IId   He *put on* a hat. (phrasal verb, transitive)
They *cleaned up* the room. (phrasal verb, transitive)
He *likes* to eat candy. (Vtto: transitive verbs having infinitive
    complements)
Glass *feels* smooth. (sense verbs, copular)
Sugar *tastes* sweet. (sense verbs, copular)
The boy *looks* sad. (sense verbs, copular)
The present *is for* your (_____ be for _____)
The cloud *looks like* an elephant. (_____ copular verb + *like* _____)

IIe   We went to the movie *yesterday*. (one-word adverb of time)
We eat *at noon*. (prepositional phrase, adverb of time)
The girl is *very* tall. (intensifier plus adjective)

IIg   The *dog* and the *cat* are friends. (subject conjuncts)
The boy *hopped* and *skipped*. (verb conjuncts)
He walked *to school* and *to the store*. (phrase conjuncts)

IIh The bird is *not* in the tree. (T-negative)
The dog did *not* chase the cat. (T-negative)
How many dogs do you have? (T-*how many?*)
What did the dog *do*? (T-*what . . . do?*)
What is the *dog doing*? (T-what *(be) . . .* do*(ing)*?
Where is the bird? (T-*where?*)
Whose cat saw a dog? (T-*whose?*)
First the boy brushed his teeth, *then* he went to bed. *(first . . . then)*
He *likes to eat* candy. (Vtto: transformation, embeds infinitive phrase)
He *wants to play* baseball. (Vtto: embeds an infinitive phrase)

IIIa *One of* the cats is black. (pre-article)
Some of the boys are swimming. (pre-article)
None of the children likes school. (pre-article)

IIIb *Her* bike is new. (possessive pronoun)
Hers is new. (possessive pronoun)
Our bike is old. (possessive pronoun)
Ours is old. (possessive pronoun)
Father brought *them*. (personal pronoun)
Mother brought *us*. (personal pronoun)

IIIc We *will* go to the movie tomorrow. (modal, *will*)
We *should* brush our teeth. (modal, *should*)

IIId We *saw* a man painting our room. (Vting: transitive verbs having
  complements with active verb forms)
We *found* a frog swim*ming* in the pool. (Vting: transitive verbs having
  complements with active verb forms)

IIIe He broke the window *with* a rock.
He washed the dishes *for* father. (helping *for*)
She threw the ball *to* him. (*to* with indirect object)
She bought candy *for* her friend. (*for* with indirect object)
She ran *fast*. (adverb of manner)
They watch television *everyday*. (adverb of frequency)

IIIf He has *more* marbles *than* she does.
She is *taller than* he is.

IIIg *He ran* and *she walked*. (sentence conjuncts)
He ran *and* she ran *too*. (sentence conjuncts with *and . . . too*)

IIIh   *What* does a fireman *do? (what does . . . do?)*
What do bees *do? (what do . . . do?)*
The boy *said,* "I like dogs." (direct discourse)
What is the paint *for?* (T-*what for?*, purpose)
Who is the present *for?* (T-*who for?*, purpose)
The boy saw the dog *that the cat chased.* (the dog: relative clause with a
    direct object the same as in the main clause)
The boy *who has the cat* is my friend. (relative clause with a subject that is
    the same as in the main clause)
The *black* cat is in the tree. (adjectives placed in the noun-modifier
    position)
The cat climbed the tree *because the dog chased it.* (T-adverbial clause,
    because)
We took the horses to the river *for them to drink.* (T-*for . . . to*)
We *saw* the boy *pulling* a wagon. (T-VTing embeds a sentence as the
    complement of the transitive verb *saw.*)

IVa   The *first* car was red. (ordinal)
The *last* car was green. (ordinal)
Both of the apples are yellow. (pre-article)
Several of the boys are scouts. (pre-article)
One of the balls is red. (pre-article)
The *other* ball is green. *(other)*
The boy wants *another* apple. *(another)*

IVb   Does *anybody* want an apple? (indefinite pronoun)
Everyone likes apples. (indefinite pronoun)

IVc   The boy *is going to* go home Friday. (quasi-modal)
We *have to* do our homework. (quasi-modal)
We *must* go to bed now. (modal)

IVd   We *saw* the boy (   ) draw the picture. [Vt(to): transitive verb having
    complements with infinitive verbs but no *to* markers]
She *made* him (   ) leave. [Vt(to)]

IVe   The girl can run *very fast.* (intensifier plus adverb of manner)
It was raining *very hard.* (intensifier plus adverb of manner)

IVf The boy is *as* tall *as* the girl.
The boy has *as many* marbles *as* his friend.
I have *as much* ice cream *as* you have.
My bike is *different from* yours.

IVg You should brush your teeth often, *or* you might get cavities.
Either eat your vegetables, *or* do without dessert.
The boy likes football, *but* he does not like basketball.

IVh *How* did the boy break the window? (T-*how?*)
How many apples do you have? (T-*how many?*)
How much ice cream did you eat? (T-*how much?*)
Why did the cat climb the tree? (T-*why?*)
What did the cat climb the tree for? (T-*what . . . for?*)
How come the cat climbed the tree? (T-*how come?*)
If you eat your vegetables, *(then)* you can have ice cream. (T-adverbial
    clause, *if . . . then*)
Which bike is yours? (T-*which?*)
The boy knew that *the cat was in the tree.* (noun clause used as object of
    transitive verb)
The boy threw the ball to the girl *who threw it to the pitcher.* (T-relative,
    the indirect object of the main clause is the subject of the relative
    clause.)
The bike *that has a red seat* is mine. (T-relative, the relative pronoun is
    that.)
We heard *the boy ( ) leave.* [T-Vt(to) sentence embedded as the
    complement of the transitive verb, no *to* marker used]

Va *Neither of* the dogs is big.
Does *either of* the boys like apples?

Vd The umbrella *keeps* us ( ) dry. [Vt(be): transitive verbs having sentence
    complements from which the *be* verb has been deleted]
The present *made* him ( ) happy. [Vt(be)]

Ve Did you *ever* see an elephant?
He *never* saw the elephant.
I will go home *now.*
He went to bed *then.*
I will build a house *here.*
He went to school *there.*

Vf   The boy has *fewer* marbles *than* the girl.
We had *less* rain *than* they did.
I have *enough* money *to* go to the show.

Vg   I will buy a dog *and* a cat *also*.
I will buy a dog *and also* a cat.

Vh   1. The boy liked the girl *whose father had a motorcycle*. (T-rel. *whose*)
2. The girl brushed her teeth *before she went to bed*. (T-adverbial clause, *before*)
3. The girl went to bed *after she brushed her teeth*. (T-adverbial clause, *after*)
4. The sun went down *so they turned the lights on*. (T-adverbial clause, *so*)
5. He moved *so that the boy could sit down*. (T-adverbial clause, *so that*)
6. I know *what your name is*. (T-noun clause, *wh?*)
7. The present made *him (   ) happy*. [T-Vt(be): *be* deleted as sentence is embedded as complement of these transitive verbs]

VIa   Fred is the *tallest of* the boys. (*-est of*)
The cat drank *most of* the milk. (*-est of*)
Helen is the *taller of* the two girls. (*-er of*)

VIb   *For the boy to come early* is unusual.
For them to win the race was a surprise. (*for/to* structure used as nouns)

VIe   He *almost* fell.
He arrived at *about* noon.
Just (only) one boy helped.
Even the boy passed the test.

VIg   *Neither* the cat *nor* the dog ran away.
The boy had *neither* a cat *nor* a dog.

VIh   The soup was *too* hot *for us to* eat.
Mother had *enough* money *for* us *to* buy ice cream.
There were some marbles on the floor. (T-*there*, from *some marbles were on the floor*)
When the boy arrived he let the cat out. (T-adverbial clause, *when*)
The cat was in the tree *that was by the house*. (T-rel. o.p.—object of preposition, the noun *tree* is an object of preposition in the main clause.)
They lived in the town *where the president was born*. (T-rel. *where*)
Helen, *who lives upstairs,* has a snake.

VIIb Don't hurt *yourself*.
He fanned *himself*.

VIIe *Maybe* I will get a new bike. (sentence adverb, modal)
They will *probably* win the game. (sentence adverb, modal)
He bought the red bike *instead* of the blue one.

VIIg Joe doesn't like fried bananas, and *neither does* Fred. (T-conjunction—
and *neither do*)
Joe likes apples *and* Fred *does too*. (T-conjunction—*and* _____ *do*
_____ *too*)
Joe likes apples *and so does Fred*. (T-conjunction—*and so do*)

VIIh The boy was *so* tired *that* he fell asleep. (T-so . . . that)
They ate *while they watched television*. (T-adverbial clause, *while*)
He worked *until he was tired*. (T-adverbial clause, *until*)
A present was given to Joe. (T-passive, indirect object becomes subject)
It is *such* a fast car *that* it will win the race. (T-such _____ that)
Whistling merrily, he walked home. (T-participial phrase)
The girl climbed the tree, *didn't she?* (tag question)
You will leave early, *won't you?* (tag question)
He didn't leave, *did he?* (tag question)

VIIIb *His singing* was beautiful. (T-possessive *-ing*)
They were awakened by *the carpenter's hammering*. (T-possessive *-ing*)

VIIIc He *has finished* the paper. *(have + en)*
They *had run* home. *(had + en)*

VIIIe *Fortunately,* he found his key. (sentence adverb, evaluative)
Joe got an A, *strangely (enough)*. (sentence adverb, evaluative)

VIIIg *All of* the apples *but/except* two had worms. (T-conjunction -*all of* . . .
but/except)
None of the cars *but/except* the red one is an import. (T-conjunction—
none of . . . *but/except*)
I would *rather* have a bike *than* a horse. (T-*rather* . . . *than*)
I would like a car *other than* an import. (T-*other* . . . *than*)
Joe *says that* he likes fried bananas. (T-indirect discourse, *says that* . . .)
Joe *told* Fred *that* he likes fried bananas. (T-indirect discourse,
told . . . *that* . . .)

VIIIh Joe *asked* Fred *if* he would help. (T-indirect discourse, *asked* . . . *if* . . . embeds *yes/no* questions)

Joe *asked* Fred *where* the car was parked. (T-indirect discourse, *asked* . . . *wh* . . . embeds *wh* questions)

She *asked* the policeman *where to* park her car. (T-indirect discourse, *wh* _____ *to*)

He *asked* the mechanic *how to* fix his bike. (T-indirect discourse, *wh* _____ *to*)

"I like candy," said Fred. (T-word order, subject verb word order altered)

On the wall hangs a picture of the president. (")

It is unusual *for Fred to get an* A. (T-extra position)

It is true *that Fred got an* A. (T-extra position)

What Fred got was an A. (T-cleft sentence)

Where Fred went was to a movie. (T-cleft sentence)

What Fred did was go to a movie. (T-cleft sentence)

Night approaching rapidly, they made camp. (T-nominative absolute)

Fred kept the job *although the pay was poor.* (T-adverbial clause, *although*)

Fred, *however,* decided not to go. (conjunctive adverb)

Translations of passages
in Chapter 4

1

The fear of famine was becoming widespread, and the old man had been uncertain that he could maintain his position of authority in the village. However, the chance events of the previous night gave him just the opportunity that he needed. He could now argue forcefully that he was the one who pleased the gods. How else could the people explain the sudden appearance the night before of the vast number of ducks?

2

The work had been especially fatiguing that season. The peasants once again trudged silently home through the humid lingering heat of the day. A few had lined up to get a refreshing drink from a peddler who was apparently stingy with his portions. One young peasant who felt cheated argued belligerently. But for the appearance of a peacemaker, some violence might have erupted. Heat and weariness further slowed the tempo of emotion, and the slow march home resumed.

3

Joe pulled the covers tightly over his head. He wished that he had left the light on in the hall. He was sure now that what he had thought was a pile of dirty clothes in the corner of the room was in fact a grotesque person. Possibly, he thought, if he remained completely still until morning, the thing might miss him. At that moment, when he was just beginning to feel somewhat secure, he heard a soft creaking noise. This must be a monster. He wished then that he had taken the flashlight to bed with him. Jeff had told him that if you shone a light on a monster it would go away.

5

Mary wanted a new bike for her birthday. She understood how impractical a bike would be for her. She lived with her parents on the fifteenth floor of a tall apartment building. Not only would it be difficult to get the bike up and down the elevators and out through the lobby; it would be difficult to get the bike to the park that they could see from their apartment. Also, there were almost no sidewalks, and the street traffic around the building seemed heavy all the time. At least she knew how to ride a bike. She had learned at her cousin's who lived in a house in a quiet suburb. It seemed as though bikes were everywhere out there. Oh well, she would try to be happy with the skates that she was sure her parents had already bought for her.

6

Some of the old cows were not producing milk enough to pay for their keep. The farmer remembered their big production days and thought of how much they had contributed to his and his family's present prosperity. Each of the old cows had produced more than 150 thousand pounds of milk since they came into production. The calves that they produced made up most of the rest of the herd. These old cows seemed like old friends. He couldn't bring himself to haul them to the slaughter house to become just a bunch of hamburger. Most of the ideas he had didn't seem good enough. The only thing that he could think of was to put off any decision for one more season.

Figures of speech

This appendix is comprised of two sections. The first provides definitions of familiar figures of speech and examples of such nonliteral structures that might be used in teaching.

The second section directs teachers to publications used in preparing a reading program for use at the Tennessee School for the Deaf. In these books, abundant use is made of figurative and idiomatic structures.

Definitions and examples

DEFINITIONS

Simile an explicit comparison between two things of different kind or quality that have some characteristic in common.

Metaphor an implied comparison between two things of different kind or quality that have some characteristics in common.

Hyperbole exaggeration for emphasis of effect.

Personification attributing human or animate qualities or abilities to nonhuman, nonanimate, or abstract nouns.

Metonymy the substitution of an attribute or suggestive word for what is meant—a part for the whole or the whole for a part (synecdoche is essentially the same type).

Periphrasis the substitution of a phrase or proper name for a quality associated with the name.

Litotes the deliberate use of understatement.

EXAMPLES

Mamie had golden hair like a bright helmet.

When he spoke it sounded like a cork coming out of a gingerbeer bottle.

I am choking with the sounds that are pulled into me, and I have to keep on coughing the sounds away as they come in, or I will smother.

Splashing and spraying the water into a white dancing foam, they dove into the waves.

Three men who were standing beside him were blown over by the force of his voice.

I would have died if Mama had left it.

The ladder began to sneer at him.

The houses grew tall beside it.

We need you—and especially that weight on the line.

Betty gave the prince her hand.

David Barton, the "Buffalo Bill" of the neighborhood, tossed his five-year-old sister up on the back of a colt.

"Well, it isn't," said the Pro, red in the face.

A tornado doesn't leave you very much to pick and choose from.

He looks a little old for such dangerous tricks.

Onomatopoeia the formation of words whose sound suggests its sense.

The train squealed and screeched in and out of the station.

Sam only chuckled and chattered.

Anthimeria the substitution of nouns for verbs, denominalizing verbs.

That is just what you will do if things pan out as I planned them.

Joe was always ticketed to be the politician of the family.

Apostrophe the addressing of an absent person or personified thing.

Hey wind! You forgot the doors.

Rhetorical question use of a question not to query but to assert or deny something indirectly.

Can I ever use this old music box?

Would fall never come to an end?

Oxymoron linking of two normally contradictory terms.

With spear and hook he waged pleasant war against the salmon and red trout.

Pun use of two or more words that sound alike in the same context (paronomasia);

Be it ever so bumble, there is no place like a comb.

use or repetition of a word in the same context in different senses (antanaclasis);

Two maggots were fighting in dead Ernest.

a word used in relation to two or more words that it modifies but understood differently with each relation (syllepsis).

He lost his hat and his temper.

Idiom an accepted or common phrase contrary to the usual pattern of the language or having a meaning different from the literal.

Kay stopped short.

He was out of sight.

He spent the night.

Figurative and idiomatic structures*

Big and Little, level #1
Big and little can be friends. (p. 5)
metonomy

Baker, Baker, Bake Me a Pie, level #3
"You stunning, strawberry pie," said
    Bored Baker. (p. 2) **hyperbole,
apostrophe**

Ride and Races, level #6
ran after (p. 34) **phrasal verb**

High Wires and Wigs, level #7
go after (p. 42) **phrasal verb**

Surprises and Prizes, level #8
"An Old Lady and a Pig"
    "Fire, eat the stick." (p. 36) **apostrophe**
    "Water, stop the fire." (p. 36)
        apostrophe
    go after (p. 38) **phrasal verb**
    fire went to eat the stick (p. 39)
        personification
    water went to stop the fire (p. 39)
        personification

"Rain"
    It looks like rain. (p. 55) **simile**
    The rain will not get on the books.
        (p. 57) **personification**

Upside and Down
"Did You Ever See?"
    Did you ever see a snail . . . sail?
        (pp. 36–39) **rhetorical question**

"Space Monster Gets a Job"
    a clown. He looks like a monster.
        (p. 58) **simile**

"The Fox and His Bag"
    fox took his nap (p. 68) **idiom**

"Upside Down Amy"
    look at (p. 99) **phrasal verb**
    the world (p. 99) **metonomy**

"Song of the Train"
    clickety-clack wheels (p. 112)
        onomatopoeia

"A Week of Surprises"
    Bam went the great big black ball.
        (p. 122) **onomatopoeia**
    A bulldozer was hard at work. How it
        growled. (p. 123) **personification**

Inside and Out, level #10
"Sing a Song of People" (a poem)
    when it rains and pours (p. 3) **idiom**

"George and Martha"
    cannot stand it (p. 8) **hyperbole, idiom**
    not one more drop (p. 8) **idiom**

"Katy and Sam"
    take care of (p. 13) **idiom**

"Sarah Jack"
    let out (p. 66) **phrasal verb**

"Let's Ride the Bus"
    like as not (p. 82) **idiom**
    hang on (p. 84) **phrasal verb**
    hold on (p. 84) **phrasal verb**

---

*Ruddell, R. B., Shogren, M., & Strickland, R. *Pathfinder reading program,
levels 1-14.* Boston: Allyn & Bacon, 1978. Reprinted by permission of the
publisher.

"The Three Billy Goats Gruff" (a play)
tripping over (p. 110) **idiom**
gobble you up (p. 111) **phrasal verb**
gobble up (p. 111) **phrasal verb**

"The Baby Beebee"
"Quiet," roared the Lion. (p. 117)
personification
"Quiet," yelled all the animals. (p. 118)
personification
come up (p. 122) **phrasal verb**

"The Fat Cat"
look after (p. 127) **phrasal verb**

"I Read It in a Book!"
The little town looked sad. (p. 173)
personification, metaphor

"The Weather Is Full of the Nicest
Sounds" (p. 190) **personification**
it sings and rustles (p. 191)
personification
it rustles (p. 191) **onomatopoeia**

"Who Has Seen the Wind?"
the leaves hand trembling (p. 205)
personification
trees bow down their heads (p. 205)
metaphor, personification

"Quiet on Account of Dinosaur"
on account of (p. 226) **idiom**

Moon Magic, level #11
"The Moon's the North Wind's Cooky"
The Moon is a cooky. (p. 2) **metaphor**
North Wind bites the moon. (p. 2)
personification
South Wind is a baker. (p. 2)
personification
He kneads clouds. (p. 2)
personification
He bakes a moon. (p. 2)
personification
North Wind eats again. (p. 2)
personification

"Moon Mouse"
The moon is sitting on top of a
building. (p. 13) **personification**
The moon is hiding. (p. 16)
personification

"Squaps, the Moonling"
He saw what looked like a pair of
eyes. (p. 18) **simile**
Squaps knew her way around.
(p. 23) **idiom**

"Make a Pair"
go with (p. 30) **phrasal verb**
The trees looked like small dots.
(p. 30) **simile**
upside down (p. 30) **idiom**

"How You Talk"
voice box (p. 36) **idiom**
make believe (p. 36) **idiom**

"Sia Lives on Kilimanjaro"
look after the little ones (p. 44)
phrasal verb
He looks like a fine king. (p. 49)
simile

"Thief in the Hall"
"I wish you would get out of my
dream." (p. 60) **apostrophe**
A vacuum is as an animal that ate
dirt. (p. 63) **metaphor**
Garbage truck sounds like a hungry
stomach. (p. 68) **simile**
Garbage truck is playing. (p. 68)
personification
It was soft, like cloth. (p. 70) **simile**

"Happy Birthday"
covered with (p. 75) **phrasal verb**
two-wheeler (pp. 75–76) **metonomy**
made a face (p. 76) **idiom**
My falling is doing better. (p. 79)
oxymoron
It looks as if it got left out in the
rain.(p. 81) **simile, idiom**
after all (p. 85) **idiom**
How about pets? (p. 86)
rhetorical question

"Jobs for All"
  made of (p. 90) **phrasal verb**

"The Orchard Toy Shop"
  took over (p. 98) **phrasal verb**

"Busy Carpenters"
  song of the saw (p. 90)
    personification, metaphor
  song of the plane (p. 90)
    personification, metaphor
  song of the hammer (p. 90)
    personification, metaphor

"Take This Hammer"
  knock off (p. 104) **idiom, phrasal verb**
  The ball sends bricks flying. (p. 105)
    personification

"Pancakes, Pancakes!"
  turned to (p. 113) **phrasal verb**
  to go with (p. 114) **phrasal verb**
  Jack made room. (p. 119) **idiom**
  Watch out. (p. 121) **phrasal verb**

"Busy Wheels"
  Wheels are turning. (p. 124)
    metonomy
  Cans bang. (p. 124) **onomatopoeia**
  People wheel their babies. (p. 124)
    metonomy
  Everyone is on the move. (p. 125)
    idiom
  Cars get out of the way. (p. 125)
    idiom, phrasal verb
  Wheels bring children. (p. 125)
    metonomy
  rolling along (p. 126) **phrasal verb**
  Mail moves on wheels, too. (p. 127)
    metonomy
  take off (p. 129) **phrasal verb**
  end of the day (p. 129) **idiom**
  roll around (p. 130) **phrasal verb**
  Busy wheels are turning. (p. 130)
    metonomy

"Jacques Cousteau: Underwater Pioneer"
  grow up (p. 137) **phrasal verb**
  open up (p. 137) **phrasal verb**

It was like a tiny spaceship. (p. 139)
  simile
sea animals that look like flowers
  (p. 140) **simile**
gives off a sound (p. 141) **phrasal
  verb**
pick up (p. 141) **phrasal verb**
He heard whales talk. (p. 142)
  personification

"The Dragon Island"
  came out (p. 146) **phrasal verb**
  keep on (p. 147) **phrasal verb**
  so sweet that the evening star would
    stand still and listen (p. 147)
    personification
  to her song hold up (p. 147) **phrasal
    verb**
  roll back (p. 147) **phrasal verb**
  right away (p. 150) **idiom**
  after a time (p. 150) **idiom**
  Small islands look like dragons.
    (p. 151) **simile**

"The Monster of Loch Ness"
  Loch Ness runs into the sea. (p. 154)
    idiom
  get out of (p. 154) **phrasal verb**
  played on (p. 159) **phrasal verb**
  laughed at (p. 160) **phrasal verb**

"Infinity"
  The world is like a spaceship. (p. 165)
    simile

"The Dancing Class"
  women moved like water (p. 166)
    simile
  looked out (p. 168) **phrasal verb**
  could not wait to see (p. 169)
    hyperbole
  back and forth (p. 170) **idiom**

"Enuk, My Son"
  ran out (p. 175) **phrasal verb**
  put up (p. 177) **phrasal verb**
  made camp (p. 177) **idiom**

kept watch (p. 178) **idiom**
red sun sank (p. 180) **personification**
icy wind burned (p. 180) **oxymoron,
    personification**
close in (p. 182) **phrasal verb**
cut up (p. 183) **phrasal verb**
He ate so much he could hardly
    move. (p. 184) **hyperbole**
in time (p. 185) **idiom**

"A Pet for Rosita"
    used to (p. 187) **phrasal verb**
    laugh at (p. 188) **phrasal verb**
    come on (p. 188) **phrasal verb**
    the ball flew (p. 188) **personification**
    What's the use? (p. 189) **rhetorical
        question**
    out loud (p. 192) **idiom**
    street was noisy (p. 193)
        personification
    music floated (p. 193) **personification**
    stuck out (p. 193) **phrasal verb**
    squeeze in (p. 195) **phrasal verb**
    squeeze out (p. 195) **phrasal verb**
    found her voice (p. 199) **idiom**

"I Wonder If Herbie's Home Yet"
    one big fink (p. 203) **idiom**
    no-good friend (p. 203) **idiom**
    fall over his feet (p. 203) **idiom**
    just don't happen to like (p. 203)
        idiom
    my treat (p. 206) **idiom**
    butterfingers (p. 210) **idiom**

"Put on a Thinking Cap"
    put on a thinking cap (p. 214) **idiom**
    go with (p. 214) **phrasal verb**

"How the Brazilian Beetles Got Their
Beautiful Coats"
    Beetles have hard coats. (p. 216)
        personification
    laughed long and loud till gray sides
        were shaking (p. 219)
        personification
    don't judge by looks alone (p. 221)
        idiom

"The Way of an Ant"
    as high as the blue sky (p. 224) **simile**
    the gold ring of a sunflower (p. 225)
        metaphor

"In a Few Words"
    caught some stars (fireflies) (p. 230)
        metaphor
    came from far and wide (p. 232)
        phrasal verb, idiom
    birds filling the air with music
        (p. 233) **idiom**
    web of life (p. 234) **idiom**
    listen to the wind whistle (p. 239)
        phrasal verb, personification

Riding Rainbows, level #12
"What's Your Name?"
    stand for (p. 2) **phrasal verb**
    make up (p. 4) **phrasal verb**
    have to (p. 4) **phrasal verb**
    dry up (p. 4) **phrasal verb**

"Zeek Silver Moon"
    name after (p. 12) **phrasal verb**
    make out of (p. 12) **phrasal verb**
    all dressed up (p. 13) **phrasal verb**
    set out for (p. 15) **phrasal verb**
    turn over (p. 17) **phrasal verb**
    make up . . . mind (p. 18) **phrasal
        verb**

"How Hummingbird Earned Her
    Name"
    give out . . . first cry (p. 23)
        phrasal verb
    run after (p. 24) **phrasal verb**
    run far ahead (p. 24) **phrasal verb**
    couldn't keep up (p. 24) **phrasal verb**
    as far as (p. 24) **idiom**
    as small as (p. 25) **simile**
    What good? (p. 26) **rhetorical
        question**
    straight face (p. 27) **idiom**
    heart race (p. 29) **idiom**
    line up (p. 29) **phrasal verb**
    come for (p. 29) **phrasal verb**

go on (p. 30) **phrasal verb**
hold up (p. 31) **phrasal verb**
turn back (p. 31) **phrasal verb**
out of one's head (p. 31) **idiom**
raise one's head (p. 32) **idiom**
as quick as a hummingbird's wing
  (p. 33) **simile**
as big as a whale (p. 33) **simile**
as strong as the bear (p. 34) **simile**
as important as the chief (p. 34) **simile**

"Muhammad Ali—a Champion"
  make friends (p. 35) **idiom**
  run up to (p. 35) **phrasal verb**
  loud mouth (p. 38) **metonomy**
  couldn't believe it (p. 38) **hyperbole**
  make good pets (p. 38) **idiom**
  as fast as lightning (p. 40) **simile,
    hyperbole**
  float like a butterfly (p. 40) **simile,
    hyperbole**
  sting like a bee (p. 40) **simile,
    hyperbole**
  punches flew hard and fast (p. 41)
    personification
  make a better world (p. 42) **idiom**

"No Time for School, No Time for Play"
  "Late, are you?" (p. 48) **rhetorical
    question**
  It's out with you. (p. 48) **idiom**
  one wrong step (p. 50) **idiom**
  rock back and forth (p. 50) **idiom**
  keep from (p. 53) **phrasal verb**

"Jasper Makes Music"
  turn away sadly (p. 56) **phrasal verb**
  That's not it. (p. 56) **idiom**

"Riding Rainbows"
  took it out on (p. 57) **idiom**
  sing the same song (p. 57) **idiom**
  no matter how (p. 57) **idiom**
  belong to (p. 57) **phrasal verb**
  go by (p. 58) **phrasal verb**
  store up (p. 59) **phrasal verb**
  point out (p. 59) **phrasal verb**

laugh out loud (p. 59) **metonomy**
pull out (p. 61) **phrasal verb**
kind of like a treasure hunt (p. 61)
  simile
make a business call (p. 63) **idiom**
make music with (p. 66) **idiom**
carry out (p. 66) **phrasal verb**

"A Lazy Thought?"
  subway rush (p. 67) **idiom**
  traffic crush (p. 67) **idiom**
  no wonder (p. 67) **idiom**

"Susan Gordon, Private Detective"
  take one's case (p. 68) **idiom**
  look for (p. 68) **phrasal verb**
  full of (p. 69) **hyperbole**
  pick up (p. 69) **phrasal verb**
  stick out from (p. 71) **phrasal verb**
  take off (p. 71) **phrasal verb**
  stay out late (p. 75) **phrasal verb**
  drive out (p. 75) **phrasal verb**
  write up (p. 77) **phrasal verb**
  day is over (p. 77) **idiom**
  never miss anything (p. 77) **idiom**
  neat (p. 77) **slang, idiom**
  super (p. 77) **slang, idiom**

"New Uses for Old"
  used for (p. 80) **phrasal verb**

"Narcisa"
  First she is an ancient queen. (p. 82)
    personification
  She is a singing wind. (p. 82)
    personification
  She is a nightingale. (p. 82)
    personification

"Steffie and Me"
  school . . . like a castle (p. 84) **simile**
  call for (p. 84) **phrasal verb**
  give a punch (p. 85) **idiom**
  not around (p. 86) **idiom**
  pull up (p. 86) **phrasal verb**
  come to (a stop) (p. 86) **phrasal verb**

"I'll Be a Baker"
  can't go wrong (p. 106) **idiom**
  always look up (p. 109) **idiom**
  at last (p. 109) **idiom**
  have to do without (p. 113) **phrasal
    verb**

"Eric Plants a Garden"
  break up (p. 124) **phrasal verb**
  nothing tastes as good as (p. 127)
    simile, hyperbole
  things—corn plants (p. 128)
    anthimeria
  nothing like (p. 129) **hyperbole**
  pollen like a yellow dust (p. 130)
    simile
  take a long time (p. 130) **idiom**
  just in time for (p. 130) **idiom**

"The Garden"
  look out of (the window) (p. 139)
    phrasal verb
  Toad sang songs. (p. 141)
    personification
  come up out of (p. 142) **phrasal verb**

"Where Does Your Garden Grow?"
  made of (p. 146) **phrasal verb**
  add to (p. 146) **phrasal verb**
  ground up (p. 146) **phrasal verb**
  See for yourself. (p. 147) **idiom**
  wash away (p. 151) **phrasal verb**
  blow away (p. 151) **phrasal verb**

"Every Insect"
  in a fix (p. 152) **idiom**

"Going on a Nature Hunt"
  no matter where (p. 154) **idiom**
  take along (p. 155) **phrasal verb**
  turn into (p. 156) **phrasal verb**
  web reach across (p. 157)
    personification
  get caught (p. 158) **idiom**
  let it go (p. 162) **idiom**

"Sumi's Prize"
  ask for (quiet) (p. 168) **phrasal verb**
  could hardly wait (p. 171) **hyperbole**

if only (p. 171) **idiom**
run ahead (p. 173) **phrasal verb**
tongue would not move (p. 175)
  hyperbole
keep back tears (p. 178) **phrasal verb**
popped up (p. 178) **phrasal verb**
with a zing (p. 178) **onomatopoeia**
help . . . to . . . feet (p. 178) **idiom**

"Benjamin and Tulip"
  beat . . . up (p. 181) **phrasal verb**
  Benjamin and Tulip (p. 181)
    personification
  get the worst of it (p. 182) **idiom**
  zip up the nearest tree (p. 190)
    anthimeria
  got all night (p. 191) **hyperbole/idiom**

"The Fence"
  did no good (p. 201) **idiom**
  make . . . pay (p. 203) **idiom**

"The Beach"
  make a face (p. 212) **idiom**
  couldn't help laughing (p. 216) **idiom**

"On the Sand Dune"
  take off into space (p. 218) **phrasal
    verb**
  witching mountain (p. 218) **anthimeria**
  go on all fours (p. 220) **metonomy**
  one of these days (p. 222) **idiom**
  laugh at (p. 224) **phrasal verb**
  feel like (p. 224) **idiom**
  Annie watched them go storming up.
    (p. 227) **anthimeria**
  hand on to . . . hand (p. 229) **phrasal
    verb**
  make it (p. 230) **idiom**

Sunshine Days, level #13
"Elephant Rhymes"
  jumped so high he reached the sky
    (p. 3) **hyperbole**

"Eletelephony"
  drop the song (p. 6) **idiom**

"The Magic Pot"
  pot begins to speak (p. 7)
    personification
  make its way (p. 8) **idiom**
  will be off (p. 12) **idiom**
  fall asleep (p. 12) **idiom**

"Words of Laughter"
  can hardly stand it (p. 15) **hyperbole,
    idiom**

"Dragon Stew"
  to make up (p. 18) **idiom**
  set foot in (p. 24) **idiom**
  minding my own business (p. 25)
    idiom
  dragon crying and talking (p. 25)
    personification

"Christina Katerina and the Box"
  one sleepy summer day (p. 30)
    oxymoron
  wouldn't mind a bit (p. 36) **idiom**

"Free as a Frog"
  make fun of (p. 42) **idiom**
  a large warm sound (p. 42) **metaphor**
  it was soft like her voice (p. 42) **simile**
  feel like a bird; free as a bird (p. 42)
    simile
  back and forth (p. 45) **idiom**
  let in (p. 47) **phrasal verb**
  right out loud (p. 50) **idiom**

"Dr. Penny Walters"
  take care of (p. 52) **idiom**

"The Grasshopper"
  rope that dangled some hope (p. 62)
    personification
  sure as molasses (p. 63) **idiom**

"Lucky Ladybugs"
  turn into (p. 65) **phrasal verb**

"Muffin"
  shrank away (p. 72) **phrasal verb**
  drew away (p. 74) **phrasal verb**

"Rain Up, Rain Down"
  a cloud is a puddle (p. 82) **metaphor**
  so the puddle could fly (p. 82)
    personification

"Nate the Great Goes Undercover"
  catch up (p. 102) **phrasal verb**
  her list of 2,000 things (p. 104)
    hyperbole
  crossed out (p. 108) **phrasal verb**
  garbage can was crunchy, crackly, and
    klunkey (p. 109) **onomatopoeia**
  detective work is garbage cans (p. 109)
    metaphor
  get rid of (p. 111) **idiom**
  no matter (p. 112) **idiom**

"Lysbet and the Fire Kittens"
  go out (p. 120) **phrasal verb**
  up Harlem way (p. 121) **idiom**
  fire crackled and roared (p. 124)
    onomatopoeia
  kept nagging at the back of mind
    (p. 125) **idiom**
  burn up (p. 129) **phrasal verb**
  flames, licking at the roof thatch
    (p. 129) **personification**
  went up (p. 130) **phrasal verb**

"Miguel's Mountain"
  keep back (p. 135) **phrasal verb**
  face lit up (p. 140) **idiom**
  got his tongue back (p. 140) **idiom**

"Molly's Woodland Garden"
  dug up (p. 146) **phrasal verb**
  cabin will belong to the field mice
    (p. 151) **metaphor**
  plopped into the water (p. 155)
    onomatopoeia

"Tortoise, Hare, and the Sweet Potatoes"
  drank his fill (p. 159) **idiom**
  run for your life (p. 163) **hyperbole**
  take off (p. 163) **phrasal verb**
  run my head off (p. 165) **hyperbole**
  rooted up (p. 166) **phrasal verb**

"Andrew Wyeth: Painter"
   head for (p. 171) **phrasal verb**
   world of make-believe (p. 174) **idiom**
   magic touch like a key (p. 175) **simile**
   stretch their minds (p. 175) **idiom**
   and the wind told stories (p. 176)
      personification
   Nature became a friend. (p. 177)
      personification
   let their imagination fly (p. 178) **idiom**
   He thundered orders. (p. 181)
      anthimeria

"Gordon Parks: Photographer"
   being black makes a difference
      (p. 202) **metonomy**
   win at life (p. 214) **idiom**

"Sam Bangs and Moonshine?"
   stepped out (p. 221) **phrasal verb**

"Andrew Henry's Meadow"
   rigged up (p. 231) **phrasal verb**
   looked the ground over (p. 233) **idiom**
   looked over (p. 233) **phrasal verb**
   the ladder climbed (p. 234)
      personification

"No Nonsense"
   no nonsense (p. 242) **idiom**
   on the timid side (p. 242) **idiom**
   hair standing on end (p. 242)
      hyperbole
   put up with them (p. 243) **phrasal
      verb**
   had caught on (p. 243) **phrasal verb**
   beat around the bush (p. 243) **idiom**
   make some pin money (p. 243) **idiom**
   throw a scare in (p. 245) **idiom**
   went dead (p. 248) **idiom**
   went off (p. 248) **phrasal verb**

"The Army of Two"
   night is falling (p. 254)
      personification, idiom
   rings out (p. 255) **phrasal verb**
   keeps a sharp eye peeled (p. 259)
      idiom

sets off (p. 259) **phrasal verb**
tight as glue (p. 260) **simile**
coming in (p. 260) **phrasal verb**
run off (p. 262) **phrasal verb**
come on (p. 262) **phrasal verb**

"The Freedom Ship of Robert Smalls"
   Be sassy with your work, but not with
      your tongue. (p. 268) **pun**
   fell in love (p. 270) **idiom**
   gone up (p. 272) **phrasal verb**
   make his move (p. 273) **idiom**
   cast off (p. 275) **phrasal verb**

"Susan Bearskin"
   I will run home like the wind.
      (p. 281) **simile**
   They are like bear traps on my feet.
      (p. 281) **simile**
   went on and on (p. 281) **idiom**
   held on (p. 282) **phrasal verb**
   watch out (p. 282) **phrasal verb**
   There are more children around it
      than needles on a pine tree. (p. 282)
      metaphor
   him . . . . panting like a dog (p. 286)
      simile
   she would run as swift as an arrow
      (p. 286) **simile**
   her moccasins seemed to carry
      her . . . like a bird (p. 286) **simile**
   He's like a bear. (p. 288) **simile**
   run as fast as a deer (p. 289) **simile**

"Joanna Runs Away"
   television was gabbling loudly
      (p. 227) **personification**
   She heard Costanza's clip-clop.
      (p. 227) **personification**

"Maxie"
   tired squeak (p. 237) **oxymoron**
   reached out (p. 237) **phrasal verb**
   sing out for one full minute (p. 238)
      personification

"The Beauty Way"
   he rides as fast as the wind. (p. 251)
      simile

"Paper Airplanes"
soft as a feather (p. 278) **simile**

"The Culprits" (pp. 286–300)
personification
They're a great bunch. (p. 288) **idiom**
Oh, we've been around. (p. 289) **idiom**
It was a rotten shot and rotten thing
to do. (p. 290) **pun, idiom**
Aw, you gotta be teasing. (p. 292)
slang
What are you? A weirdo or
something? (p. 292) **rhetorical
question**
hit the water (p. 299) **idiom**
tangling with (p. 299) **phrasal verb**

"Sounding Off"
carry on (p. 142) **phrasal verb**
run out (p. 142) **phrasal verb**
Some words sound like what they
mean—bang, buzz, pop . . . (p. 302)
onomatopoeia

"Laura Bridgman"
the look on Laura's face made it quite
clear (p. 157) **idiom**
playing games with letters and words
almost the way a trained dog does
tricks (p. 163) **metaphor**
didn't get a bite to eat (p. 164)
metonomy
Can you imagine what it must have
been like for her? (p. 164)
rhetorical question

"The Lady Who Builds Giants"
talents are like seeds (p. 168) **simile**
father ran a chicken farm (p. 169)
idiom

"Baba Yaga and the Kind Little Girl"
hinges of the gate cried out (p. 182)
personification
cried out (p. 182) **phrasal verb**
he drove her away (p. 188) **idiom**

"The Sorcerer's Apprentice" story line
(pp. 189–200) **personification**

"Pigs and Pirates"
ran helter-skelter (p. 209) **idiom**

"In Time of Silver Rain" story line
(pp. 210–211) **personification**

"Persephone and Demeter"
sprang up (p. 212) **phrasal verb**
died out (p. 213) **phrasal verb**
so sad that she turned into a gray old
woman (p. 215) **metaphor**

"The Monkey and the Crocodile"
(pp. 102–111) **personification**

"The Black Snake"
snake roll like a rubber tire (p. 112)
simile
glides like a wave (p. 112) **simile**
limp as a licorice whip (p. 112) **simile**
ribbed and round (p. 112) **anthimeria**

"Otto at Sea"
waves gurgled (p. 117) **onomatopoeia**
when the good ship gave its last sad
toot (p. 118) **onomatopoeia,
personification**
sailors wept like babies (p. 118) **simile**
he's as tall as a mountain (p. 121)
simile, hyperbole

"The Useful Dragon of Sam Ling Toy"
ring his bell, clang-a-dee-clang (p. 125)
onomatopoeia
the trolley go rattly-bump (p. 125)
onomatopoeia
in a dragonish sort of way (p. 126)
anthimeria
dragon was sometimes doggish, cattish,
pigeonish (p. 127) **anthimeria**
his green eye just like a traffic light
(p. 127) **simile**
so frightened their hats popped
straight up into the air (p. 128)
hyperbole
so angry his ears turned red (p. 128)
hyperbole

"The Mayo Brothers"
It had never entered his head.
  (p. 138) **idiom**
fresh out of medical school (p. 140)
  idiom
building opened its doors (p. 142)
  personification
dump in (p. 25) **phrasal verb**
Could you eat a friend? (p. 26)
  rhetorical question
He saw what I meant. (p. 28) **idiom**
I'm sorry for the trouble. (p. 31)
  idiom

"Shrimp's Soccer Goal"
come in handy after all (p. 41) **idiom**
game was a slaughter (p. 45) **idiom**
everyone was pretty down (p. 45)
  idiom
lining up (p. 46) **phrasal verb**

"Jackie"
check out (p. 48) **phrasal verb**
sneak out (p. 49) **phrasal verb**
Wonder why? (p. 50) **rhetorical
  question**
springing off (p. 51) **phrasal verb**

"Harvestman"
hand-me-down legs (p. 56) **idiom**
creature looks a lot like a tiny bright
  pebble (p. 56) **idiom**

"Daddy Longlegs"
legs so long seem to be standing on
  stilts (p. 57) **hyperbole**

"The Biggest House in the World" title
(p. 72) **personification, hyperbole**

"Me and My Bones"
fence of bones (p. 86) **metaphor**

Hand Stands, level #14
"Peter Perfect"
I beg your pardon. (p. 3) **idiom**
I never have a moment's trouble
  with him. (p. 4) **idiom**
never has to raise his voice (p. 10)
  idiom

"Sumi's Special Happening"
looking all bones and white whiskers
  (p. 13) **metaphor**
something to make his heart sing
  (p. 15) **personification**
searching for (p. 16) **phrasal verb**
happening that will warm his heart
  (p. 17) **metonomy**
a jeep so red it looked like a ripe
  tomato (p. 18) **simile**
the world had turned white over-
  night (p. 18) **metonomy**
a thin voice that sounded like the
  song of a winter ricket (p. 19)
  simile
they roared down the road like a
  noisy red bull (p. 20) **simile**
the horn bellowed, the siren screamed,
  bells clanged (p. 20) **onomatopoeia**
wondering faces (p. 21) **metonomy**
blaze of glorious noise (p. 23)
  oxymoron
bumped over lumpy roads (p. 23)
  anthimeria
the heart is singing (p. 23)
  personification

"The Race Driver"
sent back (p. 296) **phrasal verb**
figure out (p. 297) **phrasal verb**
take part (p. 298) **idiom**

Publishers of high-interest, low-vocabulary material

Allyn & Bacon, Inc., 470 Atlantic Avenue, Boston, Massachusetts 02210.

American Education Publications, 245 Long Hill Road, Middletown, Connecticut 06457.

Benefic Press, 10300 West Roosevelt Road, Westchester, Illinois 60153.

Bobbs-Merrill Co., Inc., 4300 West 62nd Street, Indianapolis, Indiana 46206.

Book-Lab, Inc., 1449 Thirty-seventh Street, Brooklyn, New York 11218.

Bowmar Publishing Corp., 622 Rodier Drive, Glendale, California 91201.

Childrens Press, 1224 West Van Buren Street, Chicago, Illinois 60607.

John Day Co., 666 Fifth Avenue, New York, New York 10019.

Doubleday & Co., Inc., 501 Franklin Avenue, Garden City, New York 11530.

Field Educational Publications, Inc., 2400 Hanover Street, Palo Alto, California 94304.

Fearon Publishers, Inc., 6 Davis Drive, Belmont, California 94002.

Finney Co., 3350 Gorham Avenue, Minneapolis, Minn. 55426.

Follet Publishing Company, 1010 West Washington Boulevard, Chicago, Illinois 60607.

Garrard Publishing Company, 1607 North Market Street, Champaign, Illinois 61820.

Globe Book Co., Inc., 175 Fifth Avenue, New York, New York 10010.

Grosset & Dunlap, Inc., 51 Madison Avenue, New York, New York 10010.

E. M. Hale & Co., 1201 South Hastings Way, Eau Claire, Wisconsin 54701.

Harper & Row, Publishers, Inc., 10 East Fifty-third Street, New York, New York 10022.

D. C. Heath & Company, 125 Spring Street, Lexington, Massachusetts 02173.

Laidlaw Brothers, Thatcher and Madison Streets, River Forest, Illinois 60305.

Mafex Associates, Inc., 111 Barron Avenue, Johnstown, Pennsylvania 16906.

McGraw-Hill, Inc., 1221 Avenue of the Americas, New York, New York 10020.

McGraw-Hill, Inc., Webster Division, Manchester Road, Manchester, Missouri 63011.

William Morrow & Co., Inc., 105 Madison Avenue, New York, New York 10016.

Pyramid Books, 919 Third Avenue, New York, New York 10016.

Random House, Inc., 201 East Fiftieth Street, New York, New York 10022.

Reader's Digest Services, Inc., Educational Division, Pleasantville, New York 10570.

Frank E. Richards, Publisher, 324 First Street, Liverpool, New York 13088.

Scholastic Book Services, 50 West Forty-fourth Street, New York, New York 10036.

Simon & Schuster, Inc., 630 Fifth Avenue, New York, New York 10020.

Steck-Vaughn Company, Box 2028, Austin, Texas 78767.

Franklin Watts, Inc., 845 Third Avenue, New York, New York 10022.

Albert Whitman & Company, 560 West Lake Street, Chicago, Illinois 60606.

Xerox Education Publications, Education Center, Columbus, Ohio 43216.

INDEX